HIZMET IN AFRICA

HIZMET IN AFRICA

*The Activities And Significance
Of The Gülen Movement*

David H. Shinn

Hizmet in Africa: The Activities and Significance of the Gülen Movement
Copyright © 2015 by Tsehai Publishers. All rights reserved.

Apart from any fair dealing for the purpose of private study, research, criticism or review, as permitted under the Copyright Act, no part of this publication may be reproduced in any form, stored in a retrieval system or transmitted in any form by any means—electronic, mechanical, photocopy, recording or otherwise—without the prior permission of the publisher. Enquiries should be sent to the undermentioned address.

Tsehai books may be purchased for educational, business, or sales promotional use. For more information, please contact our special sales department.

Tsehai Publishers
Loyola Marymount University
1 LMU Drive, UH 3000, Los Angeles, CA 90045

www.tsehaipublishers.com
info@tsehaipublishers.com

ISBN: 978-1-59-907121-3 (Paperback)
ISBN:978-1-59-907122-0 (Hardcover)

First Edition: September 2015

Publisher: Elias Wondimu
Book Layout and Cover Design: Sara Martinez
Copy Editor: Jeffrey Nazzaro

Cover images from Dreamstime: © Kierran1, Pg-images, and Yakthai

Library of Congress Catalog Card Number
A catalog record for this book is available from the Library of Congress.

British Library Cataloguing in Publication Data
A catalogue record for this book is available from the British Library.

10 9 8 7 6 5 4 3 2 1

Printed in the United States of America

To everyone on this planet who works on behalf of religious tolerance and interfaith dialogue.

CONTENTS

FOREWORD	By the Most Reverend Archbishop Thabo Makgoba	i
PREFACE	By David H. Shinn	iii
ABBREVIATIONS		v
CHAPTER 1	Introduction	1
CHAPTER 2	Fethullah Gülen, the Gülen Movement, and *Hizmet*	9
CHAPTER 3	TUSKON, Business, and Banking	27
CHAPTER 4	Gülen-affiliated Schools and Related Programs	43
CHAPTER 5	*Hizmet* Dialogue Centers	71
CHAPTER 6	*Hizmet* Humanitarian Activities	85
CHAPTER 7	Gülen-affiliated Media and Outreach Programs	101
CHAPTER 8	*Hizmet*, the AKP, and Turkey-Africa Relations	115
CHAPTER 9	Conclusion	129
APPENDIX	Gülen-affiliated Schools in Africa	137
SELECTED BIBLIOGRAPHY		149
INDEX		153

FOREWORD

BY THE MOST REVEREND ARCHBISHOP THABO MAKGOBA

Primate of the Anglican Church of Southern Africa & Anglican Archbishop of Cape Town

Hizmet in Africa is a comprehensive and important work, giving the reader insight and more understanding into the valuable work and social investments of the *Hizmet* Movement, inspired by the teachings of Fethullah Gülen, in Africa. The book gives us a brief but insightful introduction to the *Hizmet* Movement in Africa. It pays testimony to the vital work being done by *Hizmet* Movement teachers, business people, academics, and volunteers in uplifting communities and contributing to the broader development of our societies within postcolonial Africa and, more specifically, postapartheid South Africa.

The book encounters and accounts firsthand for the holistic approach of Fethullah Gülen and the *Hizmet* Movement in solving global issues through education, dialogue, and humanitarian aid. The challenges facing us in the twenty-first century are vast and immense, especially in the continent of Africa; however, *Hizmet in Africa* sheds light on a movement that has a holistic and universal approach to solving global challenges, and that is committed to building new partnerships, the promotion of cultural exchanges, and universal values—concepts that are needed more than ever before. The book displays by example through action that the *Hizmet* Movement has a broad-based approach in dealing with different communities, embracing diversity as a bond for social cohesion—not being selective of who they serve, but rather serving all communities and societies regardless of their faith, culture, ethnicity, race, class, gender, or linguistic grouping.

From my personal interactions with members and volunteers of the *Hizmet* Movement, and engaging with the texts, teachings and philosophical ideas of Fethullah Gülen, I can recommend this book as a long overdue—sound and important—work on the *Hizmet* Movement and its activities in Africa. In our continent, which is ravaged by poverty, conflict, and underdevelopment—the *Hizmet* Movement brings with it a new holistic and universal approach to solving the challenges, contributing to dialogue and seeking solutions, not merely by just teaching, but also by being willing to share and exchange with Africa's diverse traditions, cultures, and societies.

The *Hizmet* Movement has a multifaceted and holistic approach in attempting to solve global challenges, and this book pays testament to the broad spectrum of the Movement's involvement in Africa, which has had an immensely positive impact on our societies and broader communities. The Movement's activities of promoting education, interfaith and intercultural dialogue, humanitarian aid, and community service are highlighted in great detail. This book also gives us a broad overview of the Turkish business community and volunteers who donate funds, dedicate resources, and give personal time to ensure the Movement can promote new projects and continue to sustain existing projects—a revolutionary selfless approach to giving to and servicing humanity.

This book engages the reader to better understand the teachings of Fethullah Gülen, the *Hizmet* Movement, and its activities in Africa. It puts into perspective the holistic approach to solving challenging global issues in the twenty-first century, by providing solutions which champion education, dialogue, humanitarian aid, charitable giving, conflict resolution, and social development. The activities and projects of this transnational civic movement are much needed in the continent of Africa, and in countries such as South Africa. Our communities and society have already witnessed firsthand the positive impact of the *Hizmet* Movement in contributing to building a better future for all of humanity.

PREFACE

BY DAVID H. SHINN

My area of specialization is East Africa and the Horn and, more recently, China-Africa relations. Four years ago I didn't expect to be researching and writing a book on the Gülen Movement in Africa. I had attended a few events at the Rumi Forum, a Gülen-affiliated dialogue center in Washington, and participated in 2010 in one of the Forum's sponsored trips to Turkey. The director of the Rumi Forum, Emre Celik, asked if I would do a study of *Hizmet*'s activities in Africa. He agreed to organize meetings in a number of African countries and Turkey with persons associated with and knowledgeable about the Movement. The Rumi Forum covered the cost of my travel to Africa and Turkey. I insisted on complete control over the final manuscript and accepted no reimbursement for the time I put into this project. All of the analysis contained in this book is my own and based on information I collected from both *Hizmet* and third-party sources.

I knew Africa well before undertaking this study, having specialized in African affairs academically since the early 1960s at George Washington and Northwestern universities. I also spent 37 years in the U.S. Foreign Service, where most of my assignments dealt with Africa, both on the continent and at the State Department in Washington. I had tours of duty at U.S. embassies in Kenya, Tanzania, Mauritania, Cameroon, and Sudan, and served as ambassador to Burkina Faso and Ethiopia. I have been teaching African affairs at George Washington University since 2001.

The Gülen Movement is a generally opaque organization. While much has been written about the philosophy of Fethullah Gülen, from whom the Movement has evolved, there is little documentation about its global activities, especially in Africa. I had to learn a great deal about Gülen's ideas and the way in which they are being applied in Africa. This required visits to Africa and Turkey and access to individuals who are active in the Movement. This access would not have been possible without the assistance of the Rumi Forum. Most of my *Hizmet* contacts seemed genuinely pleased to share information about their activities and, on some occasions, willing to acknowledge problems and challenges. It was also apparent to me, however, that some contacts were concerned as to how I would use their information.

The Gülen Movement is controversial; a quick search of the Internet will demonstrate the point. It has many critics. It became even more controversial after disagreements began to emerge in 2012 between the Movement and Turkey's ruling Justice and Development Party (AKP). This subsequently resulted in a nasty confrontation between the Movement and the AKP, with implications for the Movement's activities outside Turkey. While I summarize the changing relationship between *Hizmet* and the AKP, my purpose is to describe and analyze the Gülen Movement only in Africa. This book does not deal with *Hizmet* programs in Turkey or any other part of the world. I have made every effort to offer a factual and dispassionate analysis. Readers can judge for themselves whether I have achieved this goal.

I believe both supporters and critics of the Gülen Movement will agree on one thing after reading this book. They will be surprised at the magnitude of *Hizmet* activities in Africa. It is important, however, to keep these activities in perspective. Africa is a continent three-and-a-half times the size of the United States, has 54 countries, and more than one billion inhabitants. It can absorb with minimal obvious impact the activities of a single organization such as *Hizmet*, especially one that tends to operate quietly and often opaquely. But in at least a small way, *Hizmet* is probably found in every country in Africa and, in a few, is the best known symbol of Turkey, even when its activities are not understood by local residents to be associated with the Gülen Movement.

David H. Shinn
May 2015
Washington, D.C.

ABBREVIATIONS

ABITAT	Association of Businessmen and Industrialists of Tanzania and Turkey
AKP	Justice and Development Party
ANTE	Association Nigéro-Turque d'Entrepreneurs
ATSA	Atlantique Turquie-Sénégal Association pour le Dialogue Culturel entre les Civilisations
BBC	British Broadcasting Corporation
CIA	Central Intelligence Agency
CSITT	Complexe Scolaire International Tchado-Turc
DEiK	Foreign Economic Relations Board
DRC	Democratic Republic of the Congo
ECOWAS	Economic Community of West African States
EGESADER	Aegean Health Volunteers' Association
ESAFED	Aegean International Federation of Health
ICD	Islamic Corporation for the Development of the Private Sector
IDB	Islamic Development Bank
IDP	internally displaced person
JWF	Journalists and Writers Foundation
KARDESLIK	Senegalese-Turkish Businessmen's Association
KYM	Kimse Yok Mu
MAF	Mohammed Al Fatih
MOZTÜRK	Association of Mozambican and Turkish Merchants
MÜSIAD	Independent Industrialists' and Businessmen's Association
NGO	non-governmental organization

NTIC	Nigerian Turkish International Colleges
NTNU	Nigerian Turkish Nile University
PAGAD	People against Gangsterism and Drugs
SATBA	South African Turkish Business Association
SBC	Samanyolu Broadcasting Company
TAH	Tamweel Africa Holding
TIKA	Turkish Cooperation and Coordination Agency
TUDEC	Ghana-Turkey Cooperation and Development Association
TÜFIAD	Turkish-Moroccan Businessmen's Association
TURCABA	Turkish and Cameroonian Businessmen's Association
TÜSIAD	Turkish Industry and Business Association
TUSKON	Confederation of Businessmen and Industrialists of Turkey
UTBA	Uganda-Turkey Business Association

CHAPTER 1

INTRODUCTION

Hizmet, or "service" in Turkish, is the name that the followers of Fethullah Gülen prefer to use in reference to the global social movement that is better known as the Gülen Movement. Gülen is the Turkish-born Sunni Muslim spiritual leader who inspired this movement of mostly Turkish nationals. In 1991, he left Turkey for health reasons for the United States, where he continues to live. While his health has worsened over the years, he also now has serious political differences with the government in Turkey and might not be allowed to return and move freely in the country.

Hizmet contains a strong strain of Turkish nationalism.[1] Gülen Institute board member Y. Alp Aslandoğan explains, however, that while most *Hizmet* followers are Turkish Muslims, the Movement includes non-Turkish nationals and even non-Muslims. It is a social phenomenon that defies easy definition.[2] There is no accurate count of the number of followers of Fethullah Gülen and/or those who support *Hizmet* activities. The estimated number varies widely; it ranges between two and eight million Turks inside Turkey and in the diaspora, in addition to modest numbers of non-Turks. Bayram Balci, a visiting scholar at the Carnegie Endowment for International Peace, concluded that "the Gülen movement is the single most influential socioreligious movement that Turkey has ever seen."[3]

One Senegalese interlocutor who knows the organization well emphasized that *Hizmet* programs do not distinguish between Muslims and non-Muslims.[4]

---

1   Michael J. and Karen A. Fontenot, "The Characteristics and Appeal of the *Hizmet* Movement," in *The Gülen Hizmet Movement and its Transnational Activities*, ed. Sophia Pandya and Nancy Gallagher (Boca Raton, FL: BrownWalker Press, 2012), 22–23.

2   Author's notes on remarks made 6 February 2013 at Georgetown University in Washington.

3   Bayram Balci, "The Gülen Movement and Turkish Soft Power," 4 February 2014, http://carnegieendowment.org.

4   Author's meeting on 7 January 2013 in Dakar, Senegal, with Thierno Ka, presidential adviser on religious affairs.

South Africa's ambassador to the United States and former premier of the Western Cape, Ebrahim Rasool, also made an effort to learn about *Hizmet*. He concluded that the Gülen Movement is an effort to internalize the core values of Islam. He said *Hizmet* came to the Western Cape without a template but in an effort to inspire Muslims. It supported education, dialogue, and the policy of inclusion.[5]

A great deal has been written about the Gülen Movement as it pertains to Turkey and even beyond Turkey's borders. There is, however, no book length work on *Hizmet*'s activities in Africa, which, in any event, only have a 20-year history. This book is limited to *Hizmet* in Africa's 54 countries. It touches on the broad outlines of Gülen's Sufi philosophy and ideas, especially as they play out in Africa, but it is not another book about Fethullah Gülen or his contribution to Islamic thinking. It is the first comprehensive effort to document and analyze the totality of the *Hizmet* effort in Africa.

I approach this project as a specialist on Africa, not an expert on Turkey. The vast majority of my 37-year career in the U.S. Foreign Service dealt with Africa and included assignments at American embassies in Kenya, Tanzania, Mauritania, Cameroon, Sudan, Burkina Faso, and Ethiopia. I spent shorter periods in the Seychelles and Chad, and have travelled extensively throughout the continent. While assigned to the State Department in Washington, I had responsibility at various times for all of the countries in East Africa, the Horn of Africa, and the Indian Ocean islands. Since retiring from the Foreign Service, I began in 2001 teaching African affairs in the Elliott School of International Affairs at George Washington University. I continue to teach, write extensively on African affairs, and return regularly to Africa.

This book began at the suggestion of the Rumi Forum, a Gülen-affiliated dialogue center located in Washington. The Rumi Forum agreed to arrange access to Gülen-affiliated organizations in Africa and Turkey and cover my travel costs if I would donate my time for researching and writing the book. I agreed to do so only if I had complete editorial control over the book's content, which has been the case. It also became apparent that without the assistance of the Rumi Forum, I never would have received on my own the open access accorded by Gülen-affiliated organizations at every stop in Africa and Turkey.

Review of the Literature

There is a wealth of material on the Gülen Movement, most of it written by followers or sympathizers. In fact, much of it has been published by the Gülen-affiliated press. The largest publisher is the Kaynak Publishing Group in Turkey. *Hizmet* has two English-language publishing houses in the United States: Tughra

---

5 Author's meeting on 19 October 2012 in Washington with Rasool.

Books in New York City and Blue Dome Press in Clifton, New Jersey. Dar al-Nile Publishing is the Arabic-language and Editions du Nil the French-language publishing house under Kaynak.

There is considerable public criticism of Fethullah Gülen and *Hizmet*. As an Islamic thinker with Sufi values, he has made many enemies, especially in the world of Islamic Salafism. He is also viewed skeptically by many non-Muslims and Turkish secularists. Much of the concern seems to be related to the fact that *Hizmet* lacks transparency. The most outspoken criticism appears on the Internet and is rarely well documented. Much of it is anonymous. There is at least one book—*Strategic Defamation of Fethullah Gülen: English vs. Turkish* (2012) by Doğan Koç—that is intended explicitly to refute the negative information about the Gülen Movement. I discuss several criticisms of *Hizmet* activities in Africa that seem to have merit but try to take a neutral position on Gülen's interpretation of Islam.

The starting point of a literature review is Gülen's body of work. He has published about 50 books in Turkish; the key ones have been translated into English and other languages. Gülen's books are collections of articles that he has written over the years and then given book titles such as *Pearls of Wisdom*, *Essentials of the Islamic Faith*, and *The Messenger of God: Muhammad*. Those that have been translated into English are accessible free of charge at *http://en.fgulen.com/gulens-works*. His writing tends to be dense, sometimes almost impenetrable. My focus was on those articles that have an impact on *Hizmet* activities in Africa such as schools, dialogue centers, and *Kimse Yok Mu*, *Hizmet*'s humanitarian arm. Gülen's thoughts have been nicely summarized by a number of authors and organizations. A case in point is *Understanding Fethullah Gülen* (no date) published by the Gülen-affiliated and Istanbul-based Journalists and Writers Foundation.

Most of the book length accounts of the Gülen Movement have been written by followers or persons who are inclined to treat it sympathetically. Examples include Muhammed Çetin's *The Gülen Movement: Civic Service without Borders* (2010) and *Hizmet: Questions and Answers on the Gülen Movement* (2012). Other favorable accounts are *Tradition Witnessing the Modern Age: An Analysis of the Gülen Movement* (2008) by Mehmet Enes Ergene; *Beginnings and Endings: Fethullah Gülen's Vision for Today's World* (2013) by Walter Wagner; *A Dialogue of Civilizations: Gülen's Islamic Ideals and Humanistic Discourse* (2007) by B. Jill Carroll; *Embracing the World: Fethullah Gülen's Thought and Its Relationship to Jalaluddin Rumi and Others* (2013) by Ori Z. Soltes; and *Cross-cultural Dialogue on the Virtues: The Contribution of Fethullah Gülen* (2014) by Trudy D. Conway.

A couple of sympathetic books deal with narrower aspects of the Movement. One title is *Wrestling with Free Speech, Religious Freedom, and Democracy in Turkey: The Political Trials and Times of Fethullah Gülen* (2011) by James C.

Harrington. Another is *The Gülen Movement: Building Social Cohesion through Dialogue and Education* (2010) by Gürkan Çelik. Helen Rose Ebaugh wrote *The Gülen Movement: A Sociological Analysis of a Civic Movement Rooted in Moderate Islam* (2010). A useful overview of the Gülen Movement, it includes a section on the criticisms of *Hizmet*, but then refutes each one. *The New Turkish Republic: Turkey as a Pivotal State in the Muslim World* (2008) by Graham E. Fuller contains ten laudatory pages devoted to the Gülen Movement. The author is a former vice chairman of the U.S. National Intelligence Council.

There have been a number of conferences devoted to the Gülen Movement, often organized or at least supported by *Hizmet* organizations that result in the publication of the papers delivered at the event. The collections tend to be sympathetic to the Movement, but do offer some diversity of opinion.

One of the first collections was *Turkish Islam and the Secular State: The Gülen Movement* (2003), edited by M. Hakan Yavuz and John L. Esposito. The book represents papers presented at a conference on the Gülen Movement hosted by The Center for Muslim-Christian Understanding at Georgetown University in Washington. A journal devoted to the study of Islam and Christian-Muslim relations, *The Muslim World*, devoted its July 2005 edition to "Islam in Contemporary Turkey: The Contributions of Fethullah Gülen."

Muslim Citizens of the Globalized World: Contributions of the Gülen Movement (2006) resulted from papers presented at two conferences hosted by the Graduate Program in Religious Studies at Southern Methodist University and Rice University's Boniuk Center for the Study and Advancement of Religious Tolerance. The first conference took place in Houston, Texas, in 2005 and the second in Dallas, Texas in 2006. Robert A. Hunt and Yüksel A. Aslandoğan edited the book.

One of the most massive collections of papers appeared as the *Muslim World in Transition: Contributions of the Gülen Movement* (2007), edited by Ihsan Yilmaz and others. The conference took place in London, 25–27 October 2007 and was hosted by the House of Lords, the School of Oriental and African Studies at the University of London, and the London School of Economics.

John L. Esposito and Ihsan Yilmaz edited *Islam and Peacebuilding: Gülen Movement Initiatives* (2010). It reflects papers presented at the 2007 conference in London cited above; the International Conference on Peaceful Coexistence: Fethullah Gülen's Initiatives for Peace in the Contemporary World, Erasmus University in The Netherlands, 22–23 November 2007; and Islam in the Age of Global Challenges: Alternative Perspectives of the Gülen Movement, Georgetown University in Washington, 14–15 November 2008.

The South Africa-based Turquoise Harmony Institute, a Gülen-affiliated dialogue center, published *Gülen Movement: Its Essentials in Thought and Practice and Potential Contributions to Reconciliation in South African Society* (2010). It contains the proceedings of panel discussions held in Cape Town, South Africa on 13 March 2010.

Heon Kim and John Raines edited *Making Peace in and with the World: The Gülen Movement and Eco-Justice* (2012). It uses the Gülen Movement as a case study. The book contains the papers delivered at a conference at Temple University in Philadelphia, Pennsylvania in 2010. *The Gülen Hizmet Movement and its Transnational Activities: Case Studies of Altruistic Activism in Contemporary Islam* (2012) was edited by Sophia Pandya and Nancy Gallagher. It emphasizes the ways in which followers of Gülen have interpreted and implemented his message around the world.

There are two books by authors who have a thorough understanding of the Gülen Movement that stand out in their effort to analyze the Movement critically while, at the same time, acknowledging the positive contributions. The first is *Toward an Islamic Enlightenment: The Gülen Movement* by Hakan Yavuz (2013). A professor of political science at the University of Utah, Yavuz focuses on the impact of the Gülen Movement in Turkey; his book says little about *Hizmet*'s international activities. The second book, by Joshua D. Hendrick, is *Gülen: The Ambiguous Politics of Market Islam in Turkey and the World* (2013). Hendrick is an assistant professor of sociology and global studies at Loyola University Maryland in Baltimore. While the book goes beyond Turkey, it has little to say about *Hizmet* in Africa.

Research on *Hizmet* in Africa is limited to a half-dozen book chapters or short monographs dealing with South Africa, Nigeria, and Kenya, cited in the footnotes. There is also a master of Islam dissertation from St. Paul's University in Kenya titled *Gülen-inspired Schools and Their Contribution to Christian-Muslim Relations in Nairobi, Kenya* (2012) by Fatih Akdogan. The author is the director of the *Hizmet* dialogue center in Nairobi. *Hizmet* activities in Africa have received minimal attention by researchers.

State of the Question

Because it is a recent phenomenon and so little has been written about *Hizmet* in Africa, the primary sources of information are interactions with persons engaged in *Hizmet* activities and journalistic accounts. While the African press has done a good job in some countries covering *Hizmet*, it seems to have ignored the subject in others. The most complete coverage appears in the Istanbul-based *Today's Zaman*, which is affiliated with *Hizmet*. This means that most of the information available about *Hizmet* in Africa comes from *Hizmet* sources. Inevitably, this tends to result in a positive bias. For the most part, however, African sources confirmed the positive impact of *Hizmet*'s engagement in Africa.

From an Africa-wide research point of view, this is virgin territory. It is not a question of building on previous work except for those few country-specific monographs. It is the beginning point. There was not even a complete list, at least not one available to the public, of the Gülen-affiliated schools in Africa. One of the most frustrating and time-consuming components of this book was building the list of more than 100 *Hizmet* schools cited in the appendix. In spite of my best effort, there are undoubtedly a few omissions and errors in this list. In effect, the state of the question, at least as it applies to the Gülen Movement in Africa, is based mostly on anecdotal information, with analysis made on the basis of extrapolated research from Turkey and other parts of the world.

Thesis

My thesis is both modest and basic. It has become apparent in recent years that the Gülen Movement has significantly increased its engagement in Africa. But there is no comprehensive documentation of this engagement and what it means for Turkey and Africa. The purpose of this book is to document the engagement and explain its significance.

I continue to interact frequently with specialists on Africa around the world. I am astounded how few of them have even heard of Fethullah Gülen, the Gülen Movement, or *Hizmet*. Those few who are at least familiar with the name have no more than a rudimentary understanding as to what the Movement is doing in Africa. While it is important not to overstate the significance of the Gülen Movement in Africa, African specialists should understand what it is and what impact it now or potentially has in any given country.

By singling out this topic, the book probably implies that *Hizmet* has a greater importance in Africa than is, in fact, the case. I don't have a solution to this problem except to urge readers to keep the Movement in perspective. For example, *Hizmet* schools are the best known part of its program in Africa and 18 or 19 countries do not have a single school. Several countries have only one school.

Methodology

The methodology for this book was straightforward and uncomplicated. It consisted of learning the basics of Gülen's philosophy and reading the key works in English about the Movement. It then involved interviews, mostly with *Hizmet* followers and organizations, during two visits to Turkey—one of about ten days in 2010 and another for a week in 2013. There were also meetings with academics, government officials, and think tank personnel, some of whom were not part of *Hizmet*.

The core of the research took place during two visits to Africa and meetings with *Hizmet* members and organizations, government officials, religious figures, media representatives, civil society representatives, academics, and students who attend *Hizmet* schools and their parents. The first visit took place in August–September 2012, with stops in Johannesburg, Pretoria, and Cape Town in South Africa; Dar es Salaam and Zanzibar in Tanzania; Nairobi and Mombasa in Kenya; and Addis Ababa in Ethiopia. The second visit occurred in December 2012 and January 2013, with stops in Abuja, Kaduna, and Lagos in Nigeria; Dakar in Senegal; and Casablanca, Marrakech, and Rabat in Morocco. I also took advantage of visits to and public lectures in Washington by experts on the Gülen Movement.

The research involved a search of the Internet, including *Hizmet* organization websites, for media and other coverage of *Hizmet* activity in Africa. This involved drawing on both English- and French-language material. This information was invaluable in documenting *Hizmet* activities in many of those countries that I was not able to visit. Journalistic and think tank accounts were also important for chapter 8 on *Hizmet*, Turkey's ruling Justice and Development Party, and Turkey-Africa relations. This relationship changed dramatically while writing the book and continues to evolve.

The analysis of all of this information then depended on my involvement in African issues dating back to the early 1960s and a physical presence in Africa for 17 years. I followed no formulae or theories; I just collected data and did my best to analyze the data on the basis of long experience in and with Africa.

Argument

Chapter 2 begins with a brief look at the background of Fethullah Gülen and his Islamic philosophy, drawing on both his writings and analysis of them by experts. It discusses *Hizmet* or the Gülen Movement from a global perspective and touches on major criticisms of this social phenomenon.

Chapter 3 focuses on *Hizmet*'s global commercial arm, known as The Confederation of Businessmen and Industrialists of Turkey. It describes its activities in Africa and analyzes the importance of local *Hizmet* business organizations. The chapter also has a section on one of the most recent *Hizmet* efforts in Africa—Islamic banking.

Hizmet involvement in education is at the center of its Africa effort. After discussing Gülen's educational philosophy in chapter 4, there is a section on name selection of the schools and an overview of the number of schools in Africa. This is supplemented by an appendix that identifies by name all the schools known to exist in Africa. The chapter discusses the financing of the schools and their link to Turkish business and the degree to which Islam plays a role in the schools. It documents an impressive list of complimentary remarks about the schools by African leaders and notes there has also been criticism of the schools. The chapter describes the evolving relationship between the Turkish government and the schools. It concludes with a deeper analysis of the schools in five countries: South Africa, Kenya, Nigeria, Senegal, and Morocco.

Chapter 5 documents and analyzes the significance of *Hizmet*'s small dialogue centers. Most African countries do not have a center. Those countries that do have a center tend to be those where Turkish business interests are greater. As a result, the chapter discusses in greater detail the dialogue centers in South Africa, Tanzania, Kenya, Nigeria, Senegal, Morocco, and Egypt.

Hizmet has its own global humanitarian arm, known as *Kimse Yok Mu*, which is especially active in Africa. Chapter 6 evaluates *Kimse Yok Mu*'s structure and organization, the value of its aid to Africa, and especially its largest programs in Sudan, Somalia, Uganda, Ethiopia, and Kenya. The chapter provides limited information on *Kimse Yok Mu* programs in other African countries and identifies several affiliated *Hizmet* humanitarian efforts.

Chapter 7 deals with the *Hizmet* media and outreach effort in Africa. It identifies the magazines, journals, newspapers, news agencies, and Internet resources that one finds in Africa. It discusses book publishing relevant to Africa and the role of *Hizmet*'s Ebru television. The chapter concludes with an analysis of the Journalists and Writers Foundation and Gülen conferences as they apply to Africa.

Chapter 8 takes *Hizmet* in Africa back to Turkey and assesses the impact of the Movement's programs on policies in Africa by the Turkish government and its ruling political party. It begins with the early relationship between *Hizmet* and the Justice and Development Party (AKP). Continuing chronologically, it moves to the high point in the relationship and then the development of cracks between *Hizmet* and the Justice and Development Party. The chapter concludes with a discussion of the factors that led to a breakup of the relationship and the impact of that breakup on *Hizmet* in Africa.

The conclusion, chapter 9, ties together the previous chapters and analyzes the overall impact of *Hizmet* and the philosophy of Fethullah Gülen in Africa.

CHAPTER 2

FETHULLAH GÜLEN, THE GÜLEN MOVEMENT, AND HIZMET

Fethullah Gülen the Man

The key figure in this book is Fethullah Gülen, a Turkish-born Muslim leader who inspired a following of mostly Turkish nationals. These followers have fanned out around the globe to engage in service activities and to encourage others to consider his moderate Islamic philosophy. Often called the Gülen Movement, especially by outsiders, persons within the Movement prefer to refer to it as *Hizmet,* the Turkish word for voluntary service. While *Hizmet* has religious overtones, the primary focus of Gülen's followers both inside Turkey and outside is the development of altruistic service organizations.

Born in the eastern Anatolian province of Erzurum in 1941, Fethullah Gülen attended religious schools or *madrasas*.[1] He was shaped by his family, Sufism, and the writings of Bediüzzaman Said Nursi, one of Turkey's most prominent Sufi thinkers, who died in 1960. Gülen became aware of the writings of Said Nursi in 1957–1958 and is now often regarded as Nursi's successor, although there are important differences in their thinking. Gülen became a congregational prayer leader or imam in 1959 and subsequently taught and administered courses on Islamic sciences in a Qur'anic school. He grew up holding a conservative religious worldview.[2]

---

1   A student and biographer of Gülen, Tuğrul Hoca, says he was actually born in 1938. See Joshua D. Hendrick, *Gülen: The Ambiguous Politics of Market Islam in Turkey and the World* (New York: New York University Press, 2013), 71. Pages 62–88 of Hendrick's book offer a non-traditional biography of Gülen.

2   M. Hakan Yavuz, *Toward an Islamic Enlightenment: The Gülen Movement* (Oxford: Oxford University Press, 2013), 25–36. There is a wide body of literature on Fethullah Gülen and his extensive writings. While the Internet is replete with criticism of Gülen and his ideas, most of the published works are laudatory and often commissioned by followers of the Gülen Movement. The book by Yavuz is largely sympathetic. Yavuz is in regular contact with the followers of Gülen, but he is not a member of the

Sufism is at the core of Gülen's beliefs. As he explained in an interview published in *The Atlantic* in 2013, "although I do not belong to any Sufi order and I have never attempted to establish one, I can say that the righteous masters of Sufism have influenced me greatly."[3]

Following the 1971 military coup, Gülen was indicted and convicted of violating Article 163 of the Turkish Penal Code, which criminalized ideas and activities perceived as critical of the secular Turkish state; he spent seven months in prison. Gülen received an amnesty and in 1972 resumed his religious work. In the 1970s, Gülen offered intellectual support to center-right and nationalist Turkish political parties opposed to the Kemalist Republican People's Party. In 1979, Gülen began to extend his ideas more broadly in Turkey with the publication of *Sizinti* magazine, which synthesized scientific knowledge and Islam. He saw Islamic morality as a solution to Turkey's problems.[4]

Gülen supported the 1980 coup but still faced an arrest warrant by the military leadership. He maintained a low profile; a state security court revoked the arrest warrant in 1986. Gülen used this period to disseminate his theology by distributing audiocassettes throughout Turkey. Gülen developed close ties with Prime Minister Turgut Özal and emerged in the 1980s as one of the dominant figures in Turkish Islamism. He created a nationwide educational and cultural movement. Kemalist elements stepped up their campaign against Gülen and were joined by radical Islamists who charged he was too "accommodating" and "pro-American."[5]

The 1997 military "soft coup" led unexpectedly to the liberalization of Turkey's leading Islamic groups. Gülen and his followers tried to portray themselves as moderate vis-à-vis other Islamic organizations in Turkey. Prior to the national elections in 1999, both President Süleyman Demirel and Prime Minister Bülent Ecevit defended Gülen's activities and worldview. Kemalists and Gülen's secular critics concluded, however, that he intended to end the secular nature of Turkish society. The prosecutor of the Ankara State Security Court requested an arrest warrant on charges that Gülen was plotting to overthrow the state by creating a

---

Movement. His stated goal is "neither to praise nor to condemn but to understand a religious and sociopolitical movement with the potential for enormous influence not only in Turkey but also in much of the wider Islamic world" (Yavuz, 12). For a brief "authorized" biography of Gülen, see Gülen Institute, *Fethullah Gülen: Biographical Album* (Houston, TX: Gülen Institute, undated). For early influences on Gülen, see Mehmet Enes Ergene, *Tradition Witnessing the Modern Age: An Analysis of the Gülen Movement* (Somerset, NJ: Tughra Books, 2008), 6–9. See also Ori Z. Soltes, *Embracing the World: Fethullah Gülen's Thought and Its Relationship to Jalaluddin Rumi and Others* (Clifton, NJ: Tughra Books, 2013), 60–65.

3   Interview with Jamie Tarabay in *The Atlantic* (14 August 2013).
4   Yavuz, 36–38.
5   Ibid., 38–41.

clandestine organization. Although the State Security Court rejected the request, a Kemalist group launched an attack against him and his media organization. In 1999, Gülen left Turkey for the United States because of this campaign against him and for medical reasons. He has been living ever since, never married, at the Golden Generation Worship and Retreat Center in Saylorsburg, Pennsylvania, about 100 kilometers north of Philadelphia.[6]

In 2000, Turkey's state prosecutor filed for the arrest of Gülen on the grounds that he and his followers intended to overthrow the secular government and create a theocratic state. The High Criminal Court in Ankara finally dismissed the case in 2006.[7] The same year, Gülen filed for permanent residency in the United States. Rejected initially by the Department of Homeland Security, the United States eventually granted permission for him to remain permanently in 2008. Since arriving in the United States, Gülen recreated himself as a "global imam" who quietly established close ties with many prominent Americans.[8] According to University of Utah political science professor M. Hakan Yavuz, he "has emerged as the leader of one of the most dynamic, transnational, and wealthy faith-based Islamic movements in Turkey."[9]

In 2008, the American magazine *Foreign Policy* included Gülen on its list of the world's top 100 public intellectuals. *Foreign Policy* then asked readers to vote on the list. Some 500,000 persons responded and Gülen came in first. *Foreign Policy* commented that members of the Gülen Movement consider him an inspirational leader who encourages a life guided by moderate Islamic principles. His detractors, on the other hand, believe he represents a threat to Turkey's secular order.[10] In 2013, *Foreign Policy* included Gülen on its list of the world's 500 most powerful individuals in fields that included politics, high finance, media, military, and religion.[11]

In 2013, *Time* magazine produced a list of the 100 most influential people in the world, from artists and leaders to pioneers, titans, and icons.

---

6   Ibid., 41–43.

7   Helen Rose Ebaugh, *The Gülen Movement: A Sociological Analysis of a Civic Movement Rooted in Moderate Islam* (Heidelberg: Springer, 2010), 32. This period is dealt with in detail by James C. Harrington, *Wrestling with Free Speech, Religious Freedom, and Democracy in Turkey: The Political Trials and Times of Fethullah Gülen* (Lanham, MD: University Press of America, 2011).

8   Yavuz, 44–45.

9   Ibid., 45–46.

10 www.foreignpolicy.com/articles/2008/06/16/the_world_s_top_20_publc_intellectuals?print=yes&hidecomments=yes&page=full.

11 www.foreignpolicy.com/articles/2013/04/29/the_500_most_powerful_people_in_the_world.

Gülen appeared on this list under the category of leaders. Some of the other leaders were Barack Obama, Xi Jinping, Abdullah Ocalan, Kim Jong Un, and Pope Francis.[12]

The Islamic Philosophy of Fethullah Gülen

Gülen has produced an enormous range of commentary on religious, social, and political issues. His grounding for this work did not come from university training but from his reading of Sufi writings, self-education, and his personal experiences in Turkey. It is not the purpose of this book to comment extensively on his writings or theology. But it is necessary to outline some of Gülen's core beliefs, especially those that have had an impact on his followers who implement *Hizmet* activities in Africa.

Gülen believes that Islam requires a combination of self-development and glorification of God through communal actions. The main purpose of life for Muslims is sacrifice and service to God. Commenting on Gülen's ideas, Yavuz explains that "Muslims need to engage in building communities, obeying the Sharia, and responding to socioeconomic challenges through religiously sanctioned actions."[13] Gülen's writings stress sacrifice as a religious virtue, which is an important motivating force of his followers. Gülen is effectively calling on them to "act collectively for the betterment of their own communities."[14] Gülen believes Islam should be used to change people and their relationships with others through "transformative action" in the here and now. His goal is to empower Muslims to liberate themselves from confining, existing conditions.[15]

There are several themes in Gülen's writings that are especially relevant to *Hizmet's* global activities. They include Gülen's views on education, science, tolerance, and interfaith dialogue. *Hizmet* began in Turkey in the early 1980s with the development of Gülen-affiliated schools. According to Gülen, "Education always has been the most important road of serving the people."[16] From the standpoint of *Hizmet* in Africa, Gülen's emphasis on education is his most significant contribution.

---

12 "The 2013 Time 100," *Time* (29 April–6 May 2013), 64. *www.time100.time.com/2013/04/18/time-100/slide/all/*. For a mostly sympathetic account of Fethullah Gülen and the Movement, see Suzy Hansen, "The Global Imam," *The New Republic* 241, issue 19 (2 December 2010): 10–15.

13 Yavuz, 48.

14 Ibid., 48.

15 Ibid., 49–50.

16 Fethullah Gülen, interview in the *Daily Nation* (Nairobi, Kenya) on 30 July 2004.

Gülen considers the absence of education or inferior education as the most important problem of the century.[17] He sees education as a lasting solution for society's problems such as ignorance, poverty and division. Education not only offers knowledge but provides people with a sense of purpose in life and allows them to become productive members of the economy. The purpose of learning is to satisfy human and community needs that contribute to solving global problems.[18] He argues that the Muslim community is not in urgent need of additional mosques, but of knowledge that can be provided by schools. He put education at the center of his efforts, also realizing that schools bring people together from different backgrounds.[19]

Gülen-inspired schools emphasize math, science, language, arts, sports, and high moral values. Operationally, Gülen strongly believes there should be tripartite cooperation among the schools' teachers, parents (most of whom pay upper end tuition rates), and sponsors (usually Turkish business persons). Gülen also encourages scholarship programs for highly qualified students of parents who cannot afford the fees.[20]

Gülen-affiliated schools are sometimes located in regions, including some countries in Africa, that are predominantly non-Muslim or that have significant minorities from other religions. This raises the question of the role of Islam in the instruction of non-Muslims. The Gülen Movement generally does not teach Islam in schools outside Turkey and even in Turkey religious courses are only taught one hour per week.[21] Rather, teachers, and some of them outside Turkey are not Muslim, are expected to demonstrate exemplary behavior and lead by example with the objective that students will internalize their behavior and see them and other Muslims as good people. There is no overt effort to convert students of other religions, but there is a desire to present Islam in the best possible light.[22] David Tittensor at La Trobe University in Melbourne, Australia, concluded that what Gülen-affiliated schools are doing "is not so different" from their Christian counterparts.[23]

---

17 Ergene, 96. For a discussion of the role of education in *Hizmet*, see Soltes, 103–123.

18 Yüksel A. Aslandoğan and Mohammed Çetin, "The Educational Philosophy of Gülen in Thought and Practice," in *Muslim Citizens of the Globalized World: Contributions of the Gülen Movement*, ed. Robert A. Hunt and Yüksel A. Aslandoğan (Somerset, NJ: The Light and IID Press, 2006), 31–36.

19 Bekim Agai, "Fethullah Gülen and His Movement's Ethic of Education," *Middle East Critique* 11, no. 1 (2002): 38.

20 Aslandoğan and Çetin, 44–45.

21 Agai, 30.

22 Yavuz, 109.

23 David Tittensor, "The Gülen Movement and the Case of a Secret Agenda: Putting the

Although Gülen was a product of Turkish *madrasa* schooling, he became a critic of some of its practices, such as the way it taught basic Islamic sciences, the insufficiency of its curriculum, its repetitive technique, and the way the tradition of commentary and interpretation hindered reform, innovation, and improvement. His major concern was the omission from the curriculum of natural sciences. Gülen argues that the Qur'an actually encourages the combination of religious and natural sciences.[24]

The Gülen approach to education has its critics, especially in Turkey. Kemalist and secular groups charge that Gülen-affiliated schools are Islamizing society and that the movement eventually seeks to control the state. This argument has little or no relevance to schools established outside Turkey. While there is no single organization that manages this global educational network, the schools tend to emphasize similar subject matter and follow common policies and objectives, including strong discipline, a dress code, and proper moral conduct. There is also some evidence that Gülen is actively involved in setting broad goals and perhaps even strategies for the schools, or at least those in Turkey.[25]

While there are many positive aspects of *Hizmet* schools, the system focuses on conformity with tradition rather than encouraging critical thinking. They seek to foster a certain worldview and way of conduct, which limits consideration of alternative lifestyles and values.[26] Yavuz concludes that the system does not liberate students from tradition, authority, or conservative morality. He also wonders if some individuals within the movement are seeking to further Islam or their own ambitions.[27]

Closely linked to Gülen's views on education is the importance he attaches to science and its relationship to Islam. He believes that science is an essential instrument for comprehending the power and nature of God. Gülen-affiliated schools emphasize science rather than the humanities or liberal arts, which, in any event, may undermine the foundations of Islam's moral and religious worldview.[28]

Debate in Perspective," *Islam and Christian-Muslim Relations* 23, no. 2 (2012): 174.

24 Ergene, 120–124. For a discussion of Gülen's philosophy of education, see Gürkan Çelik, *The Gülen Movement: Building Social Cohesion through Dialogue and Education* (Delft, Netherlands: Eburon, 2010), 97–116.

25 Yavuz, 94–97. For an uncritical account of Gülen-affiliated schools in Turkey, see B. Jill Carroll, *A Dialogue of Civilizations: Gülen's Islamic Ideals and Humanistic Discourse* (Somerset, NJ: The Light, Inc. and The Gülen Institute, 2007), 72–78.

26 Yavuz, 105–106.

27 Ibid., 115.

28 Ibid., 96–97. Walter Wagner, *Beginnings and Endings: Fethullah Gülen's Vision for Today's World* (New York: Blue Dome Press, 2013), 142–144.

Students from Gülen-affiliated schools have an impressive record in national and international science and math competitions.

Gülen believes that science and religion are both compatible and complementary and insists that science not be separated from religion.[29] But according to Gülen, science needs to be seen in the context of principles and values cited in the Qur'an.[30] Gülen wrote that "the Qur'an and *hadith* are true and absolute. Science and scientific facts are true as long as they are in agreement with the Qur'an and *hadith*, and are false inasmuch as they differ or lead away from the truth of the Qur'an and *hadith*."[31] While science cannot replace the role of religion, Gülen believes that science will become dominant in the twenty-first century.[32] On another occasion, Gülen wrote that "science without religion is crippled, while religion without science is blind."[33]

Tolerance is a key concept in Gülen's thinking, although he approaches the issue broadly and in recent years has used the term more selectively.[34] Gülen argues that "we should have such tolerance that we are able to close our eyes to the faults of others, to have respect for different ideas, and to forgive everything that is forgivable . . . ."[35] Tolerance is one of Gülen's four "pillars of dialogue," the others being love, compassion, and forgiving. By combining a commitment to faith and tolerance, Gülen creates a paradigm in Islamic dialogue. His philosophy is committed to Islam, but reaches out to non-Muslim believers and even nonbelievers.[36]

Gülen's attention to tolerance is demonstrated in the Gülen-affiliated schools, which encourage a more tolerant citizenry where people can pursue their own faith and promote the well-being of others.[37] There are, however, some limits

---

29 Aslandoğan and Çetin, 39. Osman Bakar, "Gülen on Religion and Science: A Theological Perspective," *The Muslim World* 95, no. 3 (2005): 369.

30 Bakar, 366.

31 Fethullah Gülen, *Understanding and Belief: The Essentials of Islamic Faith* (Izmir, Turkey: Kaynak Publishing, 1997), 335.

32 Ahmet T. Kuru, "Fethullah Gülen's Search for a Middle Way between Modernity and Muslim Tradition," in *Turkish Islam and the Secular State: The Gülen Movement*, ed. M. Hakan Yavuz and John L. Esposito (Syracuse, NY: Syracuse University Press, 2003), 121–122.

33 Fethullah Gülen, "The Irresistible Power of Religion," *Leadership* (13 September 2013), *http://leadership.ng*.

34 Yavuz, 186–187. Çelik, 125–135.

35 Fethullah Gülen, *Toward a Global Civilization of Love and Tolerance* (Somerset, NJ: The Light, Inc., 2004), 33.

36 Lester R. Kurtz, "Gülen's Paradox: Combining Commitment and Tolerance," *The Muslim World* 95, no. 3 (2005): 373.

37 Ibid., 380.

to tolerance when it comes to the position of women. Many followers of Gülen have a conservative approach to women in social situations and there is some debate as to the role women play in leadership positions in the Movement itself. While Gülen-affiliated schools encourage the education of girls, there tends to be a separation of the sexes in the schools, at least beyond the primary level.[38]

Directly related to tolerance is interfaith dialogue, perhaps the most important contribution Gülen has made to modern discourse after his encouragement of Gülen-affiliated schools. Gülen argues that "interfaith dialogue is a must today." He adds that "we should always bear in mind that relationships with civilized persons must be through dialogue."[39] This effort has manifested itself in the form of Gülen-sponsored dialogue centers, which operate under a wide variety of names except for his name. These centers are expanding in Africa and are discussed in chapter 5.

Gülen is a pioneer of inter-religious understanding and traces the concept back to basic Islamic themes. He views dialogue with followers of other religions as an integral part of the Islamic ethic. He urges Muslims to be self-critical and discourages the transformation of Islam into an ideology. In fact, he argues this effort has politicized Islam and prevented Muslims from engaging in dialogue with adherents of other religions. Gülen has been sharply criticized by some Islamists for his position on interfaith dialogue and especially his 1998 meeting with Pope John Paul II.[40]

Gülen's objective in promoting interfaith dialogue is to build social relationships that promote tolerance and peace rather than reconcile theological differences. He is also more focused on demonstrating exemplary conduct, for example in the Gülen-affiliated schools, than in conversion. He operates on the assumption that preaching alienates others and hinders reconciliation between

---

38 Sophia Pandya, "Creating Peace on Earth through *Hicret* (Migration): Women Gülen Followers in America," in *The Gülen Hizmet Movement and its Transnational Activities: Case Studies of Altruistic Activism in Contemporary Islam*, ed. Sophia Pandya and Nancy Gallagher (Boca Raton, FL: Brown Walker Press, 2012), 109. Margaret Rausch, "Gender and Leadership in the Gülen Movement: Women Affiliates' Contributions to East West Encounters," in *The Gülen Hizmet Movement and its Transnational Activities*, 141. Anna J. Stephenson, "Leaving Footprints in Houston: Answers to Questions on Women and the Gülen Movement," in *Muslim Citizens of the Globalized World*, 142–144.

39 Gülen, interview in *Daily Nation*. See also Wagner, 147–150. For an in-depth analysis of Gülen's views on dialogue, see Mohamed Soffar, "The Concept of Dialogue: A Study of Fethullah Gülen and Sayyid Qutb," *Hemispheres Studies on Cultures and Societies No. 24* (Warsaw: Polish Academy of Sciences, 2009), 5–28.

40 Zeki Saritoprak and Sidney Griffith, "Fethullah Gülen and the 'People of the Book': A Voice from Turkey for Interfaith Dialogue," *The Muslim World* 95, no. 3 (2005), 329–340.

faiths. Interfaith dialogue is not confined to the mosque, church or university campus, but can take place wherever people interact. Gülen has three goals in the interfaith dialogue process: building relationships and networks, promoting social cohesion and peace, and transforming perceptions of Islam.[41]

According to Gülen, dialogue "means two or more people coming together to talk and meet on certain subjects and, by means of this, to draw closer together to one another."[42] Yavuz explains that Gülen's primary goal is to develop a framework for religious coexistence despite clear differences. He is not seeking common ground for different religions. Interfaith dialogue "becomes citizenship training with responsibilities and rights to build a shared future through collective actions."[43]

Gülen is committed to interfaith dialogue on the basis that Judaism, Christianity, Islam, and other world religions have the same theistic source and pursue the same goal. Gülen relates all major religions to each other by the same divine revelation. Gülen's inclusive approach to religion and his interfaith theology stem from the common denominators across religions that offer the foundations for an Islamic interfaith theology and a rationale for interfaith dialogue. Finally, Gülen believes the Qur'an is a universal call for dialogue that primarily, but not exclusively, targets the Abrahamic religions—Islam, Judaism, and Christianity.[44]

Gülen Movement or *Hizmet*?

Although the term Gülen Movement is frequently applied to those who support activities such as schools and dialogue centers that follow Gülen's philosophy, this is not his preference. Gülen reportedly neither approves of nor uses the term. He prefers volunteers' service or *Hizmet*. Followers of Gülen often say they use Gülen Movement for the sake of convenience. Even the term "movement" is misleading, as it implies an organization with more central authority than is in fact the case. The network does not have formal positions of authority and Gülen is not its president or leader in any formal sense.[45]

---

41 Yavuz, 173–174. Çelik, 118–125.

42 Fethullah Gülen, *Love and the Essence of Being Human*, 2nd ed. (Istanbul: Journalists and Writers Foundation Publications, 2004), 171.

43 Yavuz, 188. For an analysis of Gülen's approach to dialogue, see Karina Korostelina, "Dialogue as a Source of Peaceful Coexistence," in *Islam and Peacebuilding: Gülen Movement Initiatives*, ed. John L. Esposito and Ihsan Yilmaz (New York: Blue Dome Press, 2010), 104–106 and 118–120.

44 Turan Kayaoglu, "Preachers of Dialogue: International Relations and Interfaith Theology," in *Islam and Peacebuilding: Gülen Movement Initiatives*, 163–164.

45 Pim Valkenberg, "The *Hizmet* Movement in the Dialogue between Muslim and

Pim Valkenberg, a Christian theologian from the Netherlands, commented that "Gülen does not decide what is to be done, nor does he own the movement or one of its parts."[46] Gülen has never made, accepted or approved any claim to leadership of the Movement.[47] Journalists, academics, and persons outside the Movement probably continue to use the term Gülen Movement because it is the easiest way to describe the phenomenon. In any event, *Hizmet* is not yet a term widely understood outside the Turkish language.

The followers of Gülen have contributed to the confusion concerning the most appropriate way to describe these activities. The schools and dialogue centers, at least those in Africa, generally do not link Gülen to the name of their organization or their activities. On the other hand, Gülen is the "honorary president" of Gülen-affiliated organizations such as the Rumi Forum in Washington, the Peace Islands Institute in Newark, New Jersey, and the Niagara Foundation, which has eight branches in the United States. There is a Gülen Institute at the University of Houston in Texas dedicated to the promotion of peace and civic welfare. News stories about Gülen-affiliated schools and other activities are regularly covered in Gülen-affiliated publications such as *Today's Zaman* and its Turkish-language counterpart, *Zaman*. Most scholarly studies, including those written by Gülen followers, have the Gülen Movement in the title and rely heavily on the term in their commentary.

There have been numerous conferences and seminars, usually organized by Gülen-affiliated dialogue centers devoted explicitly to the study of Gülen's philosophy. The conference theme often includes Gülen in the title. Examples include "The Gülen Movement and the Schools' Educational Philosophy," "Establishing a Culture of Coexistence and Mutual Understanding: Exploring Fethullah Gülen's Thoughts and Actions," and "Diversité et Cohésion dans un Monde Globalisé: Contributions du Mouvement Gülen."

Individual papers presented at these conferences often have titles that refer to the Gülen Movement. While Gülen-affiliated media seem increasingly to use the term *Hizmet* Movement, they also refer to the Gülen Movement. Even the Turkish-based, Gülen-affiliated Journalists and Writers Foundation published a document titled "Understanding Fethullah Gülen" that contains a section called "The Gülen Movement."[48] It is not surprising that the public is confused about

---

Christian Religious Traditions," in *The Gülen Hizmet Movement and its Transnational Activities*, 36–37. For answers to many questions about the Movement by one of its members, see: Muhammed Çetin, *Hizmet: Questions and Answers on the Gülen Movement* (New York: Blue Dome Press, 2012).

46 Valkenberg, 37.

47 Muhammed Çetin, *The Gülen Movement: Civic Service without Borders* (New York: Blue Dome Press, 2010), 280.

48 Undated document published in Istanbul.

the most appropriate term—Gülen Movement or *Hizmet*—for referring to the activities of Gülen supporters.

Defining *Hizmet* or the Gülen Movement

Hizmet or the Gülen Movement, this book uses the terms interchangeably. *Hizmet* is not a political movement and is not formally allied with any established political party. In 2014, Fethullah Gülen stated that "we are not and will not be a political party."[49] For Gülen, religion is far above politics and serves as a source of morality and ethics, which are not in conflict with responsible politics. Gülen does not want religion to become a tool of politics because people may then blame religion when politics become abusive.[50]

Mehmet Enes Ergene, one of the key figures in the Gülen Movement, emphasized that it is not an ideologically driven organization nor is it akin to political Islamism. He added at the most basic level the Movement "has a religious, social and cultural identity which is totally independent of any political or ideological structure."[51] *Hizmet* has no special doctrines or dogmas, no secret texts, no rites, rituals, insignia, costumes, or ceremonies. There is no formal membership. Leadership is decentralized and the activities of the Movement are open to all.[52]

While Gülen has millions of followers and sympathizers, the actual number is not known. Estimates of followers in Turkey vary from two to eight million persons or less than 10 percent of Turkey's total population at the high estimate.[53] *Hizmet* is, however, the largest civil society movement in Turkey.[54]

Hizmet is a faith-based social movement that relies primarily on a bottom-up approach to civic and social activism.[55] The common thread of its followers

---

49 Gülen, "Gülen Says Gov't Cut Back on Rights and Freedoms in Turkey," *Today's Zaman* (18 March 2014).

50 Çetin, 153 and 160.

51 Ergene, 16–17.

52 Çetin, 177–178. Soltes, 98–101, argues that Gülen echoes the Socratic-Platonic ideal but takes his ambitions beyond the relatively small world of Socrates and Plato.

53 Comment by Thomas Sorlie during 17 December 2013 video presentation hosted by Cultural Knowledge Consortium Speaker Series. Claire Berlinski puts the number of followers at between 3 million and 6 million in "Who is Fethullah Gülen?" *City Journal* (Autumn 2012).

54 Ihsan Yilmaz, "State, Law, Civil Society and Islam in Contemporary Turkey," *The Muslim World* 95, no. 3 (2005): 394.

55 John L. Esposito and Ihsan Yilmaz, "Conclusion," in *Islam and Peacebuilding: Gülen Movement Initiatives*, 343–345.

is "their acceptance of the scholarly authority of Gülen."[56] It operates on the basis that altruistic service by means of education, health and welfare activities, interfaith dialogue, and peace define a true Muslim. Muhammed Çetin, who wrote his PhD dissertation on the Gülen Movement and is affiliated with the Movement, described it as an apolitical civil society movement.[57]

At the same time, there is a political component to *Hizmet*. Hüseyin Gülerce, who is personally close to Gülen and a columnist for *Zaman* and *Today's Zaman*, said that *Hizmet* is not purely a religious movement, although it encourages people to return to their origins and spiritual resources. It seeks the acceptance of universal human values, including love, dialogue, tolerance, and reconciliation to attain peace. Gülerce added, however, that "the *Hizmet* movement has always been involved in politics as a civil society organization."[58]

Y. Alp Aslandoğan, a board member of the Gülen Institute, argues that *Hizmet* is a social phenomenon that defies easy definition. It includes non-Turkish and non-Muslim followers. It began in the 1960s in Izmir, Turkey, spread throughout Turkey in the 1970s, and became transnational in the 1990s. The schools are at the center of the Movement and are especially attractive to socially conservative families who are otherwise reluctant to send girls beyond required educational levels. There are many fault lines in Turkish society and *Hizmet* tries to put religion in a position where it encourages peace.[59]

Graham E. Fuller, former vice chairman of the National Intelligence Council at the Central Intelligence Agency who has written extensively on Turkey, commented that the Gülen Movement is "more modern and influential than any other Islamic movement in Turkey today. . . . Gülen's charismatic personality makes him the number one Islamic figure of Turkey."[60] The Movement has the largest and most powerful infrastructure and financial resources of any movement in Turkey and has become international by virtue of its global network of schools, dialogue centers, and charitable activities. The Movement until recently has been accommodating of state policies and supportive of the broad goals of Turkish foreign policy. Despite the deep hostility that the Turkish military leadership has towards the Movement, Gülen's followers speak positively about the military.

---

56 Çetin, 177.
57 Ibid., 178–179.
58 Gülerce, *Today's Zaman* (31 January 2014).
59 Remarks by Yüksel A. Aslandoğan on 6 February 2013 at Georgetown University in Washington, D.C.
60 Graham E. Fuller, *The New Turkish Republic: Turkey as a Pivotal State in the Muslim World* (Washington: US Institute of Peace, 2008), 56. See also Sophia Pandya, "Introduction: The Hizmet Movement Abroad," in *The Gülen Hizmet Movement and its Transnational Activities*, 1.

Hizmet focuses on encouraging gradual social change in Turkey through the propagation of Islamic values at the grass-roots level.[61]

Service activities, especially those outside Turkey, usually operate independently and not under the direction of any central authority. There is, however, considerable informal contact among some of the supporters of the different service efforts. There is no formal membership in the Gülen Movement. Followers do not belong to any particular community or network and normally belong to a variety of associations. Most of them are introduced to *Hizmet* by friends rather than relatives.[62]

Joshua D. Hendrick, author of an academically critical book about the Gülen Movement, explained that Gülen Movement institutions emerged autonomously, connected by a loose network of social, financial, and ideational ties. He added, correctly in the author's view, that "this ambiguous organizational model" allowed school administrators, business persons, editors, and dialogue center directors to choose when they wanted to freely associate their institution's identity as part of the Movement. Alternatively, they could choose to refer to their institutions as Gülen-inspired or deny any affiliation whatsoever.[63]

The different skills required for varied *Hizmet* activities results in followers from widely diversified socioeconomic backgrounds. Most of the educated participants do not work in religiously oriented occupations but in engineering, the sciences, and business. The Movement also has a significant number of students. *Hizmet* tends to attract middle- or upper-middle-class persons from urban areas and those with a high level of academic achievement.[64] Some *Hizmet* activities overlap and followers may fulfill different functions contemporaneously within the network. Consequently, the Gülen Movement does not require an umbrella organization for coordination purposes.[65]

According to Yavuz, the Gülen Movement consists of three circles. First, there is a core group of believers who lead the *Hizmet* activities in a spirit of unconditional loyalty to Gülen. This includes numerous university graduates who come from rural areas or small towns in Turkey, a group of "elder brothers," and a new generation of leaders with American or European university educations. There is a growing debate between the older members and the new generation that is more aggressive and vocal. There is no tolerance for incompetence and mistakes. Second, there are the affiliates who support

---

61 Fuller, 56–57.
62 Çetin, 194–195 and 244.
63 Hendrick, 57.
64 Ibid., 211–212.
65 Ibid., 217.

the Movement directly and indirectly by establishing good works and charities. This group includes small and medium-size merchants and business persons who constitute the board of trustees of the Movement's numerous foundations. They do fundraising and, in Turkey, are organized horizontally in different neighborhoods. Municipal, provincial, and state-level leaders are responsible for the implementation of decisions. Third, there are sympathizers who share Gülen's goals but do not participate actively. This group includes many nominal Muslims, including agnostics and nonbelievers.[66]

Authority extends outward from the first circle. The Movement is less cohesive on the periphery but according to Yavuz has "military-like discipline at its core."[67] In recent years, there has been a decentralization of power as the Movement has grown. Many local Gülen leaders have been given more autonomy and developed "baron-like" qualities due to their control over huge funds and properties. The first circle acts like a "committee of wise men," in which there is constant rivalry. Since Gülen has no deputy, Yavuz believes some in the first circle see themselves as potential successors. The second circle is critical for fundraising. Each circle consists of a bundle of networks of ideas and practices aimed at creating the good life. The shared beliefs and goals of Gülen unite the three circles.[68]

From a practical point of view, the Gülen Movement is a conglomeration of networks concentrated around five primary activities: educational institutions, business enterprises, media and broadcasting, charitable and humanitarian projects, and religious gatherings. Helen Rose Ebaugh at the University of Houston described in her book the Gülen Movement and the Gülen-inspired institutions in Turkey.[69] Elisabeth Özdalga at Middle East Technical University in Ankara concluded that "the Gülen movement is permeated by the idea of competition, be it between individuals, enterprises and/or schools. The objective of this competitive struggle is higher profit and better academic results."[70]

Turkish business persons inside Turkey and outside the country provide most of the funding for Gülen-affiliated projects. Each project has its independent accounting system and the amount of funding varies considerably from project to project. Wealthy industrialists might provide well over $1 million for projects in Turkey or outside the country, while persons of modest means obviously contribute much less. Some donors, especially wealthier ones, provide between 10 percent and 70 percent of their income annually to *Hizmet*. On average,

---

66 Yavuz, 86–87.

67 Ibid., 87.

68 Ibid., 87–88.

69 Ebaugh, 84–103.

70 Elisabeth Özdalga, "Redeemer or Outsider? The Gülen Community in the Civilizing Process," *The Muslim World* 95, no. 3 (2005): 235.

supporters with more modest income turn over about 10 percent of their earnings annually to help fund *Hizmet*. Even some Turkish graduate students who live on small stipends offer about 10 percent of their income. There are also in-kind donations and volunteering of expertise.[71]

While the goal of the donors is not to make a profit, some business persons almost certainly benefit indirectly from their association with *Hizmet* programs. In those cases where *Hizmet* projects such as some schools make a profit, they seem to plough the money back into the project. On the other hand, business persons who help finance a particular *Hizmet* activity draw on contacts such as the parents of students attending a school in order to further their business interests. Supporters of the Gülen Movement overwhelmingly say they do not, however, have the expectation of material or personal gain.[72] It is a fascinating, perhaps unique relationship involving religion, business, and service to others.

Some analysts compare the Gülen Movement to Opus Dei, Scientology, the Masons, Mormons, Muhammadiyah of Indonesia, the Buddhist Soka Gakkai International based in Japan, and various Indian guru-led or political religious groups.[73] All of these groups have significant differences with *Hizmet*, although Soka Gakkai responds to natural disasters and emphasizes interfaith activities.[74]

One organization with some goals similar to those of *Hizmet* is the Buddhist order known as the Tzu Chi Charitable Foundation. Founded in 1966 by a Taiwan-born nun, Tzu Chi volunteers living outside Taiwan began setting up chapters in 1985. Tzu Chi now is an international non-governmental organization with more than five million members. It is devoted to charity, medicine, education, environmental protection, and the promotion of humanistic values around the world. It is among the first organizations to help out when disasters occur. It helped, for example, in Rwanda and Ethiopia. Like *Hizmet*, Tzu Chi is based on volunteer efforts but does not appear to have the same strong connection with the business community.[75]

The activities of *Hizmet* are probably closer to those of the Aga Khan Foundation and its affiliated organizations, especially the focus by both the Aga Khan and *Hizmet* on education and the establishment of schools.[76] The Aga Khan

---

71 For a good discussion of financial support for the Movement, see Ebaugh, 52–61. See also Yavuz, 80–83.

72 Çetin, 232.

73 Hansen, 10–11.

74 Soka Gakkai International website. *www.sgi.org*.

75 Richard Madsen, lecture at the San Diego Taiwanese Cultural Center. *www.taiwancenter.com/sdtca/articles/5-07/5.html*.

76 Gabrielle Angey, "Turkish Islam in Africa: A Study of the Gülen Movement in Kenya," *Mambo!* French Institute for Research in Africa 10, no. 3 (May 2012): 3.

is the spiritual leader of the Shia Ismaili Muslims. *Hizmet* has, however, a shorter history, is geographically more widespread, is less structured, and has some important operational differences. In addition, the lifestyles of the Aga Khan and Fethullah Gülen are totally different. Although *Hizmet* and the Aga Khan organizations work in many of the same countries, there is no formal cooperation between them. In Kenya, some Ismailis attend interfaith events organized by the *Hizmet* dialogue center.[77]

Joshua Hendrick described the Gülen Movement as "a transnationally active, Turkish and Muslim-identified education, media, and business network whose actors and institutions span well over one hundred countries."[78] He argues that the Movement has emerged as Turkey's most influential nonpartisan, nonmilitary social force and thus constitutes a primary player in Turkey's "passive revolution."[79] Hendrick explained that by focusing its efforts in education and the media, the Movement has cultivated an entire generation of loyal supporters and established itself as the leading private producer of "Turkish Islam" for the twenty-first century religious marketplace.[80]

Criticism of the Movement

The Gülen Movement has numerous critics and has received plenty of criticism. The most common complaint is that Gülen wants to take over the Turkish state and replace the secular government with an Islamic state. Gülen is sometimes charged with being an agent of the U.S. government, especially the Central Intelligence Agency. Another theme suggests that Gülen is taking advantage of uneducated, rural Turks and brainwashing them with his philosophy. Some are concerned that Gülen's ideas are a return to traditional customs and values that are not compatible with modern democracy. Others complain that followers of Gülen only support their own people and neglect the rest of Turkish society. Some critics argue that Gülen is leading a secret society.[81]

Yavuz suggests there are two major criticisms of Gülen's ideas. First, Gülen provides his followers with well-established views that discourage them from thinking critically. Second, Gülen's ideas are rooted in the Abrahamic tradition

---

77 Author's meeting on 31 August 2012 in Nairobi, Kenya with Fatih Akdogan, interfaith chairman of *Hizmet's* Respect Foundation.
78 Hendrick, 2.
79 Ibid., 8.
80 Ibid., 24.
81 Ebaugh, 115–128. For a similar listing of criticisms, see Özdalga, 439–440. Tittensor, 163–179.

of revelations rather than liberal and democratic values. Gülen believes revelation should guide and shape the meaning of the good life. He does not appreciate that Islam in Turkey is a more divisive than unifying factor. Yavuz implies this view ignores the reality of what is happening in Turkey today. The Gülen philosophy, as a result, may be in conflict with aspects of pluralism and individualism.[82] Summarizing, Yavuz concludes that "the movement is too *Islamist* and conservative for some social democrats and the secularist military, too *liberal* and pro-American for Islamists, too *Turkish* nationalist for the Kurdish nationalists, too *Sunni-Hanefi* for the Alevis, and too worldly for some Sufi-oriented Muslims."[83]

One need only turn to the Internet to find a wide assortment of criticisms of the Gülen Movement. One of the most comprehensive websites in English is run by Citizens against Special Interest Lobbying in Public Schools. The name of the website is "A Guide to the Gülen Movement's Activities in the US." The website discusses all aspects of the Gülen Movement and includes criticism of *Hizmet* activities outside the United States. The website says it focuses on Gülen charter schools because it believes "they constitute one of the most egregious abuses of our public education system for business/political interests."[84]

While based in Istanbul in 2012, Claire Berlinski wrote a somewhat critical analysis of the Gülen Movement that resulted in a detailed rejoinder by an organization that supports the Movement.[85] She argued, for example, that many people who had left the Movement commented that its organizational structure is strict, hierarchical, and undemocratic. She also concluded that the Movement is primarily interested in increasing its share of power.[86]

It is not the purpose of this book to refute or substantiate the numerous criticisms leveled against the Gülen Movement, but just to note that *Hizmet* has attracted a considerable amount of controversy. Those who are interested in the criticisms can find them easily on the Internet and read the counterarguments by persons who support the Gülen Movement. The remainder of this book documents *Hizmet* activities in Africa, looks dispassionately and factually at its significance, and comes to some conclusions about its impact in Africa and on Turkey-Africa relations.

---

82 Yavuz, 65.
83 Ibid., 241.
84 *www.turkishinvitations.weebly.com.*
85 Berlinski, "Who is Fethullah Gülen?" *www.city-journal.org/2012/22_4_fethullah-gulen.html.* The Alliance for Shared Values rejoinder is titled "Fact Checking 'Who is Fethullah Gülen' by Claire Berlinski." It is not on the website but was provided upon request.
86 Berlinski.

Concluding Thoughts

This brief review of Fethullah Gülen's life and philosophy emphasizes those aspects of his beliefs that influence *Hizmet* and especially its operations in Africa. Gülen has written extensively on a variety of topics that are not discussed here and are not particularly relevant to the purpose of this book. On the other hand, it is important to capture Gülen's thinking as it relates to the connection between the business community and *Hizmet*. It is also essential to consider his views on education, interfaith dialogue, tolerance, and humanitarian programs, all of which are major *Hizmet* activities and themes in Africa.

While Gülen prefers that the Movement be referred to as *Hizmet*, it is not surprising that most persons who are not part of the effort refer to it as the Gülen Movement. The general public can associate the philosophy with Fethullah Gülen the person and his writings. The Turkish word *Hizmet* is just not sufficiently widely known to serve as the common designation for the Movement.

The Gülen Movement is accused by its critics of lacking transparency, and there is some truth to this charge. Persons involved in the Movement contribute to the confusion by carefully avoiding any link between the *Hizmet* schools and business associations on the one hand, and the Gülen name on the other. The schools choose not to highlight Gülen's philosophy or name, as they prefer to lead by example; bringing attention to Gülen is not seen as a priority. Nevertheless, the Movement explicitly uses the Gülen name and enthusiastically encourages his ideas in its dialogue centers and public outreach efforts. Since 2013, persons affiliated with the Movement have been especially reluctant to acknowledge their affiliation because of the crackdown against *Hizmet* by the government of Turkey.

The following chapters document *Hizmet* activities in Africa and provide the reader with a thorough understanding as to what the Movement is doing there. Whether explicit or implicit, Gülen's philosophy is behind all of this activity.

CHAPTER 3

TUSKON, BUSINESS, AND BANKING

Hizmet may be unique among global service movements in the degree to which it relies on financial support from the business and industrial community, at least until fees cover the costs of some of its activities such as schools and student dormitories. Cash and in-kind donations by individual Turkish business persons are critical to the establishment of Gülen-affiliated schools and the Movement's other activities in Africa. This chapter discusses the connection between *Hizmet* and the Turkish business community.

The Confederation of Businessmen and Industrialists of Turkey

There is an informal connection between the Gülen Movement and the powerful Confederation of Businessmen and Industrialists of Turkey, which is widely known as TUSKON. Created in 2005, it is a non-governmental and non-profit umbrella organization with headquarters in Istanbul representing seven Turkish business federations, 212 business associations, 54,000 Turkish entrepreneurs, and more than 140,000 companies.[1] Outside Turkey, it has offices in Brussels, Washington, Moscow, Beijing, and Addis Ababa, and partner organizations in 140 countries. The Addis Ababa office works in partnership with the Gülen-affiliated Nejashi Ethio-Turkish International Schools. (See chapter 4). TUSKON's primary goal is to expand foreign markets for Turkish businesses and make the Turkish economy a more important part of the global economy.[2]

TUSKON works to achieve its goals by organizing "trade bridges" in Istanbul and other Turkish cities where foreign importers can interact with Turkish manufacturers, sending Turkish business delegations to other countries, hosting foreign business delegations, and organizing seminars and workshops in foreign

---

1 *www.tuskonus.org/tuskon.php?c=1&s=&e=396*.
2 *www.tuskoneu.org/about-tuskon/*.

countries. Africa has been an important part of this program from the beginning.[3]

For the purpose of this analysis, the key question is the extent to which TUSKON is part of the Gülen Movement. There is considerable evidence of a strong link between TUSKON and *Hizmet*. Hakan Yavuz asserts that pro-Gülen business persons established TUSKON.[4] The president and chairman of TUSKON, Riza Nur Meral, in a 2013 interview subsequently carried on the *Hizmet* website, acknowledged that the Gülen-affiliated schools in Africa are behind Turkey's trade initiatives on the continent.[5] In an earlier comment in 2011, Meral said TUSKON is happy to make use of the network of schools established by the Gülen Movement; there is a clear synergy between the schools and TUSKON. He added that "we benefit from the Gülen network. They are a source of support and contacts with markets and government officials in countries where Turkey often may have no official links. In Africa's 53 [now 54] countries, Turkey has 25 [now 35] embassies."[6]

When specifically asked about TUSKON's institutional role in the Movement's organization, a TUSKON representative replied that we don't say that we are part of *Hizmet*. We have our own board and interests. There is no direct partnership, but many of our members are Gülen Movement people and they feel that as an organization TUSKON is a Movement institution.[7]

A *Hizmet*-affiliated Turkish entrepreneur in the printing business in Istanbul explained that he is considering opening a printing business in Senegal because the market for advertising flyers and commercial products is almost untapped. Senegal would be his first investment outside Turkey. When asked why Senegal, a country he knew little about, rather than some other part of the world, he responded that Europe's falling economy makes it less attractive. In addition, Senegal has a strong presence of Gülen-affiliated schools that underscores Turkish interest in the country and offers an existing infrastructure for helping to set up a business.[8]

In March 2011, Turkish President Abdullah Gül led a large TUSKON delegation to Ghana and Gabon. At the time, Turkey did not have an embassy

---

3 Author's meeting on 12 January 2013 in Istanbul, Turkey with TUSKON Secretary-General Mustafa Günay.

4 Hakan Yavuz, *Toward an Islamic Enlightenment: The Gülen Movement* (Oxford: Oxford University Press, 2013), 126.

5 Interview in *Rotahaber* (20 February 2013).

6 Wendy Kristianasen, "Turkey's Growing Trade Network," *Le Monde Diplomatique* (May 2011), *http://mondediplo.com/2011/05/09turkeytrade*.

7 Joshua D. Hendrick, *Gülen: The Ambiguous Politics of Market Islam in Turkey and the World* (New York: New York University Press, 2013), 167.

8 Author's meeting on 11 December 2010 in Istanbul, Turkey with Turkish entrepreneur.

in Gabon. As a result, TUSKON networked with teachers at the Gülen-affiliated school in Gabon for help with advance planning and business contacts. The frequent involvement in TUSKON-organized events by President Gül and other senior government officials also underscored the close ties between TUSKON and the government. Meral pointed out that many TUSKON members support financially Gülen-affiliated schools, including those in Gabon. He also defended publicly the transparency of *Hizmet*, emphasizing that it "provides a useful network for TUSKON."[9] Hakan Taşçı, TUSKON's representative in Washington, said that "most of our members admire Gülen."[10]

In 2013, there was a falling out between Fethullah Gülen and the government of Prime Minister Recep Tayyip Erdoğan (see chapter 8). The impact was quickly felt on TUSKON's relationship with the Turkish government. Early in 2014, TUSKON criticized what it called a "systematic campaign of defamation" against it. The TUSKON statement came a few days after a recording of a telephone conversation surfaced in social media in which Gülen and TUSKON Secretary-General Mustafa Günay discussed an oil refinery opportunity in Uganda. The monitored conversation mentioned gifts of pineapples. Government officials and Erdoğan himself subsequently ridiculed Gülen and TUSKON, emphasizing that Turkey will not become a pineapple republic.[11]

TUSKON filed 60 lawsuits, alleging illegal wiretapping of a phone conversation, and won all of them in court. It announced that it will use the money won in the lawsuits to build an orphanage in Uganda.[12]

Relations between TUSKON and the government subsequently worsened. TUSKON Chairman Meral charged that the Erdoğan government was threatening to wipe the confederation "off the market" following critical remarks it made about government policies.[13] Meral added that companies close to *Hizmet* "were contacted by some top government figures—by Erdoğan in person in certain cases—and they received threats to cut relations with the Movement."[14]

TUSKON's website and publications make no reference to the Gülen Movement or *Hizmet*. TUSKON is not formally part of the Gülen Movement

---

9 Ibid.
10 Suzy Hansen, "The Global Imam," *The New Republic* 241, issue 19 (2 December 2010): 11.
11 "TUSKON Says Systematic Campaign of Defamation Under Way, *Today's Zaman* (26 January 2014).
12 "Compensation Used to Develop Uganda," 1 April 2014. www.tuskonus.org.
13 "TUSKON's Fifth Board Meeting," 2 March 2014. www.tuskonus.org. "Erdoğan Gov't Threatened to 'Wipe TUSKON off Market Map," Says Chairman," *Today's Zaman* (28 February 2014).
14 "President Meral Speaks to WSJ," 2 March 2014. www.tuskonus.org.

and some of TUSKON's members have no affiliation with *Hizmet*. TUSKON accepts all reputable companies, irrespective of their interest in, or connection with, the Gülen Movement. Most TUSKON members, however, probably do support one or more *Hizmet* activity. TUSKON is usually on the agenda of visits to Istanbul organized by Gülen-affiliated organizations, and its newspapers, Turkish-language *Zaman* and English-language *Today's Zaman*, accord TUSKON significant coverage. Consequently, it is instructive to review TUSKON's activities in Africa with the knowledge that it has close links to *Hizmet*.

TUSKON's first international event was the Turkish-African Foreign Trade Bridge held in Istanbul in 2006. The event was attended by 500 business persons from 33 African countries, 20 ministers, 40 other officials, and 1,500 Turkish business persons.[15] TUSKON subsequently organized a series of these trade bridges. For example, the seventh Turkey-Africa Trade Bridge in 2011 put 350 African business persons from 54 African countries in touch with 600 Turkish company representatives. TUSKON has expanded the trade bridges to locations outside Istanbul. In 2014, the Turkey-East Africa Trade Bridge took place at Gaziantep in southern Turkey. Some 127 companies from 11 African countries participated with the goal of increasing trade and investment with Turkey.[16]

Together with the London-based Chatham House and Sabanci University's Istanbul Policy Center, TUSKON organized in 2011 a Turkey-Africa seminar that emphasized investment possibilities in Africa. Most of the TUSKON events are not Africa-specific but global in focus. For example, TUSKON's 2013 World Trade Summit hosted 1,343 foreign firms and 800 Turkish companies. African companies were, however, well represented.[17] TUSKON has had some kind of contact with all 54 countries in Africa.[18]

In addition, TUSKON is engaging Africa at the regional level. In 2014, it hosted in Lagos, Nigeria the Economic Community of West African States (ECOWAS)-Turkish Export Expo. The exposition showcased textiles, machinery, furniture, cosmetics, and household materials from Turkey, Ghana, and Nigeria. The goal was to attract representation from all 15 ECOWAS members.[19] TUSKON subsequently hosted a trade bridge for 110 business persons from

---

15 TUSKON, Pamphlet titled *TurkiyeAfrica2 Foreign Trade Bridge* (May 2007).
16 "Turkey-East Africa Trade Bridge," 2 March 2014. *www.tuskonus.org*.
17 "TUSKON's 'African Wave' Makes Splash at Istanbul Summit," *Today's Zaman* (26 November 2013).
18 Author's meeting on 12 January 2013 in Istanbul, Turkey with TUSKON Secretary-General Mustafa Günay.
19 "Turkish Entrepreneurs Develop Business Ties at ECOWAS-Turkish Expo," *Vanguard* (7 March 2014). *www.ecowasexpo.com*.

eight West African countries in Turkey's western province of Bursa, where they met with 300 local business persons.[20]

One of TUSKON's most innovative efforts occurred in 2014 when it hosted the first Turkey-Africa Women Entrepreneurs Trade Bridge in Istanbul. More than 350 women from 39 African countries participated in the conference. TUSKON and the African Union Commission signed a memorandum of understanding, which created a strategic partnership for focusing on trade between female entrepreneurs in Africa and their counterparts in Turkey. TUSKON Chairman Meral commented at the conference that from the standpoint of economic growth, Africa is the most promising continent in the world. The second Turkey-Africa Women Entrepreneurs Trade Bridge is expected to be held in Africa.[21]

TUSKON is optimistic about the future of Turkish business in Africa. While Turkey faces strong competition from countries such as China, TUSKON believes the quality of Turkish products is generally higher and its companies are willing to take risks. Secretary General Mustafa Günay believes Turkish companies are especially well equipped to compete in the areas of clean energy, environment, service sector, and water supply.[22]

There are two similar Turkish business organizations that have no relationship with the Gülen Movement. One is the Independent Industrialists' and Businessmen's Association (MÜSIAD), a non-profit group of 5,560 members representing more than 15,000 companies. It has an international network with affiliates in 47 countries, including most countries in North Africa and in a few Sub-Saharan African countries.[23] The second group is the Turkish Industry and Business Association (TÜSIAD), a civil society organization with 600 members from the industrial and service sectors representing some 3,500 companies. It has five offices outside Turkey, but none in Africa.[24]

Businessmen sympathetic to Gülen established TUSKON to compete with the more Islamic-oriented MÜSIAD and the secularist TÜSIAD. TUSKON has emerged as the most activist business organization in Turkey and has become especially engaged in Africa.[25]

---

20 "Turkey-West Africa Trade Bridge," 1 May 2014. *www.tuskonus.org*.

21 Teguest Yilma, "African, Turkish Women Entrepreneurs Merge at B2B Conference," *Capital* (11 March 2014).

22 Author's meeting on 12 January 2013 in Istanbul with Günay.

23 *www.mir-initiative.com/updates/speakers/omer-cihad-vardan/about-musiad/*.

24 *www.tusiad.org*

25 Yavuz, 126.

TUSKON's Bilateral Activity in Africa

TUSKON's bilateral engagements in Africa are especially impressive. Since 2005, the organization has crisscrossed the continent. The following analysis offers a sampling of what it does. In North Africa, Morocco has been a recent focus of attention. In 2010, TUSKON coordinated a Turkey-Morocco Trade Forum in Casablanca and hosted a Turkey-Morocco Trade Bridge in Istanbul in 2011. Some 200 Turkish and 80 Moroccan business persons attended the event. In 2013, TUSKON sent 44 Turkish members from the textile sector to meet in Morocco with 310 counterparts at the Turkey-Morocco Textile Business Forum. This resulted in $30 million of textile deals.[26]

Not surprisingly, TUSKON has paid special attention in West Africa to Nigeria, the largest economy in Africa. In 2011, it organized in Istanbul the Turkey-Nigeria Trade and Investment Forum attended by Nigerian President Goodluck Jonathan and Turkey's Deputy Prime Minister Cemil Çiçek. In 2013, in an effort to reach out to more countries, TUSKON organized the Economic Community of West Africa States' Summit in Lagos, Nigeria that promoted investment in member states. The same year, 150 Nigerian entrepreneurs attended the TUSKON-hosted Turkey-Nigeria Trade and Investment Forum in Istanbul with 350 Turkish business representatives.

Ghana, another strong economic performer in Africa, was also a top priority for TUSKON, which in 2010 hosted an investment seminar in Istanbul for a 20-member Ghanaian delegation. In 2011, President Abdullah Gül headed a business forum organized by TUSKON in Accra. Most members of the Turkish delegation were interested in trade and investment. In 2013, Ghanaian President John Dramani Mahama attended TUSKON's Turkey-Ghana Trade and Investment Forum in Istanbul.

TUSKON does not neglect the smaller economies in West Africa. In 2012, Gabon's President Ali Bongo Ondimba participated in TUSKON's Turkey-Gabon Trade and Investment Forum in Istanbul. Benin's President Thomas Yayi Boni has been a frequent TUSKON visitor. In 2012, he addressed a TUSKON trade and investment forum in Istanbul. He returned in April 2013 on a business trip when he made another visit to TUSKON. In December 2013, he returned again to meet with President Gül and attend a TUSKON Turkey-Benin Trade and Investment Forum.

In 2010, President Gül led a TUSKON delegation of 130 Turkish business persons to the Democratic Republic of the Congo (DRC) and Cameroon. While in the DRC, Gül visited the Gülen-affiliated school. In 2013, Cameroon

---

26 "TUSKON Sees $30 mln in Morocco Textile Contracts," *Today's Zaman* (6 March 2013).

President Paul Biya presided over the TUSKON Cameroon-Turkey Economic Forum in Istanbul. In 2012, Rwandan President Paul Kagame addressed the Turkey-Rwanda Trade and Investment Forum in Istanbul. The following year, Rwanda's trade minister led a delegation of business persons to a similar event.

Turning to East Africa, TUSKON organized in 2011 a trade forum in Addis Ababa, Ethiopia attended by four members of the Turkish parliament, 84 Turkish business persons, and 600 Ethiopian and 400 Tanzanian business representatives. In 2014, speaking at the Ethiopia-Turkey Trade and Investment Forum in Addis Ababa, Ethiopian Prime Minister Hailemariam Desalegn commented that TUSKON has contributed positively to Ethiopia's development. TUSKON signed a commercial partnership with the Ethiopia Chamber of Commerce and a bilateral commercial agreement that will provide advantages for TUSKON members with both Ethiopia and the 22-member Common Market for Eastern and Southern Africa.

In 2011, Zanzibar's President Ali Mohamed Shein led a delegation of 20 business persons to participate in TUSKON's Seminar on Investment Opportunities in Zanzibar held in Istanbul. In 2010, TUSKON organized a Turkey-Uganda Business Forum in Kampala. Turkish Minister of State Bülent Arinç and 40 business persons from Turkey participated. In 2012, Ugandan President Yoweri Museveni received a TUSKON delegation in Kampala.

In 2012, TUSKON even held a Somalia-Turkey Business Forum in conflict-plagued Mogadishu. Somali President Hassan Sheikh Mohamud subsequently participated in a Turkey-Somalia Trade and Investment Forum in Istanbul. TUSKON has extended its activities to Africa's Indian Ocean island nations. In 2013, the foreign minister of Mauritius led a business delegation to Istanbul where the Mauritius Chamber of Commerce and Industry signed a framework agreement on trade and economic cooperation with TUSKON.

South Africa, which represents Africa's second largest economy, has received special attention from TUSKON. In 2010, Turkey's minister of foreign trade led a 100-strong TUSKON delegation to participate in the Turkey-South Africa Business Forum. In 2012, Turkey's minister of economy headed another delegation to the Turkey-South Africa Business Forum in Johannesburg. The meeting took place at a large complex built by a Turkish friend of Fethullah Gülen. More than 20 members of this TUSKON delegation continued to Mozambique, where they participated in the International Trade Fair of Maputo. In 2012, 95 TUSKON member companies took part in the International Fair of Luanda in Angola.

South Africa's former premier of the Western Cape and subsequent ambassador to the United States, Ebrahim Rasool, had a cordial relationship with the Gülen Movement during his time as premier. He commented perceptively that the Movement fully understands the importance of Turkish businesses and investments operating through TUSKON.[27]

Local Turkish Business Associations

Almost every African country that has a significant representation of Turkish businesses also has a locally organized Turkish business organization. As in the case of TUSKON, these are not formal Gülen organizations and members are not required to support *Hizmet* programs, but they tend to have a preponderance of members who do contribute to *Hizmet*. There is a particularly close link between these business organizations and the *Hizmet* schools, which are often initiated by the Turkish business community.[28] (See chapter 4.) In addition, the schools attract the children of wealthier and higher status African parents, often business persons and senior civil servants. This provides the Turkish business community with a useful group of professional contacts and the prospect of hiring quality African graduates who have learned some Turkish. The schools also offer an education with which expatriate Turks are often comfortable for their own children.

These business associations that tend to be closely associated with Gülen-affiliated schools and that support *Hizmet* activities are not to be confused with the 17 Turkish business councils in Africa such as the Turkish-Sudanese Business Council or the Turkish-Kenyan Business Council. The business councils come under Turkey's Foreign Economic Relations Board (DEiK), a private sector institution for developing Turkey's economic, commercial, industrial, and financial relations with foreign countries.[29] In a few African countries, Sudan for example, the business council seems to be more active than the *Hizmet*-related businessmen's association. In others, the *Hizmet*-related businessmen's association is more visible. In any event, there are more *Hizmet*-linked organizations than DEiK business councils in Africa.

There is no public, central registry of the Gülen-affiliated associations of business persons in Africa, although TUSKON probably maintains a listing of all the associations in Africa with which it partners. Like so much of global *Hizmet* activity, the associations develop informally and operate independently. Some have informative websites, when you can identify them; others have marginally useful websites or none at all. Some countries, Liberia for example, do not have any Gulen-affiliated business associations. Sudan, which has a large number of Turkish companies in the country, does not appear to have an active Gülen-

---

27 Author's meeting on 19 October 2012 in Washington, D.C. with Ebrahim Rasool.

28 David Tittensor, *The House of Service: The Gülen Movement and Islam's Third Way* (New York: Oxford University Press), pp. 164.

29 *http://en.diek.org.tr/*.

affiliated business association. The best way to obtain information about the associations is to visit the cities where they are located and speak with someone who is involved with the organization or is knowledgeable about the Turkish community. There are also occasional useful articles in the media concerning the presence and activities of the associations.

Perhaps the most sophisticated local Turkish business organization in Africa is the South African Turkish Business Association (SATBA). A non-profit organization founded in 2007, it has a professional website, board of directors, and executive committee.[30] It partners with TUSKON and is responsible for a wide range of Turkish commercial activity in South Africa, where there is about $1 billion in Turkish investment. It works closely with South African chambers of commerce and has some 50 Turkish companies and 20 South African companies as members. The annual membership fee is $2,000. SATBA also promotes Turkish companies in nearby Mozambique, Angola, Zambia, Zimbabwe, Angola, Madagascar, Namibia, and the DRC.[31]

According to its secretary general, SATBA is open to members holding any political or religious beliefs. While many members support *Hizmet* projects in South Africa, some do not and a few don't even know about Fethullah Gülen. Many SATBA members have been, however, strong supporters of Gülen-affiliated schools in South Africa, the activities in South Africa of the *Hizmet* humanitarian organization *Kimse Yok Mu*, and the *Hizmet* dialogue centers.[32]

Tanzania offers a contrast to the more developed Turkish business organization in South Africa. The Association of Businessmen and Industrialists of Tanzania and Turkey (ABITAT) was founded in 2012 by six Gülen-affiliated Turkish companies and some 200 Tanzanian companies. It serves as the official representative of TUSKON in Tanzania and is "selective" in its membership, which presumably means member companies must follow Gülen business principles based on honesty.[33]

In 2012, members of the Turkish business community in Kenya associated with *Hizmet* established the Turkish-Kenya Businessmen's Association. Some 15 of the 35 Turkish companies in Kenya and about 100 Kenyan companies initially expressed interest in joining. While getting established, it had good cooperation from the Turkish embassy in Nairobi and benefited significantly

---

30 *http://satba.org/*

31 Author's meeting on 25 August 2012 in Johannesburg, South Africa with SATBA Secretary General Serkan Ergul.

32 Ibid.

33 *www.abitat.org/*. Author's meeting on 28 August 2012 in Dar es Salaam, Tanzania, with Ibrahim Biçakçi, director of the Gülen-affiliated Feza Schools and board member of ABITAT.

from contacts the *Hizmet* schools arranged with students' parents who were also engaged in business. As is often the case in Africa, the *Hizmet* schools preceded the establishment of the business organization; the two organizations then worked hand-in-hand.[34] Turkish business persons help fund the Gülen-affiliated Light Academy schools and organize meetings between Turkish and Kenyan businessmen at school facilities.[35]

Hussein Parmaksiz, previously a teacher in Siberia, came to Ethiopia unfamiliar with Gülen-affiliated schools. After arrival in Ethiopia, he stayed in the school's guest house and realized that school personnel were an important source of information and advice for getting involved in business. After drawing on their assistance, he concluded that the relationship could be mutually beneficial and became an active supporter of the schools. In 2011, seven large Turkish investors in textiles asked Parmaksiz to set up the Ethio-Turkish Entrepreneur Association. He began with 25 Turkish companies, not all of which are linked to Gülen, and no Ethiopian companies. Some of the Turkish business members meet periodically at the Gülen-affiliated school dormitory to view videos about Fethullah Gülen's values and then discuss them afterwards. Other Gülen-affiliated business persons established in 2012 the Rainbow Charity Association that provides free food packages and meat during Ramadan. Estimates of Turkish investment in Ethiopia range from $500 million to $1.6 billion.[36]

Yavuz Zemheri spent ten years as a teacher and principal with Gülen-affiliated schools before establishing in 2011 the Association of Businessmen and Investors of Nigeria and Turkey (ABINAT) in Abuja and an informal branch office in Lagos. The association arranges trips for Nigerian business persons to Turkey and Turkish investors to Nigeria. It works with the Nigerian Association of Chambers of Commerce, Industry, Mines and Agriculture, as well as the Nigerian Investment Promotion Commission. As of late 2012, ABINAT had 50 Nigerian companies as members but no Turkish companies. Most but not all of the Nigerian companies follow Gülen business principles. ABINAT set as an early goal the establishment of a skills center to teach computer science, carpentry, electrical work, plumbing, and auto mechanics. The intention is to send 40 Nigerian students to Turkey for a year of training and then have them return to teach. Nigerian state governments sponsor the students and a Turkish construction company provided a $25 million gift for building the center as part of a $400 million contract that it had won.[37]

---

34 Author's meeting on 1 September 2012 in Nairobi, Kenya with Ahmet Ökmen, secretary general of the Turkish-Kenya Businessmen Association.

35 Gabrielle Angey, "Turkish Islam in Africa: A Study of the Gülen Movement in Kenya," *Mambo!* French Institute for Research in Africa 10, no. 3 (May 2012): 2–3.

36 Author's meeting on 4 September 2012 in Addis Ababa, Ethiopia with Hussein Parmaksiz.

37 Author's meeting on 31 December 2012 in Abuja, Nigeria with Yavuz Zemheri,

Tuncay Tas, also a former teacher at a Gülen-affiliated school, is the general secretary of ABINAT. Tas emphasized that ABINAT partners with TUSKON, for example organizing in 2013 the Economic Community of West African States-Turkish Exports Products Fair in Lagos. Although supporters of the Gülen Movement were instrumental in organizing the event, it was open to all interested companies. He underscored ABINAT's assistance to visiting Turkish business delegations. Turkey's Ministry of Commerce funded 70 percent of the visiting Turkish delegations and TUSKON issued the invitations. According to Tas, more than 1,000 Turkish textile companies were selling their products in Nigeria.[38]

The Ghana-Turkey Cooperation and Development Association (TUDEC) was founded in 2011 by a group of business, educational, medical, and legal professionals to facilitate educational, cultural, commercial, and humanitarian ties between Ghana and Turkey. While the major objective is to support education and scholarships for Ghanaians, TUDEC also establishes partnerships among businesses in both countries, implements small development projects, and encourages cultural exchanges. It works closely with TUSKON and organizes visits to Turkey for Ghanaian business persons and trips to Ghana by Turkish business representatives from around the world.[39] The president of TUDEC, Yusuf Temizkan, is also the general manager of the Gülen-affiliated Galaxy International School.[40] As a result, the *Hizmet* school-business connection is especially close in Ghana.

Moving to Senegal, Sami Karasin is the coordinator of the Senegalese-Turkish Businessmen's Association known as *Kardeslik* (Turkish for brotherhood). He has a long background with Gülen-affiliated businessmen's groups, including the Izmir Businessmen's Association. He responded to an advertisement for the opening in Dakar. *Kardeslik* was established in 2006 and now has 20 member companies, ten from Turkey and ten from Senegal. It arranges exchange visits, helps organize trade fairs, and coordinates with TUSKON. *Kardeslik* sponsors Senegalese students at the Gülen-affiliated dormitories in Senegal. Karasin also serves as the honorary and unpaid coordinator in Senegal and nearby countries for *Hizmet's* humanitarian arm, *Kimse Yok Mu*.[41]

One of the projects encouraged by *Kardeslik* was the construction by a Turkish investor in Dakar of a $3.5 million eye hospital complete with operating

---

president of ABINAT. "Nigerian, Turkish Businessmen to Strengthen Ties for Increased Productivity," *National Mirror* (15 April 2013).

38 Author's meeting on 2 January 2013 in Lagos, Nigeria with Tuncay Tas.

39 *www.tudec.org*.

40 William Yaw Owusu, "Ghana-Turkey Friendship Deepens," *Daily Guide* (16 December 2013).

41 Author's meeting on 8 January 2013 in Dakar, Senegal with Sami Karasin.

theaters and clinics. *Hizmet* persuaded Cavit Kalkan, who had ties with *Hizmet* in Ankara, to make the investment. It opened in 2013 with 30 staff, including eight from Turkey. The goal is to turn a profit, although as the most advanced eye hospital in Senegal it also fills an important void. In addition, Kalkan owns an electronic company in Dakar that has not yet been successful because of strong competition from Chinese and French products. Kalkan is chairman of *Kardeslik*, on the board of the *Hizmet* schools, and volunteers for *Kimse Yok Mu* activities.[42]

The Turkish-Moroccan Businessmen's Association (TÜFIAD) began in 2006 in Casablanca and now has four branch offices. TÜFIAD has five full-time and five part-time staff according to its secretary general, Gökmen Ertas. It has 500 members, 90 percent of whom are Moroccan and 10 percent Turkish. The association emphasizes Moroccan membership. Some 15 of the 65 Turkish business persons living in Morocco have *Hizmet* connections and are members. An estimated 50 percent of the Moroccan members have some interest in *Hizmet*. It partners with TUSKON. It arranges on average each month visits to Morocco by three groups (10 to 25 persons) of Turkish business persons and sends one group of about 20 Moroccan business persons each month to Turkey. It maintains close ties with the Turkish embassy in Rabat.[43]

One of the more unusual Gülen-affiliated companies in Morocco is Cebelitarik, a for-profit travel agency established in 2007 and based in Casablanca that runs, among other investments, a guest house in Casablanca for *Hizmet* visitors. It provides travel services to both *Hizmet* and non-*Hizmet* customers between Morocco and Turkey and Europe. Its manager, Selahattin Senal, says that it receives a share of the Moroccan student traffic headed for Turkey under *Hizmet* programs because of its competitive prices.[44]

The business associations described above suggest how these groups began, are organized, their purpose, and their links to *Hizmet*. While it is not possible to identify all of them in Africa based on visits to seven countries, press reports suggest there are many more. For example, the Turkish-Egyptian Businessmen's Association cooperates with TUSKON, although the extent of its ties to *Hizmet* is not clear.[45] In 2012, TUSKON played a role in the creation of the Somali-Turkish Businessmen's Association in Mogadishu.[46]

---

42 Author's meeting on 8 January 2013 in Dakar, Senegal with Cavit Kalkan.

43 Author's meeting on 5 January 2013 in Rabat, Morocco with Gökmen Ertas. http://tufiad.org.

44 Author's meeting on 5 January 2013 in Casablanca, Morocco with Selahattin Senal.

45 "Turkey-Egypt Business Forum Improves Trade Ties," *New Europe Online* (18 April 2010).

46 "Somalia Sees Recovery with New Turkish Investments," *Today's Zaman* (8 April 2012).

In 2010, another TUSKON-related organization, the Uganda-Turkey Business Association (UTBA), began operations in Kampala.[47] The Turkish and Cameroonian Businessmen's Association (TURCABA) cooperated with TUSKON, the Turkish embassy, and other organizations in preparing the 2010 visit of President Gül to Cameroon.[48] There is a Mali-Turkish Businessmen's Association in Bamako where there are an estimated 200 Turkish investors.[49] Next-door neighbor Niger has the Association Nigéro-Turque d'Entrepreneurs (ANTE), which encourages interaction between Nigerien and Turkish business persons. The president of ANTE also serves as the director general of the Gülen-affiliated school in Niger.[50] The Association of Mozambican and Turkish Merchants (MOZTÜRK) worked with TUSKON in organizing the 2012 Mozambique-Turkey Trade and Investment Forum in Maputo.[51]

The Turkish business presence in Africa is arguably the most important aspect of the Turkey-Africa relationship and those business persons affiliated with *Hizmet* are a significant part of the effort. The close linkages between Gülen-affiliated business persons and the numerous *Hizmet* programs, especially the schools, in so many African countries make this relationship especially unique.

Hizmet Islamic Banking

A Gülen-inspired financial institution, Bank Asya, began operations in Turkey in 1996 when 346 business persons bought shares to form a bank that does not charge interest and operates on Sharia principles in that it does not finance gambling or alcohol. Many of the 346 investors were indifferent to Gülen business principles but still saw a good investment opportunity. Some of the Gülen-affiliated schools and hospitals in Turkey finance their projects through Bank Asya, which must work hard for their business, as other banks are highly competitive.[52]

Many of the original Bank Asya shareholders subsequently sold their holdings; the bank is now public and owned by numerous individuals and companies who have purchased shares. It is impossible to determine how many shareholders

---

47 *www.utba.or.ug/*.

48 *http://turcaba.org/*.

49 "Turkey Should Support ECOWAS as Key Player to Resolve Mali Crisis," *Today's Zaman* (27 January 2013).

50 "Complexe Scolaire Bedir de Niamey: Symbole d'une Presence Turque Reussie au Niger," *http://lesahel.org*.

51 Eva Meignen, "Mozambique-Turkey Trade and Investment Forum," *AllAfrica.com* (10 October 2012).

52 Helen Rose Ebaugh, *The Gülen Movement: A Sociological Analysis of a Civic Movement Rooted in Moderate Islam* (Heidelberg: Springer, 2010), 84–86.

today are inspired by Gülen. The chairman of the board of Bank Asya is a wealthy business person who owns several companies in the shipping industry and is a supporter of Gülen-affiliated projects. There are, however, no official ties between Gülen and the board of directors of the bank, the bank officers, or clients of the bank. The bank's president contends that although it remains an Islamic bank, Gülen's ideas do not have a significant impact on bank operations.[53] A frequent contributor to the Gülen paper, *Today's Zaman*, wrote that Bank Asya is "owned mostly by movement sympathizers."[54] Until problems with the AKP, Bank Asya was Turkey's largest of four participation banks, with about 30 percent of the market share.[55]

About half of 55 Gülen Movement leaders interviewed in Turkey responded there is no question that Bank Asya is the Movement's bank. Others explained there is no "organic connection" between the bank and the Movement.[56] The fact is that Bank Asya is the primary underwriter of all TUSKON trade summits as well as all conferences organized by the Movement's Journalists and Writers Foundation and Turkish Language Olympics. It is also a major advertiser in the Movement's *Zaman* and *Today's Zaman* papers.[57]

The end of cooperation in 2013 between the Gülen Movement and the Erdoğan government resulted in a campaign by Erdoğan to shut down Bank Asya, thirteenth largest among Turkey's 51 banks. Bank Asya shares lost 40 percent of their value in September 2014 and it lost 25 percent of deposits during the second quarter. Disagreement over this campaign within the Turkish government and a counter offensive by Movement supporters briefly righted Bank Asya.[58] Early in 2015, however, Turkey's banking regulator seized control of the bank and appointed a new chief executive officer and board of directors. This was quite a change from 19 years ago when Erdoğan, then mayor of Istanbul, was present alongside Gülen at the opening of the bank.[59]

In 2009, Bank Asya acquired for $15 million a 40 percent stake in the Senegal-based Tamweel Africa Holding (TAH) SA owned by the Islamic

---

53 Ibid.

54 Oguzhan Tekin, "Coming Soon: Operation against the Hizmet Movement," *Today's Zaman* (1 January 2014).

55 Ebaugh, 84.

56 Hendrick, 168.

57 Ibid., 170.

58 "Erdoğan Steps Up Attacks on Bank Aysa, Raising Risks of Banking Crisis," *Today's Zaman* (18 September 2014). Giorgio Buttironi, "The Dispute over Bank Aysa: What Lies Ahead in Erdoğan's Turkey?" *Today's Zaman* (15 October 2014).

59 Isobel Finkel and Ercan Ersoy, "Turkey Takes Over Bank Aysa as Erdoğan Exerts Power," *Bloomberg* (3 February 2015).

Corporation for the Development of the Private Sector (ICD), a subsidiary of the Islamic Development Bank (IDB). Bank Asya, the IDB, and the ICD all promote Islamic finance in Africa. ICD created TAH as a structure with legal ownership and management rights of the affiliates. It brought in Bank Asya to strengthen the technical expertise of the affiliates, enhance their product offerings, and extend the network. The mission of TAH was to promote Islamic finance in Africa by building modern, Sharia-compliant banks.[60]

TAH held about 69 percent of the shares of the Islamic Bank of Senegal, which was capitalized at 15 million Euros and almost 100 percent of the Islamic Bank of Mauritania, which was capitalized at 17.5 million Euros. TAH held just over 50 percent of the shares of the Islamic Bank of Niger and the Islamic Bank of Guinea; each one was capitalized at about 8 million Euros. These four banks had six branches when TAH bought shares in them; by early 2013, there were 25 branches. There was also very little profit when TAH bought shares in the banks. By 2012, the bank in Senegal made $10 million, the bank in Niger $2.5 million, the bank in Guinea $300,000, and the bank in Mauritania, the newest one, broke even.[61]

The banks charged no interest but partnered with the borrower and shared the profit or loss. If the borrower made a profit, the bank made a profit; if the borrower lost money, the bank lost money. The bank had an incentive for the loan to be successful. When a person borrowed money for a house, the borrower rented the house from the bank until the loan was paid off. The banks did not transfer loans from one bank to another and they were permitted to provide loans to non-Muslims.[62]

TAH had every intention of increasing its operations in Africa. It expected to open in Benin and had intended to open in Mali until conflict there cancelled the plan. It was looking at the possibility of expanding into Algeria, Tunisia, Libya, Ghana, and Kenya.[63] Like Bank Asya, TAH was not a Gülen institution, but it was clearly inspired by his banking principles and it had close ties in Africa to *Hizmet* activities. Islamic banking in Africa linked to *Hizmet* was at an early stage of development and accounted for a minuscule amount of available capital. It was, nevertheless, one more indication of the impact that Fethullah Gülen was having, in this case almost unbeknown to borrowers, in Africa. The problems experienced by Bank Asya in Turkey forced TAH to sell its 40 percent stake to ICD early in 2015.[64]

---

60 *www.ta-holding.com/*.

61 Ibid. Author's meeting on 8 January 2013 in Dakar, Senegal with Ihsan Basyigit, consultant to the general manager of Tamweel Africa Holding SA.

62 Author's meeting with Ihsan Basyigit.

63 Ibid.

64 "Bank Asya Sold Subsidiaries Worth TL 568M within Past Year," *Daily Sabah* (13

Concluding Thoughts

Gülen Movement members of the business community in Turkey and Turkish business persons residing in Africa are central to the success of *Hizmet*. The key organization in Turkey is TUSKON; independent Gülen-affiliated business associations in Africa are also essential to *Hizmet* efforts. Without the financial support of this sector and the volunteer efforts of its members, it would be nearly impossible for *Hizmet* to carry out its activities in Africa.

While the motivation of the business persons is mostly altruistic, many of them have developed a symbiotic relationship with *Hizmet* institutions in Africa. As explained in this chapter, the business community funds initial construction of the schools, which, in turn, provide useful information and contacts to the Turkish business community. Business persons largely fund *Hizmet* dialogue centers (chapter 5) and humanitarian programs (chapter 6), which assist the business community more indirectly. While there is nothing sinister about this relationship, *Hizmet* institutions collectively offer important advantages for many members of the Turkish business community as it expands its engagement in Africa.

The Gülen Movement's initiative to engage in Islamic banking in Africa accomplished two goals. It underscored the Movement's support for the concept of Islamic banking, and in those areas where it was established, it offered a service to Turkish business persons generally and *Hizmet* supporters in particular. The Movement's Islamic banking activities were available in only a small number of countries when Bank Asya ran into problems with the Turkish government.

January 2015).

CHAPTER 4

GÜLEN-AFFILIATED SCHOOLS AND RELATED PROGRAMS

The most visible component of the Gülen Movement in Africa is the Gülen-affiliated school. As of 2014, there were more than 100 primary, middle, and secondary schools, or some combination thereof, in 35 of Africa's 54 countries; the number continues to increase. Ironically, few Africans have ever heard of Fethullah Gülen and most students attending *Hizmet* or Gülen-affiliated schools and their parents are also unfamiliar with Gülen's philosophy and do not associate the schools with him. Those Africans who are aware of the schools usually refer to them as Turkish schools. By design, the schools never contain Gülen's name or *Hizmet*.

There seems to be no central registry of the schools; each school or school system operates independently. At the same time, they have certain characteristics in common. They emphasize ethics and strict discipline, the general themes of Gülen's philosophy, interaction with parents, and the teaching of science, math, and technology. They operate according to the laws of the country where they are located and teach a curriculum approved by the host government. Organizationally, they are usually established as NGOs, foundations, trusts, or companies, depending on local laws. While there is no centralized control of the schools, there is an informal network whereby *Hizmet* administrators and teachers often move from one school to another—within a country, from one African country to another, and from one continent to another.[1]

Gülen's Educational Philosophy

The concept of *Hizmet* schools followed Gülen's belief that secular schools were unable to remove themselves from the prejudices of modernist ideology. Islamic *madrasas* largely ignored technology and scientific thought, and consequently lacked flexibility and the ability to break with the past and offer

---

1 Based on author's visits to about three dozen schools in Africa.

an education needed for the modern world. The Turkish Sufi-oriented *tekkes*, which were suppressed during the rule of Mustafa Kemal Atatürk, traditionally emphasized the development of spiritual values. In any event, they lost their dynamism. The challenge, as Gülen saw it, was to find a system in which these different pedagogical concepts could overcome the tendency to regard each other as rivals so they could work together and learn from each other.[2]

Gülen's answer was the *Hizmet* school. He wanted a program that offered a well-rounded education that included respect for human rights and tolerance toward others. He believed that religious scholars should have a sound background in the sciences and scientists should be exposed to religious and spiritual values. In this manner, he hoped the conflict between religion and science would end, or at least its absurdity would be acknowledged. As a result, *Hizmet* schools are well known for their scientific fairs, mathematics Olympiads, and high-technology equipment. The school's goal is the integration of the study of science with character development, social awareness, and active spirituality, in which Gülen includes ethics, tolerance, openness, pluralism, psychological health, and logic.[3]

For Gülen, human needs and the solving of human problems are part of education. This requires committed teachers who are inspired to serve humanity rather than themselves. Teachers should provide wisdom and moral guidance by serving as examples rather than preaching values. Teachers should demonstrate that they can coexist comfortably with all people, irrespective of their class, ethnic, cultural, or religious affiliation. They are expected to avoid smoking, alcohol, and drugs. Gülen believes a good school protects students from bad habits and teaches concepts for this life and the next. Students should not only learn theoretical information but should be prepared for adulthood.[4]

The Movement's first schools started in Turkey in the early 1980s. Following the breakup of the Soviet Union, Gülen's disciples began to open schools in the

---

2   Thomas Michel, "Identifying Our Partners in Dialogue," paper given on 28 May 2012 at the African Union headquarters in Addis Ababa on the occasion of a conference on "Establishing and Sustaining the Culture of Coexistence and Mutual Understanding," 2–3.

3   Thomas Michel, "The Thinking behind the Gülen-Inspired Schools," paper given on 19 October 2010 in Jakarta, Indonesia, on the occasion of a Gülen conference, 3–4. Adama Diop, "Fethullah Gülen's Idea on the Relationship between Science and Religion," paper delivered at the same conference. Muhammed Çetin, *Hizmet: Questions and Answers on the Gülen Movement* (New York: Blue Dome Press, 2012), 23–28.

4   Ahmet Orhan Polat, "The Key Factors behind the Success of Gülen-Inspired Schools," paper given on 19 October 2010 in Jakarta, Indonesia on the occasion of a Gülen conference. For a good discussion of this topic as it is practiced in the *Hizmet* schools in Kenya, see Gabrielle Angey, "Turkish Islam in Africa: A Study of the Gülen Movement in Kenya," *Mambo!* 10, no. 3 (May 2012), 2.

predominantly Muslim parts of Russia, the Balkans, and newly independent nations in the Caucasus and Central Asia. They subsequently began appearing in largely Muslim inhabited regions of China, Southeast Asia, Africa, and even North America and Europe.[5]

Naming *Hizmet* Schools

There are distinct patterns in the naming of the *Hizmet* schools and other Gülen-affiliated institutions, which are strong indicators of their link to the Gülen Movement.[6] The overwhelming majority of Turkish-financed schools in Africa are part of the *Hizmet* network. The government of Turkey and Turkish NGOs, including the Gülen Movement's *Kimse Yok Mu*, have financed the construction of several schools that were subsequently turned over to African governments for staffing and operation.

The galaxy theme is popular, as in the Feza (Space) Schools in Tanzania, Star International in South Africa, and Galaxy International School in Ghana. Light is another common theme, as in the Light Academy in Kenya, International Light College in Madagascar, Şafak (Dawn) École Internationale Turco-Congolaise in the Democratic Republic of the Congo, and Groupe Scolaire Şafak in Côte d'Ivoire. A number of the schools in Africa use a water theme. The Fountain Educational Trust operates the Nizamiye Schools in South Africa and the Nile Foundation runs the *Hizmet* schools in Somalia. The only *Hizmet* university in Africa is the Nigerian Turkish Nile University.[7]

The horizon theme is common in Africa, as in L'École Internationale Ufuk (Horizon)-Benin, Le Collège Horizon International in Burkina Faso, and Horizon School in Zambia. Friendship and hope appear frequently as themes. There is Colégio Esperança International (Hope International College) in Angola, Hope Kids Academy in Rwanda, and Amity International College in Cameroon. Strength is occasionally a theme, as in Nejashi (King) Ethio-Turkish International Schools and Collège de la Citadelle in Guinea. Ottoman heroes sometimes provide school names in Africa. In Morocco, there are the Mohammed Al Fatih Schools and in Senegal the Yavuz Selim Schools. Some of the school names contain no hint of words that connect them to Gülen, but make reference to Turkey. Examples include École Internationale Turco Gabonaise, International Libyan Turkish School, Sudanese-Turkish School, and the Nigerian Turkish International College.[8]

---

5 Thomas Michel, "Identifying Our Partners in Dialogue," 4.
6 "Name Symbolism in the Gülen Movement," *http://turkishinvitations.weebly.com.*
7 See appendix for list of schools in Africa.
8 Ibid.

Hizmet Schools Come to Africa

Hizmet schools in Africa only have a 20-year history. The first one opened in Tangier, Morocco, in 1994. The first school in Sub-Saharan Africa appeared in Senegal in 1997, followed by schools in Kenya, Tanzania, and Nigeria in 1998. By one count, Africa had 33 *Hizmet* schools by 2001 and 95 by 2010. As of 2011, there were 24,868 African students in the schools, which had a total staff of 2,422 African teachers and 698 Turkish staff.[9]

It is difficult to count the *Hizmet* schools and almost impossible to compare numbers used by different researchers. The appendix in this book attempts to identify all of the schools in Africa as of 2014. The major problem in counting schools concerns the degree to which schools located on the same campus are truly separate. In some cases, boys and girls occupy the same facility but are said to have separate schools. In other cases, the primary, middle, and secondary school are in the same complex and considered to be one school while in other cases they are treated as three schools. This analysis tries to determine if a school has a separate principal and, if so, it is counted as a separate school. If not, the complex is considered as one school. Using this methodology, and acknowledging there is guesswork in several cases, the total number of *Hizmet* primary, middle, secondary, or some combination thereof in Africa as of 2014 was 113. There were an additional eight independent kindergartens and several special teaching centers. The number continues to grow and it often takes months for new schools to come to the attention of the public outside the country where they have been established.

Of the 35 African countries that had *Hizmet* schools in 2014, nearly all of them are predominantly Muslim or have a Muslim population of 10 percent or more. The exceptions are South Africa, Angola, and Equatorial Guinea, which have a *Hizmet* school or schools and a small percentage of Muslims. South Africa is sufficiently populous that even its 3 percent Muslim population is significant. Cape Verde may be another exception, although it is not certain whether it has a *Hizmet* school. Six African countries—Botswana, Republic of the Congo, Lesotho, Namibia, São Tomé and Principe, and Seychelles—have a Muslim minority of 5 percent or less and none has a *Hizmet* school. The fact that they also have tiny Turkish communities may be a more important explanation for the absence of a school. Two Arab countries—Algeria and Tunisia—in North Africa have no *Hizmet* school and Libya only obtained one in 2012. Arab countries seem to be less receptive to the Gülen Movement than non-Arab countries with large Muslim populations, but that is the subject for another study.

---

9   Oğuzhan Tekin, *Turkish Foreign Policy towards Africa: Motivations and Interests 2001–2010*, MA Thesis, Fatih University (June 2012), 73.

Financing of Schools and Links to Turkish Business

The capital for establishing a *Hizmet* school is usually provided by the Turkish business community that is resident or has an interest in a particular African country (see chapter 3). It is rare to find a *Hizmet* school in a country that has a tiny Turkish community or none at all. In a few cases, a single business person puts up the money. In most cases, a group of business representatives raises the funds. Following Turkish tradition, some donations are anonymous. There are often in-kind contributions from local Turkish construction or furniture companies. Occasionally, an African government donates land for the school in order to encourage its construction. Once the school opens, the goal is to cover operational costs by charging fees, which tend to be near the higher end of the scale for private and foreign schools in any particular country. Teacher salaries are modest; it is not unusual for a school to turn a profit. All school administrators commented that profits are ploughed back into capital improvements, school expansion, and/or scholarships for academically gifted students who cannot afford the fees.[10]

There is a return on this investment by Turkish business persons and companies. Turkish nationals sympathetic to the Gülen Movement who have children living with them in an African country have an obvious place to send their children to school. More importantly, the schools tend to attract the sons and daughters of host government officials, local business persons, and other prominent members of society. The schools emphasize the active involvement of parents in the education of their children. This results in a useful system for Turkish business persons who support *Hizmet* activities by expanding their contacts with key Africans in the local community. In many cases, the schools assist in organizing trips to Turkey for both the students and parents.

The Gülen-affiliated TUSKON (chapter 3) also works closely with the schools to increase trade between Turkey and African countries.[11] African ambassadors and business persons, for example, stressed at the TUSKON-organized Turkey-West Africa Trade Bridge at Bursa in 2014 that the *Hizmet* schools were instrumental in helping to develop trade relations between their countries and Turkey.[12]

The importance of the schools in supporting Turkish business interests was

---

10 Author's meetings with several dozen *Hizmet* school administrators and teachers in Africa. Helen Rose Ebaugh, *The Gülen Movement: A Sociological Analysis of a Civic Movement Rooted in Moderate Islam* (Heidelberg: Springer, 2010), 97–101. David Tittensor, *The House of Service: The Gülen Movement and Islam's Third Way* (New York: Oxford University Press, 2014), pp. 152–153.

11 Tekin, 73–74.

12 "Turkish Schools Help to Enhance Trade Relations with Africa," *Today's Zaman* (15 April 2014).

especially significant in the late 1990s and the first ten years of the current century. In many cases, a *Hizmet* school preceded the establishment of a Turkish embassy in African countries. At the beginning of 2009, Turkey had embassies only in the five North African countries, the Democratic Republic of the Congo, Ethiopia, Kenya, Nigeria, Senegal, South Africa, and Sudan. By the end of 2008, there was at least one *Hizmet* school in 27 African countries, well over twice the number of Turkish embassies in Africa and a few countries had multiple schools. In those countries where there was no Turkish embassy, the Turkish business community tended to rely on the schools for guidance and support.

The government of Turkey began a significant expansion of its presence in Africa in 2009 and had 35 embassies by 2014, the same number of countries that had *Hizmet* schools, although not all in the same countries. At the beginning of 2014, *Hizmet* still had schools in eight Sub-Saharan African countries where Turkey did not yet have an embassy. In addition, some Turkish embassies are thinly staffed. Even after the expansion of Turkey's embassies, the schools continued to work closely with the Turkish business community.

Hizmet Schools and Islam

Hizmet schools are sometimes accused of being Islamic *madrasas* in disguise. While there is one *Hizmet* system in South Africa operated by the Fountain Educational Trust that is clearly Islamic in character, even it does not follow the traditional *madrasa* pattern. All *Hizmet* schools teach the national curriculum of the country where they are located. Gülen supporter Muhammed Çetin argued that "no matter where situated, Gülen-inspired schools are not religious but follow secular, state-prescribed curricula and internationally recognized programs subject to state inspection."[13] Bekim Agai, a researcher at the University of Bonn, noted that *Hizmet* schools "do not teach religion, even though faith is a primary motive for their creation. Rather, they stress the teaching of ethics . . . ."[14]

In Africa, there are variations on the degree to which there is any instruction about Islam in *Hizmet* schools. Some schools offer no instruction in Islam or any other religion. The schools in Kenya and Ethiopia are a case in point.[15] In fact, student enrollment in a few schools in Africa is predominantly non-Muslim. Others present the teaching of Islam as an elective during regular teaching hours

---

13 Muhammed Çetin, *The Gülen Movement: Civic Service without Borders* (New York: The Blue Dome Press, 2010), 256.

14 Bekim Agai, "The Gülen Movement's Islamic Ethic of Education," in *Turkish Islam and the Secular State: The Gülen Movement*, ed. Hakan Yavuz and John L. Esposito (Syracuse, NY: Syracuse University Press, 2003), 48–49.

15 Mary Fitzgerald, "Ethiopian Schools Put Turkey on Curriculum," *Irish Times* (1 January 2010). Angey, 2.

or after hours. Salahaldin International School in Cairo teaches an American curriculum in English but offers Qur'anic classes. The school's academic director said the school cares about ethics and moral values but insists it is not an Islamic school.[16] The Sudanese Turkish schools offer the national Islamic curriculum mandated by the ministry of education. They provide instruction about the Qur'an and teach Turkish as one of the languages.[17]

Some African Muslims even complain that the *Hizmet* schools are not sufficiently Islamic.[18] The director general of the Yavuz Selim schools in Senegal commented that Islamic education in the country historically was religious in focus; *Hizmet* was the first to offer a "modern Muslim education."[19]

The *Hizmet* program in Morocco offers what seems in Africa to be a unique arrangement whereby some 100 Turkish university-level girls connected with *Hizmet* study English, French, Arabic, math, Islam, and Arabic literature. In 2013, 33 Turkish girls shared a dormitory in Casablanca with Moroccan girls. The focus is on English; the teachers are Moroccan. For half a day each month, they take part in a study circle or reading camp where they discuss Gülen's philosophy and Islamic topics. Moroccan girls who express an interest are welcome to join the study circle. About ten participated each session. There is a similar program for Turkish boys in Morocco.[20]

The Fountain Educational Trust in South Africa (see appendix) operates three schools that appear to be distinctive from the others operating in Africa. Known as the Nizamiye Schools, according to their website they were inspired by Gülen and they describe themselves as Islamic schools with an Islamic ethos. The language of instruction is English and they follow the South African curriculum. But they incorporate Islamic instruction and Arabic into the curriculum, including memorizing the Qur'an. In 2009, the Trust took responsibility for the failing Islamic Al-Azhar Institute in Port Elizabeth, which is now called the Nizamiye Al-Azhar Institute. The Nizamiye School in Midrand, between Johannesburg and Pretoria, is attached to the largest mosque in the southern hemisphere, which was built by a follower of Gülen.[21]

---

16 Noha El-Hennawy, "Egypt: The Turks Are Coming!" *Los Angeles Times* (19 May 2009).

17 Information provided by Marie Besancon on 24 September 2014 based on a visit to the Sudanese Turkish schools in Khartoum.

18 Author's meeting on 31 December 2012 in Abuja, Nigeria with Hamid Bobboyi, director of the Centre for Regional Integration and Development.

19 Author's meeting on 8 January 2013 in Dakar, Senegal with Adnan Demir.

20 Author's meeting on 6 January 2013 in Casablanca with five Turkish girls who were part of the program.

21 Author's meeting on 26 August 2012 in Midrand, South Africa with Isak Turan, a

African Testimonials for *Hizmet* Schools

Gülen-affiliated media like to highlight the praise given to *Hizmet* schools by senior African officials, and it has been significant. South African President Jacob Zuma, during a meeting with executives of one of the *Hizmet* school systems in the country, assured his government's continuing support for the schools, in spite of alleged pressure from the Turkish government in 2014 to shut them down. During a joint press conference in Ankara with President Abdullah Gül, Kenyan President Uhuru Kenyatta pointedly expressed appreciation for the *Hizmet* schools in Kenya.[22]

Ugandan President Yoweri Museveni, during a meeting with a TUSKON delegation in Kampala, praised the schools, adding that he closely follows their success.[23] In an interview with the Cihan News Agency, Uganda's Minister of State for Foreign Affairs said the schools paved the way for Turkey to reach out to Africa.[24] Zambian President Rupiah Banda opened the Horizon Primary and High School in Lusaka. He said on that occasion Zambia would collaborate with the schools in pursuit of quality education.[25] Former Ethiopian Prime Minister Meles Zenawi, during a meeting with backers of *Hizmet* schools, said he has only heard positive comments about the schools.[26]

During a meeting in Istanbul organized by TUSKON, Gabon's President Ali Bongo Ondimba urged Turkish volunteers to open more schools in his country.[27] At another session in Istanbul organized by TUSKON, Ghana's President John Mahama also asked Turkish investors to open more schools in Ghana.[28] Guinea's minister of state for foreign affairs, during a meeting in Istanbul with the Turkish foreign minister, said "the Guinean people are fond of the Turkish schools in

---

teacher at the Nizamiye School. *www.nizamiyeschool.co.za*.

22 "South African, Kenyan Leaders Show Support for Turkish Schools," *Today's Zaman* (8 April 2014).

23 "President Museveni Supports Turkey's Reaching Out to Africa," *Today's Zaman* (29 April 2012).

24 "Ugandan FA Minister: Turkish Schools Paved Way for Turkey to Reach Out to Africa," 4 August 2013, *http://hizmetnews.com*.

25 "President of Zambia Mr. Rupiah Banda Thanks Turkish Investors in Education," 24 May 2011, *www.hizmetnews.com*.

26 "Turkish School Officials Visit Ethiopian Prime Minister," *Today's Zaman* (15 April 2011).

27 "Gabon President: My Country Is Very Satisfied with Turkish School," *Today's Zaman* (20 July 2012).

28 "Turkish Schools Helped Start Trade with Turkey," *Zaman* (24 January 2013).

our country."²⁹ Mali's former president and its current ministers of culture and higher education and research have all praised the *Hizmet* schools. The two ministers were especially appreciative that the schools remained open following the outbreak of civil war in Mali.³⁰ Addressing a group of visiting Turkish business persons, Burkina Faso's cabinet director jokingly suggested Turkey should not waste its money establishing an embassy in Ouagadougou because it already had a Turkish school.³¹ The Tunisian minister of culture, during a symposium in the country that included Gülen's philosophy, said Tunisia could benefit from the example of *Hizmet*.³²

Travelling through Africa, the author also encountered numerous complimentary remarks about the schools from prominent Africans. In South Africa, Deputy Minister for Economic Development Hlengiwe Mkhize spoke highly of the *Hizmet* schools.³³ Former Tanzanian President Ali Hassan Mwinyi participated in the process that led to the opening of *Hizmet* schools. He said they are now among the best in Tanzania.³⁴

Mahdi Ahmed Ali, special advisor to Ethiopia's deputy prime minister, said the *Hizmet* system is one of the best in the country.³⁵ Ethiopian Minister of Federal Affairs Shiferaw Teklemariam and Minister of Defense Siraj Fegessa also spoke highly of the *Hizmet* schools.³⁶ Current Ethiopian President and former ambassador to Turkey Mulatu Teshome is knowledgeable about the *Hizmet* schools in Ethiopia and said they provide a "very satisfactory quality of education."³⁷

The executive secretary of Nigeria's National Mosque Complex, Ibrahim A. Jega, said his country had witnessed the positive impact of *Hizmet* educational

---

29 "Guinean MFA: Our People Fond of Turkish Schools," Cihan News Agency (8 April 2013).

30 "President of Mali Praises Success of Turkish Schools," *Today's Zaman* (3 July 2009). Mali Education Minister Lauds Teachers in Nation's Turkish Schools," *Sunday's Zaman* (28 July 2013). "Malian Minister Praises Turkish Schools for Persevering through War," *Today's Zaman* (15 April 2013).

31 "Turkish School like a Diplomatic Mission in Burkina Faso," *Today's Zaman* (24 November 2009).

32 "We Need the Hizmet Movement Example in Tunisia," 15 May 2013, www.hizmetmovement.blogspot.com.

33 Author's meeting on 26 August 2012 in Pretoria.

34 Author's meeting on 28 August 2012 in Dar es Salaam.

35 Author's meeting on 4 September 2012 in Addis Ababa.

36 Author's separate meetings on 5 September 2012 in Addis Ababa.

37 Author's meeting on 21 May 2014 in Addis Ababa.

facilities.[38] A presidential adviser on religious affairs in Senegal praised the *Hizmet* schools there.[39] The chairman and managing director of the daily paper *Le Quotidien* commented that many Senegalese want to send their children to *Hizmet* schools.[40] The head of Senegal's private school division in the Ministry of Primary and Secondary Education singled out the positive value of *Hizmet*'s emphasis on the teaching of ethics.[41] A prominent medical doctor in Morocco praised *Hizmet*'s effort to accord equal treatment to everyone who participates in the system.[42]

Criticism of *Hizmet* Schools

Although *Hizmet* schools in Africa have been widely praised, they do not escape criticism. Based on visits to many of the schools, the most common criticism from parents and students in Anglophone countries was that Turkish teachers are not native speakers of English and sometimes do not have an adequate command of the language. The language of instruction is English in Anglophone countries and there are few native English-speaking teachers on the staff.

A common complaint expressed by Turkish administrators was the inability to hire sufficient numbers of highly qualified local teachers, especially in countries where the *Hizmet* salary structure does not compare favorably with the salaries paid by other private schools. Well over half of the staff, including teachers, is non-Turkish in almost all of the schools.

While *Hizmet* administrators and teachers were reluctant to acknowledge individual problems in their schools other than occasional disciplinary issues, more serious allegations appear periodically, particularly on the Internet. Some of the allegations turn out to be bogus. In 2010, for example, a number of African boys at a "school" in Polokwane, South Africa, alleged they were sexually abused by three teachers. An Internet account claimed the school was part of the *Hizmet* system. The facility was actually run by another part of the Turkish community engaged in tutoring the Qur'an.

One of the strangest cases occurred in 2003, when Ibrahim Itabaci, the executive director of *Hizmet*'s Bedir International High School, was one of five persons turned over by the government of Malawi to the U.S. Central Intelligence Agency (CIA) and whisked out of the country for interrogation. The United States initially alleged that the five suspects were channeling money to al-Qaeda. After

---

38 Author's meeting on 31 December 2012 in Abuja.
39 Author's meeting on 7 January 2013 in Dakar with Thierno Ka.
40 Author's meeting on 7 January 2013 in Dakar with Madiambal Diagne.
41 Author's meeting on 8 January 2013 in Dakar with Malick Soumare.
42 Author's meeting on 5 January 2013 in Casablanca with K.G. Snoussi.

33 days of detention in several African countries, all five were released. The CIA did not acknowledge its role in the affair.[43] The president of Malawi reportedly apologized to the families of the detainees for his government's involvement in this episode.[44]

Other issues have come to light that may constitute legitimate concerns. In 2011, a group of locally hired teachers at the Yavuz Selim schools in Senegal publicly denounced low salaries and late payment, exploitation of teachers, and even a "form of racism and nepotism."[45] The author was not able to verify the validity of the allegations. In 2005, following a fire at a *Hizmet* school in Kaduna, Nigeria, another Internet account complained of inadequate fire protection measures, high fees, inadequate laboratories, and crowded dormitory rooms.[46] These issues were not raised by students or parents during the author's visit to Kaduna in 2013.

In 2011, Cameroonian teachers at *Hizmet*'s Amity International College in Ngaoundéré went on strike over the payment of allowances and late payment of salaries.[47] In 2014, a coalition of Somali groups complained that the Nile Foundation, which runs the *Hizmet* schools in Somalia, led them to believe it would provide free education because the government had provided at no cost two facilities for operating the schools.[48] All *Hizmet* schools in Africa charge fees; this was probably a misunderstanding.

One parent who had a child in a *Hizmet* primary school in Kenya withdrew the student because the parent did not believe the curriculum was sufficiently Islamic in content. In addition, most of the students were Somalis who had a poor command of English. Many of them came from homes with single mothers, who had little time for or interest in the school.[49]

---

43 Jai Banda, Anton Katz, and Annette Hübschle, "Rights versus Justice: Issues around Extradition and Deportation in Transnational Terrorist Cases," *African Security Review* 14, no. 4 (2005), 60–63.

44 Raphael Tenthani, "Muluzi 'Regrets' Terror Arrests," *BBC* (29 July 2003).

45 Fara Michel Dièye, "Colère: De Grave Accusations contre le Groupe Scolaire Yavuz Selim de Dakar," 10 May 2011, *www.rewmi.com*.

46 Kenny Ashaka, "Turkish International College on Fire," 18 December 2005, *http://nm.onlinenigeria.com*.

47 "Une Grève Paralyse Amity International College," *Mutations* (Yaounde), 2 December 2011.

48 "Complaint of Turkish Nile Organization to Somali Government," 27 March 2014, *www.yoobsannews.com*.

49 Author's meeting on 3 September 2012 in Nairobi, Kenya with parent.

The AKP-led Government and *Hizmet* Schools

The government of Turkey has never provided funding for *Hizmet* schools in Africa (or presumably anywhere else). The relationship between the government and the schools has undergone a dramatic change over the past dozen years and is still evolving. There is a track record of senior Turkish officials visiting *Hizmet* schools during trips to Africa and praising them. In 2008, then Foreign Minister Ali Babacan visited one of the Yavuz Selim high schools in Dakar, Senegal.[50] President Abdullah Gül, during a 2009 visit to Kenya, went to the Light Academy in Nairobi, where he commented that the school will strengthen relations between the two countries.[51] During a trip to the Democratic Republic of the Congo in 2010, Gül visited the *Hizmet* school, where he congratulated the Turkish business persons for contributing to its construction.[52] He continued to Cameroon, where he went to Amity International College and said the *Hizmet* schools "will make Cameroon's future bright."[53]

Deputy Prime Minister Bülent Arinç, during a visit in 2010 to the Light Academy in Uganda, said the *Hizmet* schools arrived in the country before the embassy. He added that everyone from the prime minister to the man in the street says these schools provide excellent education and that Turkey has left an indelible mark on the country thanks to the schools.[54] Also in 2010, Foreign Trade Minister Zafer Çağlayan, while on a trip to Nigeria and Ghana, visited the Galaxy International School in Accra and one of the Nigerian Turkish International Colleges in Abuja. He said wherever he goes, African ministers ask for more Turkish schools.[55] In 2011, President Gül went to Ghana and Gabon, where he visited *Hizmet* schools in both countries. During a visit to South Africa the same year, then Foreign Minister Ahmet Davutoğlu visited one of the schools in Cape Town.[56] Early in 2013, the wife of then Prime Minister Erdoğan visited the Bedir School in Niger while the prime minister conducted other business.[57] Speaking in Istanbul early in 2013, Deputy Foreign Minister

---

50 "Foreign Minister Babacan Visits Turkish School in Dakar," *Today's Zaman* (13 March 2008).
51 "Turkey Boosts Business Ties with Africa," *Today's Zaman* (23 February 2009).
52 "Gül Visits Şafak Turkish School in Kinshasa," 15 March 2010, *www.tccb.gov.tr*.
53 "Cameroonian Students Perform Song for Gül," *Today's Zaman* (19 March 2010).
54 "Turkish Schools Key to Success in Africa," *Today's Zaman* (3 December 2010).
55 "Every Minister I Met in Africa Asked for More Schools," *Sunday's Zaman* (15 December 2010).
56 "Turkey, South Africa Agree to Waive Visas, Draft Free Trade Agreement," *Today's Zaman* (21 August 2011).
57 "Erdoğan Honored with State Medal in Niger," 9 January 2013, *www.ebrunews.com*.

Naci Koru commented he had visited Turkish schools in Africa with President Gül and was moved on each occasion.[58]

As the breakup between the AKP and Gülen Movement became apparent in 2013, it resulted in a complete reversal of the AKP's position on *Hizmet* schools. The first tangible impact in Africa came in March 2014, when the government of Turkey reportedly pressured the government of Gambia to close the Yavuz Selim Anatolian School, which shut down abruptly.[59] The Gülen Movement charged that Turkey offered Gambia a $300 million loan in exchange for closing the school, and contended that Foreign Minister Ahmet Davutoğlu instructed Turkish embassies to urge host governments to shut down the *Hizmet* schools. Davutoğlu initially denied there was such an instruction but subsequently said the reason behind the request was that a number of foreign civil society representatives had sent letters to officials in their countries complaining about the schools.[60]

The Gülen Movement, aided by TUSKON, is fighting back and mobilizing African support for the *Hizmet* schools. TUSKON secretary general Rizanur Meral praised the schools for their role in increasing Turkish trade, adding that efforts by the government of Turkey to shut them down only damage its global reputation.[61] Former Minister of Industry and Trade Ali Coşkun and former Education Minister Vehbi Dinçerler have called on Erdoğan to abandon the effort to shut down the Turkish schools located overseas.[62]

The AKP attack against the *Hizmet* schools rose to a new level early in 2015 when Deputy Prime Minister Arinç announced that the government will take measures against the schools in foreign countries. He said Turkey is not legally permitted to take direct measures against the schools, but suggested the government may buy the schools so they can continue to operate without influence from *Hizmet*. On a visit to Ethiopia at the beginning of 2015, President Erdoğan is quoted as saying "we have been talking about the status of these schools and saying they should be closed down."[63]

---

58 "Turkish Schools Leading Actors in Foreign Policy," *Zaman* (17 March 2013).

59 Ralph Boulton and Orhan Coskun, "Erdoğan Takes Battle with Enemies beyond Turkish Frontiers," *Reuters* (3 April 2014).

60 "Gov't Bid to Close Turkish Schools Draws Ire," *Today's Zaman* (9 April 2014).

61 "Turkish Schools Help to Enhance Trade Relations with Africa," *Today's Zaman* (15 April 2014).

62 "Ex-ministers Call on Gov't to Abandon Efforts to Shut Down Turkish Schools," *Today's Zaman* (10 April 2014). See also "Opposition, Diplomats Slam Gov't Attempt to Shut Down Turkish Schools," *Today's Zaman* (7 April 2014).

63 "Deputy PM Says Turkish Schools Abroad May Be Bought by Turkish State," *Today's Zaman* (27 January 2015).

Malian President Ibrahim Boubacar Keita visited Turkey in February 2015. At a joint press conference in Ankara, Erdoğan said Keita pledged "to take precautions" against the activities of the Gülen Movement. Erdoğan vowed to replace the *Hizmet* schools with new ones supported by Turkey's National Education Ministry.[64] There was no indication, however, that Keita agreed to close the *Hizmet* schools in Mali. In Africa so far, Gambia is the only country to have complied with Turkey's request and other African governments will not likely take kindly to this tactic.

Hizmet Education in Five African Countries

In order to appreciate the variety of the *Hizmet* system, it is instructive to look in greater detail at how it operates in several African countries. The countries selected are among those that the author visited. All of them have some of the oldest and largest *Hizmet* programs in Africa. They are South Africa, Kenya, Nigeria, Senegal, and Morocco. They represent a diversity of geography, language, religion, and culture.

South Africa

The *Hizmet* educational program in South Africa has two distinctive features. First, it is the earliest and largest *Hizmet* effort in an African country where such a small percentage of the population—about 3 percent—is Muslim. Second, it appears to be the only country in Africa that has two completely separate *Hizmet* umbrella organizations—the Horizon Educational Trust established in 1998 that operates the non-Islamic schools and the Fountain Educational Trust established in 2000 that runs the Islamic Nizamiye schools. Under South African law, educational trusts are non-profits. If they make a profit, they must reinvest it in the organization. Trusts cannot pay dividends. The South African government also transfers a small subsidy to educational trusts. The *Hizmet* schools have contributed to the arrival of some 200 Turkish students who are studying English or attending South African universities.[65]

---

64 "Mali Pledges to Stand by Turkish Gov't over Gülen Schools Issue," *Daily Sabah* (4 February 2015).

65 For an analysis of the Horizon Educational Trust teaching theory, see Yasien Mohamed, "The Educational Theory of Fethullah Gülen and Its Practice in South Africa," in *Muslim World in Transition: Contributions of the Gülen Movement*, ed. Ihsan Yilmaz (London: Leeds Metropolitan University Press, 2007), 552–571 and "A Gülen-inspired School in South Africa" in *The Muslim World and Politics in Transition: Creative Contributions of the Gülen Movement*," ed. Greg Barton, Paul Weller, and Ihsan Yilmaz (London: Bloomsbury, 2013), pp. 180–191. See also *www.horizonedu.co.za* and *http://nizamiyeschool-pe.co.za*.

The Horizon Educational Trust operates a primary through high school in Cape Town, a high school in Johannesburg, a boys high school and a primary/girls high school in Durban, and a primary school in Pretoria. In 1999, the first school—Star International in Cape Town—opened. All of the schools teach the national curriculum, have small classes of about 20 students, and modest enrollment numbers. The school in Cape Town in 2012 had 24 pre-primary, 230 coed primary, and 129 boys only high school students. Between 40 and 45 percent of the high school students received some scholarship assistance. The fees are high compared to public schools but less than some private schools. Since 2010, the enrollment has been about 45 percent Muslim, 45 percent Christian, and 10 percent Hindu. It was previously divided equally between Muslims and Christians.[66]

One-third of the teachers in the high school are Turkish and the others South African. Turks generally teach the science, math, and Turkish language courses. Nearly all of the primary school teachers are South African. The school turns students away; there is a waiting list with 25–30 percent more students. The school is popular with parents because it is drug and alcohol free; these are serious problems in public schools. The school emphasizes universal ethical values and tries to include parents in the teaching program.[67]

The Horizon International High School in Johannesburg draws about 80 percent of its 225 students from Soweto, one of the poorest areas in the city. About 45 percent of the students live in a school dormitory; the others make it to class on their own. The average class size is 24. The teaching staff is 50 percent Turkish and 50 percent South African. The operational costs are covered 80 percent by school fees, 10 percent by South African government subsidy, and the remainder by donations. In spite of the difficulties, the teaching staff makes a serious effort to keep in contact with the parents who live in Soweto. In 2012, there were 1,000 applicants for grade 8; the school accepted 75. The school loses as many as 30 of the original class by grade 12. For those who stay, however, usually 100 percent pass matriculation, i.e. meet the minimum university entrance requirements. About 80 percent of the graduates continue in a university. The school graduated 15 students in 2004; 70 percent subsequently graduated from a university.[68]

In addition to the Horizon Educational Trust schools cited above and those in Durban and Pretoria (see appendix), the Trust has operated since 2010 a tutorial

---

66 Author's visit to Star International School in Cape Town and meeting on 23 August 2012 with Mahmut Ozer, deputy principal of the school.

67 Ibid.

68 Author's meeting on 26 August 2012 in Johannesburg with Yavuz Aydin, educational director for Horizon Educational Trust, and Nicholas Bixa, who grew up in Soweto, received a full *Hizmet* scholarship and graduated from Horizon International High School, and then returned there to teach biology after getting a university degree.

center in Polokwane. After school hours and on Saturdays, it prepares about 200 students each year for examinations in mathematics and the physical sciences.[69]

The Horizon Educational Trust was also instrumental in helping the *Hizmet* community in Zambia set up a Horizon School in 2011. The government of Zambia provided the land for the school and covered 50 percent of the construction costs. Once the school became operational, the Horizon Educational Trust in South Africa turned it over to a separate Horizon Education Trust in Zambia.[70]

The Fountain Educational Trust was established only for Muslim students and, although it teaches the national curriculum, has a distinct Islamic flavor, including Arabic and Islamic studies. Its first attempt was a primary school in Cape Town that closed in 2003 after two or three years. The students were offered positions in one of the Horizon Educational Trust schools, but all of them opted for one of the other Islamic schools in South Africa. The Fountain Educational Trust retained its separate status in order to deal with this situation, which in Africa seems unique to South Africa. The geographical location of the schools is critical. If they do not have dormitories, they usually attract students from the neighborhood where they are located. Some of the Islamic communities in South Africa are highly conservative and not comfortable with the Horizon Educational Trust schools.[71]

The Fountain Educational Trust now operates three Nizamiye schools in South Africa: a primary through high school in Johannesburg, the former Islamic Al-Azhar Institute, and now a primary through high school in Port Elizabeth, and the newest one at Midrand. The school in Midrand opened in 2012 and began with grades 1–2 and 8–9. It will add new grades each year until it offers classes in all primary and secondary grades. The high school is boys only; as of 2013, 20 were there on scholarship. It is attached to the largest mosque in the southern hemisphere and includes a clinic and shopping area. It is designed for a total of 850 students. The language of instruction is English. Most of the students in Nizamiye schools are Asian; there are few Turks. About 70 percent of the teachers are South African and 30 percent Turkish. Three of the teachers are Christian.[72]

Kenya

A small group of Turkish business persons and teachers in Kenya, supported by funding from Turkish business persons from Antalya province in Turkey,

---

69 Author's meeting on 26 August 2012 in Johannesburg with Aydin Inal, executive director of the Turquoise Harmony Institute. See also *www.horizonedu.co.za*.

70 Ibid.

71 Ibid.

72 Author's visit on 26 August 2014 to the school at Midrand and meeting with Isak Turan, teacher at the school.

established in 1997 the Omeriye Foundation. It subsequently expanded its activities and became known as the Omeriye Educational Foundation and Medical Charitable Trust. It is responsible for all of the Light Academy schools in Kenya. In 1998, the boy's secondary school opened in Nairobi with only 25 students. In 2001, it was followed by a boys secondary school and a combination coed primary and girls secondary school in Mombasa. In 2002, the Foundation opened a primary school in Nairobi based on the Cambridge system and the following year another primary school in Nairobi based on the Kenya system. In 2007, it added a girls secondary school in Nairobi. In 2012, a kindergarten in Nairobi began operations, as did in 2014 a coed primary school and boys secondary school in Malindi along Kenya's northern coast. English is the language of instruction for all schools.[73]

Kenya is a predominantly Christian country with a Muslim minority of about 10 percent concentrated along the coast and in the Somali-inhabited northeastern part of the country. In 2012, the boys secondary school (grades 8 through 13) in Nairobi had 400 students, about 75 percent Christian and 25 percent Muslim. Some 20 percent of the students were from outside Nairobi and about 60 percent lived in a school dormitory. A few were foreign students. About 30 percent were on scholarship. The school offers Turkish, French, and Swahili, but not Arabic. The school consistently ranks in the top ten in Kenya.[74]

In 2012, the girls secondary school (grades 8 through 11) in Nairobi had 135 students, about 70 percent Muslim and 30 percent Christian, with 30 students living in a dormitory. The Cambridge system primary school had 200 students divided equally between Muslims and Christians. The most recent school in Malindi is part of a larger *Hizmet* project. It includes a 24-bed hospital staffed primarily with Kenyan doctors and three or four from Turkey. Each day it distributes cooked food to about 2,000 poor Kenyans. *Kimse Yok Mu* (see chapter 6) is a partner in the project.[75]

In 2012, the primary school in Nairobi that operates on the Kenya system had 120 students, about 90 percent Muslim (almost entirely Somalis) and 10 percent Christian. It was once about half Muslim and half Christian; the

---

73 For a study of the Light Academy schools as of 2008, see Mehmet Kalyoncu, "Gülen-inspired Schools in East Africa: Secular Alternative in Kenya and Pragmatist Approach to Development in Uganda," paper presented to a conference on "Islam in the Age of Global Challenges: Alternative Perspectives of the Gülen Movement" at Georgetown University, Washington, D.C., 14–15 November 2008. See also www.lightacademy.ac.ke.

74 Author's meeting on 30 August 2012 in Nairobi with Bilal Karaduman, director general of the Light Academies, and 31 August 2014 visit to the boys secondary school and meeting with the headmaster.

75 Author's meeting with Karaduman.

headmaster would like to return to a more balanced religious mix. It offers only two or three scholarships. It has 13 teachers, four from Turkey and the rest Kenyan, all but one of whom is Christian. The school offers Swahili and Turkish, but not Somali.[76]

The coed primary and girls secondary school in Mombasa had about 370 students in 2012. The students were divided about equally between Muslims and other religions, mostly Christian. About 40 percent of the students were in the Cambridge program. Some 10 percent of the primary students had scholarships, but there were none for the secondary school. There were 12 Turkish and 28 Kenyan teachers. There is no boarding for girls in secondary school and only about 10 percent of the primary students were in school housing. There were 28 Kenyan ethnic groups or foreign nationalities represented in the school. The school offers Turkish, French, and Swahili. The parents of most students were business persons and a few government officials. Almost all of the primary school graduates continue to the Light Academy secondary schools. The headmaster said the school receives strong support from the Kenyan government.[77]

In 2012, the boys secondary school in Mombasa had 95 students in the Cambridge program and 140 in the last four years of the Kenyan program. In the Kenyan system, 55 percent of the students were Muslim and 45 percent Christian. In the Cambridge system, 60 percent were Muslim and 40 percent Christian. Fees are in the midrange for top international schools. There are no scholarships for the Cambridge system; 30 percent of the students have scholarships in the Kenyan system. Most of the students in the Kenyan program lived in a dormitory, while only 30 in the Cambridge system did so. There were 29 teachers in the combined system; 13 were from Turkey. An estimated 80 to 85 percent of the graduates continue to a university, only 5 to 10 percent to universities in Turkey.[78]

A survey of 50 students, 25 graduates, and 25 parents of Light Academy students in Nairobi, Kenya, underscores the fact that Fethullah Gülen is not well known, even among those who benefit from the *Hizmet* program. Of

---

[76] Author's visit to primary school and meeting on 31 August 2012 in Nairobi with Murat Erturk, school headmaster.

[77] Author's visit to school in Mombasa and meeting on 2 September 2012 with Mustafa Genç, school headmaster. An American couple with the Catholic Maryknoll organization in Mombasa put their two children in the school after rejecting the local Catholic school because classes were too large and another private school because the fees were too high. The Light Academy was also willing to add Swahili instruction to the Cambridge program.

[78] Author's visit to school in Mombasa and meeting on 2 September 2012 with Cenal Yavas, principal, Sakiir Cavus, deputy headmaster, and Ahmed Altindis, in charge of the Cambridge program.

the respondents, 60 were Christian and 40 were Muslim. Just over a quarter of the Christians were aware of Gülen, while less than three-quarters of the Muslims knew about him. Although Gülen's writings are widely available in the schools, 64 percent of the respondents did not believe that he had any influence in the school.[79]

The same survey looked at perceptions of the Light Academy as a Muslim or secular school. Some Muslims considered it was a Muslim school because the practice of Islam is permitted and its Turkish administrators are Sunni Muslims. On the other hand, many Muslims did not perceive it as a Muslim school because Islamic subjects are not taught. A majority of the respondents considered the Light Academy a secular school. The survey also determined that 86 percent of the students and graduates respect one another's faith and said they feel respected in return.[80]

Hizmet schools have had varying degrees of success in establishing active alumni networks. It usually requires at least one faculty member who takes a serious interest in an alumni association. Kenya not only has that, but has the advantage of being an older and larger program. The Kenyan alumni effort was not very active until 2011, when an eight-year *Hizmet* veteran in Mombasa, Ismail Küçük, was brought to Nairobi to strengthen the Light Academy Schools Alumni Association. As of 2012, the Association identified about 500 alumni from Nairobi and 250 from Mombasa and had contacted 358 of them. The Association brought parents into the organization and arranged trips for some of them to visit Turkey. It began to link students and parents more closely with the Turkish business community. The Association made a special effort to identify university scholarships, especially, but not exclusively, in Turkey. It urged members of the Association to volunteer time to *Kimse Yok Mu* activities. Since 2011, the Association has held weekly meetings for groups of 10–15 members and meetings involving 200–250 members every three months.[81]

David Mwangi graduated from the Light Academy with a class of 25 in 2001. He is an active member of the Alumni Association and says he is in contact by social media with all 25 members of his graduating class, most of whom are in business although there are a few lawyers, bankers, and accountants. After graduation, he went to Turkey for one year of university education but found it too expensive and transferred back to Kenya, where he received a BA in marketing and subsequently an MA in project management from a business

---

79 Fatih Akdogan, *Gülen-Inspired Schools and Their Contribution to Christian-Muslim Relations in Nairobi, Kenya*. MA thesis, St. Paul's University, Limuru, Kenya (July 2012), 39–40. In her brief study of the Light Academy schools in Kenya, Angey makes essentially the same point, 4.

80 Akdogan, 48–52.

81 Author's meeting on 31 August 2012 in Nairobi with Ismail Küçük.

school in Europe. Mwangi subsequently took over his father's insurance business. He says the Alumni Association has been good for his business.[82]

Nigeria

The largest *Hizmet* education operation in all of Africa is in Nigeria. It includes 17 primary or secondary schools, all known as Nigerian Turkish International Colleges (NTIC), and the only university in Africa. There are four schools in Abuja, the capital, three in Kaduna, three in Lagos, the commercial capital, three in Kano, three in Yobe State, and one in Ogun State. The university is in Abuja. (See appendix.) First SURAT Group Ltd. is a for-profit holding company that controls four *Hizmet* companies dealing with education, a hospital, and tourism. The NTIC schools and university are part of the holding company and run by SURAT Educational Institutions Ltd. under an agreement with the government of Nigeria. Any profit is put back into the schools in the form of scholarships and capital improvements.[83]

In 2012, the NTIC schools enrolled about 4,200 students and employed 130 teachers and 150 support staff. The students represented 191 ethnic groups.[84] The parents of most of the students are professionals, business persons, or civil servants because they can afford the fees. For example, four of former Nigerian President Umaru Musa YarAdua's children attended NTIC schools.

The four schools in Abuja are located on a 13-acre campus and include a girls secondary, boys secondary, coed secondary, and coed nursery/primary school. Some Muslims want boys and girls separated at the secondary school level, hence the different options.

The three schools in Kaduna in predominantly Muslim northern Nigeria were established in 2007 and include a boys secondary, girls secondary, and coed primary. As of 2013, the boy's secondary school had 305 students and 215 graduates. The girls secondary school had 215 students and about 150 graduates as of 2013. The enrollment at both schools was about 95 percent Muslim and 5 percent Christian. The two schools had 42 Nigerian and 17 Turkish staff. Nearly all of the graduates went on to a university.[85]

---

82 Author's meeting on 31 August 2012 in Nairobi with David Mwangi.

83 Author's meeting on 30 December 2012 in Abuja, Nigeria with Hikmet Coban, chairman of First SURAT Group Ltd. See also *www.nticnigeria.com*.

84 Hasan Aydin and Stephen K. Lafer, "Promoting Multicultural Harmony in Nigeria: The Gülen-Inspired Schools," in *The Gülen Hizmet Movement and Its Transnational Activities*, ed. Sophia Pandya and Nancy Gallagher (Boca Raton, FL: BrownWalker Press, 2012), 199.

85 Visit to schools and author's meeting on 1 January 2013 in Kaduna with Mahmut Fesli, NTIC principal.

The nursery/primary school had 150 students, 19 Nigerian teachers, and three Turkish teachers as of 2013. The goal is to expand to two schools and 400 students. The students are almost entirely Muslim but the teachers are evenly divided between Muslims and Christians, including a Christian vice principal.[86]

The three schools in Kano in northern Nigeria include a boys secondary, girls secondary, and coed nursery/primary. The NTIC also operates three schools—a boys secondary (boarding), girls secondary (boarding), and boys secondary (day only)—in Yobe State in northeastern Nigeria.[87]

The population in Kaduna is about 65 percent Muslim and 35 percent Christian. While Muslims and Christians generally live together in peace, there has been some Muslim/Christian conflict that resulted in a larger Nigerian military presence. As of 2013, neither these problems nor Boko Haram terrorist attacks had impacted the NTIC schools in Kaduna or the schools in Yobe State, which has seen more violent Boko Haram activity. The NTIC schools are not perceived as working against Islam even though they accept Christians. They also enforce strong discipline, which is welcomed by conservative communities in northern Nigeria.[88]

The boys and girls secondary school in Lagos opened in 2000 as a coed school but subsequently subdivided into separate boys and girls schools located on the same campus in separate buildings. At the beginning of 2013, the boys school had about 200 students and the girls school about 150. They shared a staff of 30 Nigerian and 10 Turkish teachers. Both are boarding schools and both are about equally divided between Muslim and Christian students.[89]

The nursery/primary school in Lagos opened in 2008 and had 63 students as of early 2013. It had 10 Nigerian and two Turkish teachers. There were no boarding facilities. About 60 percent of the students were Muslim and 40 percent Christian. Most of the parents were engineers or business persons, and a few were civil servants.[90] Ogun State in Nigeria's southwest corner near Lagos is the location of a NTIC secondary school at Isheri.[91]

---

86 Visit to school and author's meeting on 1 January 2013 in Kaduna with Sinan Metin, NTIC principal.

87 Author's meeting on 1 January 2013 in Kaduna with Mehmet Basturk, NTIC managing director.

88 Author's meeting with Fesli.

89 Visit to schools and author's meeting on 2 January 2013 in Lagos with Fatih Keskin, NTIC principal.

90 Visit to school and author's meeting on 2 January 2013 in Lagos with Yunus Emre Dogan, NTIC principal.

91 "We Have Security Challenge—Turkish College Principal," *Daily Independent*, 31 December 2013.

Until 2012, each NTIC school had its own alumni association. There is now a countrywide NTIC Alumni Association that serves as a network for students and parents. It especially tries to find jobs for the graduates with Turkish companies. From 2004 through 2012 there were 2,300 NTIC secondary school graduates. About 1,000 of these graduates went to universities outside Nigeria. The primary destinations were Turkey (400), United Kingdom (230), Dubai (90), United States (83), Malaysia (42), Canada (30), Egypt (25), and Cyprus (18). A significant percentage of these students continued or plan to continue with MA degrees and a small number for PhDs.[92]

In 2010, Hasan Aydin of Yildiz Technical University in Istanbul conducted extensive interviews in Abuja with 22 persons (7 teachers, 8 students, 4 parents, and 3 administrators) associated with the NTIC schools. He published the results of the interviews in three separate papers. He concluded that students in NTIC schools are learning to live peacefully with others. Christians and Muslims in the schools interact harmoniously and respect each other. Three overarching themes result from the *Hizmet* educational process: love, tolerance, and peace. He also concluded that the teachers serve as role models for the students and the focus is on academic achievement. He noted that 99 percent of all the students entering the 12th grade at NTIC secondary schools in Abuja between 2004 and 2009 actually graduated. The interviews identified, however, some concerns about gender separation, English-language weaknesses of Turkish professors, and the reluctance of teachers to allow discussion of contentious Nigerian issues in the classroom.[93]

The Nigerian Turkish Nile University (NTNU) is the only foreign university in Nigeria and one of only three private universities in Abuja. It opened in 2009 and is one of 13 *Hizmet*-affiliated universities in Turkey and 13 in other countries. Enrollment at the beginning of 2013 was 500, with less than 10 percent of the students, mostly girls, from Turkey and nearly all of the rest from Nigeria. Some 30 to 40 percent of entering students graduated from one of the NTIC secondary schools. About 65 percent of the students are Muslim and 35 percent Christian. They are divided equally between male and female. At the beginning of 2013, it had a staff of 240 that included 66 Nigerian teachers and 15 Turkish teachers. English is the language of instruction. Students must also take Turkish or French; most opt for Turkish. About 300 students live in a dormitory on campus. NTNU

---

92 Author's meeting on 31 December 2012 in Abuja with Yavuz Zemheri, Association of Investors and Businessmen of Turkey and Nigeria.

93 Aydin and Lafer, 195–211. Hasan Aydin, "Four Stakeholder's Perception on Educational Effectiveness of Nigerian Turkish International Colleges: A Qualitative Case Study," *Sage Open* (April–June 2013), 1–14. *http://sgo.sagepub.com/content/spsgo/3/2/2158244013489693.full.pdf*. Hasan Aydin, "Educational Reform in Nigeria: The Case of Multicultural Education for Peace, Love, and Tolerance," *South African Journal of Education* 33, no. 1 (2013), 1–19. *www.sajournaleducation.co.za*.

has student exchange programs with Çankiri Karatekin University and the Gülen-affiliated Mevlana University in Turkey. Fees are at the upper range of the cost structure for private universities in Nigeria.[94]

NTNU graduated its first class of 75 BA students in 2013 and second class of 181 BA students in 2014.[95] It has plans for a major expansion that includes the awarding of MA degrees. Its current capacity is 2,000 students. Although NTNU has a broad range of faculties, it plans to add a faculty of medicine and agriculture. It also intends to build a large profit-making shopping mall and hotel. It has an education center attached to the NTIC schools in troubled Yobe State. In spite of the Boko Haram activity, it is moving forward with a three-year diploma program there.[96]

Senegal

In 1997, the first *Hizmet* school in Sub-Saharan Africa opened in Senegal. The Baskent Educational Association, which is responsible for the *Hizmet* schools in Senegal, began with boys secondary and girls secondary schools in Dakar. In 2002, it added a primary school, in 2005 a nursery, and in 2008 another primary school, all in Dakar. In 2009, it opened in Thies, about 60 kilometers east of Dakar, a nursery and a primary/middle school. All of the schools are known as Yavuz Selim, sultan of the Ottoman Empire from 1512 to 1520. By 2012, the seven schools enrolled more than 1,700 students. The primary language of instruction is French, although English is used for science classes and students are required to study Turkish and Spanish. All schools follow Senegal's national curriculum.[97]

Senegal is about 95 percent Muslim, 3 percent Catholic, and 2 percent indigenous religions. Muslim schools in Senegal have traditionally offered education with a religious focus. *Hizmet* is the first program to offer a modern secular education. The Yavuz Selim schools have been popular in part because their classes do not exceed 25 students. Most public schools in Dakar have about 70 students per class. Private Catholic schools in Senegal have a long tradition of quality education. Among the more recent private schools, *Hizmet* schools rank high.[98]

---

94 Author's meeting on 31 December 2012 in Abuja with Hüseyin Sert, Vice Chancellor of NTNU. See also *www.ntnu.edu.ng*.

95 "Celebration as Nigerian Turkish Nile University Sends Out 'First Fruits'," *This Day Live* (7 July 2013). "Nigerian Turkish Nile University Offers Best Education in Nigeria," *Nigeria Spur* (30 July 2014).

96 Author's meeting with Sert.

97 Author's meeting on 8 January 2013 in Dakar with Adnan Demir, general manager of the Yavuz Selim schools. *www.gsyavuzselim.com*.

98 Author's meeting on 8 January 2013 in Dakar with Baba Ousseynou Ly, Inspector of

The Baskent Educational Association is organized as a non-profit organization. The schools were not making a profit until a few years ago. Since the schools have turned a profit, it has been reinvested in the building of two 30-bed dormitories, one for boys and one for girls. The goal is to use future profits for two more dormitories in Dakar for 80 students each and two outside Dakar for 40–50 students each. All profits go into capital projects.[99]

In 2013, the girls secondary school in Dakar had 460 students, of whom 60 were boarding. About 95 percent of the students were Muslim. There were 55 Senegalese staff and 19 Turkish or other nationalities. Most of the graduates went to universities in France, some to Turkey and North America.[100] The boys secondary school had 500 students, of whom 55 were boarding. About 2 percent of the students were Catholic and the remainder Muslim. Each class has a principal professor who the students are encouraged to turn to. Three of the Senegalese teachers were graduates of *Hizmet* schools. Administrators and parents at both schools emphasized that very few students and parents knew much about Fethullah Gülen. Some did see the impact of his views on the way the schools are run, with their emphasis on getting a good science and moral education.[101]

The nursery and two primary schools in Dakar and two schools in Thies are all about 97 percent Muslim with a 2–3 percent Catholic population. In 2013, the nursery had 200 students and a staff of 22 (two Turks and 20 Senegalese). Cascade Primary School had 270 students and a staff of 25 (two Turks and 23 Senegalese) and Ciel Primary School had 280 students and a staff of 25 (two Turks and 23 Senegalese). The nursery in Thies had about 60 students and a staff of 10 (one Turk and nine Senegalese). The primary school in Thies had 220 students and a staff of 25 (five Turks and 20 Senegalese).[102]

The Baskent Educational Association began a new and unique initiative in 2012 when it opened in Dakar the Anadolu Center, which offers courses in English, French, Turkish, computer science, and secretarial services. It opened a second center at Ziguinchor, in a poor area of the Casamance region, where it offers courses at little or no cost. Senegal's prime minister asked the Association to open these centers in each region to help reduce unemployment. The government will provide the land free of charge in most cases. Nearly all

---

the Dakar Academy, Ministry of Education.
99 Author's meeting with Demir.
100 7 January 2013 visit to College Sultan, author's meeting with parents, and meeting with Sedat Kotan, headmaster of College Sultan.
101 Ibid. Author's meeting on 7 January 2013 with the headmaster of College Bosphore.
102 Author's meeting with Demir.

of the employees are Senegalese. Outside Dakar, the centers cost only about $5,000 per month to operate.[103]

Adama Diop, an adviser to the minister of education, helped set up the *Hizmet* program in Senegal. While he is personally a fan of Fethullah Gülen and knows his works well, he said that few Senegalese have any knowledge of Gülen. He described the *Hizmet* schools as a big success, especially their focus on science. He also praised the *Hizmet* philosophy that promotes selflessness and generosity.[104]

Morocco

Hizmet schools have generally not been warmly welcomed in Arab countries. Morocco is an exception and, in fact, Tangier became the location in 1994 of the first *Hizmet* school in Africa. All the schools in Morocco are under the authority of the Mohammed Al Fatih (MAF) Company, which was established in 1992. The name is taken from an Ottoman Empire sultan from 1451 to 1481. All but one of the schools operates from rented property, which is often provided at reduced cost by Moroccans who are sympathetic to the Gülen Movement. The principal language in all except the new international school is Arabic; French is next most important. English is offered, but is less popular. Moroccan regulations do not allow the teaching of Turkish or any other language. In 2013, the schools had 300 Moroccan staff and 40 Turkish teachers and administrators. Nearly all of the students are Muslim. There are no boarding facilities except at the new international school and a small one in Tangier. None of the schools has an alumni association but a teacher is designated at each school to follow the progress of graduates. There are no organized parents' associations.[105]

The disciplinary system in Moroccan schools is much stricter, almost militaristic, than in Turkish schools. Although strong discipline and respect for family and moral values are hallmarks of *Hizmet* schools, this situation still presents a challenge. The schools work closely with parents to explain the rationale of the *Hizmet* program. Every school has a designated teacher in charge of discipline and a discipline committee composed of the principal and teachers. *Hizmet* schools send their Moroccan teachers to Turkey for two-month internships to learn the Turkish system, including the different approach to discipline. (This practice did not come up at any other *Hizmet* school visited in Africa. This situation may be

---

103 Ibid.

104 Author's meeting on 7 January 2013 in Dakar with Adama Diop. Adama Diop, "Fethullah Gülen's Idea on the Relationship between Science and Religion," paper delivered at the International Fethullah Gülen Conference in Indonesia, 19–21 October 2010.

105 Author's meetings on 3 and 4 January 2013 in Casablanca and Marrakech with Mehmet Bozoğlan, assistant director general Groupe Scolaire Mohammed Al Fatih.

unique to Morocco or perhaps certain Arab countries.) Teachers from *Hizmet* schools in Egypt and Mauritania visit schools in Morocco to exchange ideas.[106]

The kindergarten through grade 12 school in Tangier was developed through the efforts of Turkish "social entrepreneurs" based in Spain. It is an all-Muslim coed school with about 700 students. Of the 79 professional staff, only seven are Turkish. Parents of the students are primarily civil servants and business persons.[107]

The MAF middle school in Casablanca opened in 2000 and only includes grades seven through nine. In 2013, it had 217 coed, Muslim students. There were three Turkish staff and 22 Moroccans, only one of whom spoke Turkish. Most classes take place in Arabic. Students study Arabic and French five hours and English three hours each week. The students speak Moroccan Arabic on the playground. The parents of most of the students are business persons and some civil servants. Most of the graduates transfer to a government high school.[108]

The middle and high school in Fes opened in 2003 and had 230 students in 2013. The staff of 35 included seven Turks. The parents are primarily business persons. The middle and high school in Tetouan, located southeast of Tangier, started a year later and had 400 coed students as of 2013, the year of its first graduating class. The staff included 35 Moroccans and five Turks. The school in El Jadida, west of Casablanca on the coast, began operations in 2010. In 2013, it had 400 students from kindergarten through grade 9 and 45 staff, only four of whom were Turkish. Each year it adds a grade until it reaches 12 and may become a boarding high school. Enrollment is 50 percent male and female. Many of the parents teach at the local university and others are in business.[109]

The international school was scheduled to open late in 2013 in Casablanca. It is designed for 1,500 students and will begin with kindergarten, primary school, 7th grade, and 10th grade. It eventually will include all grades from kindergarten through 12. It follows the Moroccan curriculum in English. The cost is considerably higher than other *Hizmet* schools. The goal is to attract upper-middle-class Moroccans. The owner of a Moroccan bus company helped buy the property for the school.[110]

---

106 Author's meeting on 5 January 2013 in Casablanca with Dalan Huseyin, coordinating counselor for all *Hizmet* schools in Morocco.

107 Author's meetings with Bozoğlan.

108 Author's visit to MAF middle school in Casablanca on 3 January 2013 and meeting with staff.

109 Author's meeting with Bozoğlan. Author's meeting on 5 January 2013 in Casablanca with the principal of El Jadida School.

110 Author's meeting with Bozoğlan.

The *Hizmet* operation in Morocco has several components not observed in Sub-Saharan Africa. One is a for-profit company designed to place Moroccan students at both *Hizmet* and non-*Hizmet* universities in Turkey and some 20 universities outside Turkey. From its beginning in 2004 through 2012, the company placed about 600 Moroccan students; 90 percent went to Turkey and 10 percent elsewhere. Of those students who went to Turkey, 30 percent enrolled in *Hizmet* universities and 70 percent in other universities. The company also placed 80 Turkish students in Moroccan universities. Fees, which vary by service provided, cover all costs of the operation and turn a profit, which is used to fund scholarships.[111]

The *Hizmet* educational program in Morocco has a number of features that set it apart from those in Sub-Saharan Africa. In addition to the student placement service, there is the program for about 100 Turkish girls studying in Morocco discussed in the section of this chapter dealing with *Hizmet* schools and Islam. The Nilüfer Center of Languages and Culture operates a dormitory for male Moroccan and Turkish university students in Casablanca and plans to add one for girls (see chapter 5).

Concluding Thoughts

Hizmet schools have only a 20-year history in Africa and about half of them opened in the last 10 years. Consequently, the schools have had significant numbers of graduates from secondary school only in recent years. It is clear, however, that the overwhelming majority of secondary school graduates continue to a university and they are beginning to occupy meaningful positions in their own countries.

The schools are distinguished by both their similarities and diversity. They all operate using the national curriculum of the country where they are located and are structured according to local law. They maintain small class sizes, usually capping classes at about 25 students. They all emphasize the pure sciences, discipline, and ethics. Nearly all of them offer Turkish as a third language. They all try to involve parents to the maximum extent possible, which also increases the opportunity for the Turkish business community to interact with an important part of African society. Increasingly, the schools see the need for effective alumni organizations.

The larger *Hizmet* educational programs tend to have unusual or even unique features. South Africa has two separate tracks—the traditional secular program

---

111 Author's meeting on 5 January 2013 in Rabat with Mahmut Saban, general manager of the educational advisory service.

and another with a strong Islamic focus. Kenya is developing an educational/health complex in cooperation with *Kimse Yok Mu* at Malindi along the coast. *Hizmet* schools in Nigeria are coping with maintaining operations in the north where Boko Haram is active. Nigeria also has the only *Hizmet* university in Africa. At the request of the Senegalese government, *Hizmet* is setting up a number of vocational training centers in an effort to reduce unemployment. *Hizmet* in Morocco, where almost all of the students are Muslim, has programs for Turkish university students to study there.

CHAPTER 5

HIZMET DIALOGUE CENTERS

Georgetown University's Thomas Michel is a frequent and sympathetic voice on the Gülen Movement. He remarked at a conference on religious tolerance in 2012 hosted by the African Union in Addis Ababa, Ethiopia that Gülen believes the duty of Muslims working for dialogue and unity should not be limited to Christians, but extends to conscientious followers of all religions. Michel then quoted Gülen: "The very nature of religion demands this dialogue. Judaism, Christianity, and Islam, and even Hinduism and Buddhism pursue the same goal. As a Muslim, I accept all Prophets and Books sent to different peoples throughout the history and regard belief in them as an essential principle of being Muslim."[1]

The Gülen-affiliated and Istanbul-based Journalists and Writers Foundation noted that after education, dialogue and cultural centers are central to the Gülen Movement. They bring different people together around issues of common concern. Locations for engagement and discussion, the activities of these centers include conferences, seminars, dialogue dinners, organization of trips to Turkey, and outreach programs.[2] These centers are recent arrivals and usually operate with a small staff in those African countries where they exist at all, but they are appearing with increasing frequency. Their activities are similar to longer established counterparts such as the Rumi Forum in Washington, D.C.

As is the case with Gülen-affiliated schools and business associations, there is no central listing of the dialogue and cultural centers. They have different names from country to country and unless you know the name of the organization, it is difficult to identify the website, if there is one. The best way to learn about the

---

1   *http://pa.au.int/en/sites/default/files/Identifying%20our%20partners%20in%20 Dialogue%20by%20Michel,%20Thomas.pdf.* For a good analysis of the Gülen Movement's views on interfaith dialogue, see İştar B. Gözaydin, "The Fethullah Gülen Movement and Politics in Turkey: A Chance for Democratization or a Trojan Horse?" *Democratization* 16, no. 6 (December 2009), 1223–1225.

2   *http://hizmetesorulanlar.com/what_type_of_institutions_and_projects_is_hizmet_ gulen_movement_comprised_of_.html.*

existence and activities of the dialogue and cultural centers is to visit the cities where they exist and meet with the local representative.

Information is often conflicting on the status of dialogue centers. According to one account, a center has been functioning in Bamako, Mali since 2011.[3] The Cihan News Agency said the "Galaxy Dialogue and Cultural Center" opened in 2012.[4] *Today's Zaman* reported in February 2013 that the center was still in the planning stage.[5] Two months later, *Today's Zaman* ran a story that the "Galaxy Culture and Dialogue Center" co-hosted the Turkish Olympiads with the *Hizmet* schools in Bamako.[6]

Gülen representatives had registered as of early 2013 the Rainbow Intercultural Dialogue Center in Monrovia, Liberia, although it had not yet opened for business.[7] An Internet search in 2014 suggested it still was not functioning. There is reportedly a dialogue center in Cape Verde, but the author was not able to develop any information on it.[8] According to one account, there is a dialogue center in Khartoum, Sudan that offers language lessons and assists with the distribution of food packages.[9] The *Hizmet Movement News Portal* occasionally runs articles on the activities of dialogue centers in Africa and elsewhere.[10]

While a few of the *Hizmet* dialogue centers in Africa are older and more generously staffed, most are new, staffed by a single professional, and still seeking to develop the most effective role they can play. There is, nevertheless, a highly similar pattern to their activities. Funding comes almost exclusively from members of the Turkish business community who are sympathetic to the philosophy of Fethullah Gülen. The centers never contain the word Gülen in their name, but they make clear they are propagating his philosophy and values. In fact, they

---

3   Author's meeting on 7 January 2013 in Dakar, Senegal with Mesut Gökcan Ateş, *Hizmet* volunteer.

4   "These Schools Are Cultivating Future's Prominent Malians," Cihan News Agency (7 January 2014).

5   "Turkish Schools in Mali Stay Open despite Conflict," *Today's Zaman* (6 February 2013).

6   "Malian Minister Praises Turkish Schools for Persevering through War," *Today's Zaman* (15 April 2013).

7   Author's meeting on 3 January 2013 in Casablanca, Morocco with Ramazan Burak, general manager of the Liberian-Turkish Light International School.

8   Author's meeting with Mesut Gökcan Ateş.

9   Author's meeting on 12 January 2013 in Istanbul with Hasan Öztürk, research fellow at the Wise Men Center for Strategic Studies (BILGESAM) who did PhD research in Darfur, Sudan.

10 *http://hizmetnews.com/*.

often host conferences and seminars devoted to his teachings and beliefs. They also distribute publications devoted to the values of Gülen.

African countries with large Turkish communities have the critical mass and business funding that makes it possible to sustain a center. But some countries with a significant Turkish community do not have a dialogue center and occasionally a country with a small Turkish population manages to establish one. Cape Verde may be a case where a small Turkish business community has created a dialogue center.

Ethiopia has a significant Turkish business community, but no dialogue center. The Ethiopian government has enacted a strict law governing non-governmental organizations that severely limits foreign funding for advocacy groups. It is not clear how Ethiopian law would interpret local Turkish business funding for a dialogue center, which has an advocacy component. In any event, this situation has deterred any initiative to develop one. The Turkish business community created in 2012 the Rainbow Charitable Association, which serves as the local arm of *Kimse Yok Mu*, the Gülen humanitarian organization. It has no advocacy function, but has a significant program in Ethiopia, as described in chapter 6. Consequently, it avoids the strict prohibition on foreign funding of advocacy groups contained in Ethiopia's law governing non-governmental organizations. In 2012, *Hizmet* also organized a major conference at the African Union headquarters in Addis Ababa on Fethullah Gülen's principles (see chapter 7).

Turquoise Harmony Institute in South Africa

The Turquoise Harmony Institute was established in 2006 as the Interfaith Foundation of South Africa with the approval of the Ministry of Home Affairs. Subsequently renamed, it probably offers the most comprehensive program of any Gülen dialogue center in Africa. Its stated goals are to promote dialogue, tolerance, and understanding among peoples of South Africa and the world. Key program themes are interfaith relations, providing relief to those in need, and emphasizing family values.[11]

The Institute has a headquarters in Johannesburg with two professional staff, and cultural centers in Cape Town and Durban, each with one professional staff member. Although its professional staff is small, it draws considerable support from Movement volunteers. The heads of the three dialogue offices meet regularly. It has a board of trustees and functions under South African law as a non-governmental organization. Funding comes primarily from Turkish business persons living in South Africa. It does not receive funding from any government. The various Gülen activities in South Africa are interlinked. For example, the Turquoise Harmony Institute shares office space in Johannesburg with the South

---

11 *www.turquoise.org.za/*.

African Turkish Business Association discussed in chapter 3 and the organization that oversees the Gülen-affiliated schools discussed in chapter 4.[12]

In addition to maintaining a library and engaging in a media outreach program, the Institute seasonally offers *Iftar* dinners and makes dialogue awards to South African residents. It routinely hosts seminars, panel discussions, public lectures, and conferences; arranges cooking classes; organizes trips to Turkey for handpicked South Africans; and offers classes in Turkish. Recent examples of lectures include those on the Prophet Abraham, a brief history of Christianity, African traditional religion, basic first aid for mothers, fasting in different faith traditions, heroes of peace, and the Gülen Movement.[13]

In 2010, the Turquoise Harmony Institute organized a panel in Cape Town on the relevance of the Gülen Movement to South African society. The seven panelists included Ebrahim Rasool, Member of Parliament and former premier of Western Cape Province, Johnny H. De Lange, Member of Parliament and deputy minister of justice, and Michael van Heerden, president of St. Augustine College in Cape Town. The Institute subsequently published the remarks of all the panelists as part of its outreach program.[14] The same year, the Ecumenism and Interreligious Dialogue Committee of the Catholic Church of South Africa and the Turquoise Harmony Institute sponsored a conference in Pretoria on the Gülen Movement and its contributions to world peace.[15]

The Institute interacts regularly with the South African Council of Churches, Jewish Board of Deputies, Catholic Bishop's Council, universities, and the South African government's cultural department. Its focus is mainstream religious groups. Many Muslims in South Africa have been skeptical about interfaith dialogue, as they fear it may compromise their faith; one extremist Muslim leader was publicly critical of the Turquoise Harmony Institute. On the other hand, South Africa's Muslim Judicial Council has been more open to interfaith dialogue.[16]

The director of the Institute's branch in Western Cape Province stressed that the goal is to reach out to underprivileged South Africans. As a result, this branch emphasizes the distribution, often in collaboration with Gülen-affiliated schools, of food packages to needy persons. The entire program is funded by

---

12   Author's meeting on 26 August 2012 in Johannesburg, South Africa with Aydin Inal, executive director of the Turquoise Harmony Institute.

13   *www.turquoise.org.za/*. Ina Cronje, "Let's Celebrate Our Diversity," *The Mercury* (24 September 2009).

14   *Gülen Movement: Its Essentials in Thought and Practice and Potential Contributions to Reconciliation in South African Society* (Turquoise Harmony Institute, 2010).

15   "Catholic Church in South Africa Discusses Gülen Movement," *Today's Zaman* (6 February 2010).

16   Author's meeting with Aydin Inal.

the Turkish business community. The director also explained that the Institute is apolitical and makes every effort to avoid political controversy. While the South African government is flexible and does not impose oversight on the Institute's operations, the Institute has concluded that South African society is less open than commonly believed and often difficult to reach.[17]

Although the author's contacts in South Africa were limited to people who had a history of favorable contact with the Gülen Movement, their testimonials about the Turquoise Harmony Institute were sincere. Catholic Archbishop Stephen Brislin of Cape Town commented that the Institute has become the "unifying movement" of Baha'i, Hindu, Christian, Jewish, and Muslim faiths in Cape Town. He particularly praised the *Iftar* meals and said the Movement is a force for moderation.[18] Stanley Ridge, a professor at the University of the Western Cape, acknowledged that all but a few of the most educated South Africans have no idea what is the Gülen Movement. At the same time, he said *Iftar* dinners organized by the Institute bring together an extraordinary group of people.[19]

Hlengiwe Mkhize, deputy minister for Economic Development, said South Africa is seeking a cooperative relationship with organizations such as the Turquoise Harmony Institute because it emphasizes tolerance and dialogue.[20] Michael van Heerden, president of St. Augustine College of South Africa, commented that bringing together like-minded people interested in dialogue is the most important contribution of the Movement. St. Augustine does some programming on campus with the Turquoise Harmony Institute.[21] All four interlocutors had visited Turkey on a trip organized by the Turquoise Harmony Institute.

One of South Africa's strongest proponents of Gülen Movement dialogue activities is former Western Cape premier Ebrahim Rasool. He argued that the Movement came to South Africa to support education, dialogue, and the policy of inclusion. Post-apartheid South Africa exposed the soft underbelly of its society. During the last half of the 1990s, this resulted in the rise of a Muslim extremist organization in the Western Cape known as People against Gangsterism and Drugs (PAGAD). At the time, the interfaith movement in the region was weak. Although the Turquoise Harmony Institute did not yet exist, supporters of the Gülen Movement organized *Iftar* dinners and showed that it was possible to bring people of different beliefs together. Rasool said the efforts of the Movement made

---

17   Author's meeting on 24 August 2012 in Cape Town, South Africa with Savas Karabulut, director of the Turquoise Harmony Institute for Western Cape. Warda Meyer, "Turks Delight Needy with Food Donations," *Weekend Argus* (18 August 2012).

18   Author's meeting on 24 August 2012 in Cape Town, South Africa with Brislin.

19   Author's meeting on 25 August 2012 in Cape Town, South Africa with Ridge.

20   Author's meeting on 26 August 2012 in Cape Town, South Africa with Mkhize.

21   Author's meeting on 27 August 2012 in Cape Town, South Africa with van Heerden.

a significant contribution to decreasing support for PAGAD, which eventually collapsed as an organized threat.[22]

Because of its considerable experience related to dialogue, the Turquoise Harmony Institute is sometimes asked to take part in similar activities in nearby countries. In 2013, for example, the director of the Institute joined the Turkish ambassador and the Ravinala Culture and Dialogue Institute at Antananarivo State University in Madagascar for a symposium on the art of coexistence. The director briefed the attendees on the Institute's dialogue efforts in South Africa.[23]

It is difficult to measure the effect of an organization such as the Turquoise Harmony Institute. There may be impacts, however, that are not obvious until more research is done in the field. Cape Town is the location of the small International Peace College of South Africa that offers a one-year enrichment program in Islamic studies and a three-year accredited BA degree in Islamic studies. It operates much as a seminary functions. The college wants to make interfaith dialogue part of its program and, as a result, draws on Gülen principles. The Turquoise Harmony Institute also shares its views on curriculum development with the International Peace College.[24] The impact of this kind of collaboration could have long-term implications for South Africa's Muslim community.

Kilimanjaro Dialogue Center in Tanzania

Tanzania is home to only about 300 Turks and did not have a fully active Gülen dialogue center as of late 2012. The Kilimanjaro Dialogue Center remained largely in the planning stage, although it had hosted some *Iftar* dinners. It shared rented office space with the other Gülen-affiliated institutions in Tanzania and did not have a full-time director. Responsibility for oversight of the dialogue center rests with the same organization that oversees the Gülen-affiliated Feza Schools and the association of business persons.[25] As of 2015, the Kilimanjaro Dialogue Center did not have an identifiable website.

Respect Foundation in Kenya

The Respect Foundation Interfaith and Intercultural Centre opened in 2007 in Nairobi. From the beginning, its focus was on interfaith and intercultural

---

22 Author's meeting on 19 October 2012 in Washington, D.C. with Rasool.

23 *http://hizmetnews.com/5994/the-art-of-coexistence-discussed-in-madagascar/*.

24 Author's meeting on 24 August 2012 in Cape Town, South Africa with M. Ighsaan Taliep, deputy principal of the International Peace College and vice president of the Muslim Judicial Council. *www.ipsa-edu.org*.

25 Author's meeting on 28 August 2012 in Dar es Salaam, Tanzania with Ibrahim Bicakci, director of Feza Schools in Tanzania.

dialogue. An early goal was countering the educational backwardness of the Muslim minority by organizing seminars and computer courses for imams in the Nairobi slums of Kibera. Early efforts at interfaith dialogue in the slums were challenging, as both Muslims and Christians feared they would lose their followers to the other side. The Foundation had better success, however, in organizing interfaith conversation groups among Christian and Muslim students at Jomo Kenyatta University.[26]

The Foundation became dormant for several years until its revival following the arrival of Fatih Akdogan, the interfaith chairman. The Foundation offers conferences, seminars, and panel discussions, arranges trips to Turkey, and makes available Gülen publications. It promotes conflict resolution and hosted in 2012, for example, a conference on peace and dialogue. The Respect Foundation welcomes people of different cultures, faiths, and ideologies.[27]

Sister Lilian M. Curaming of the Franciscan Family Association in Kenya has had experience with Gülen dialogue centers in the Philippines, South Africa, and now Kenya. She also participated in a trip to Turkey sponsored by a Gülen-affiliated organization. Sister Lilian commented that her organization operates on the basis of the principles of St. Francis of Assisi, which are compatible with those of the Respect Foundation. The two organizations now collaborate. She explained there is growing extremism in both Kenya's Muslim and Christian communities. One goal of her organization is to bring Catholics and Muslims closer together.[28]

It is the hope of the Respect Foundation to reach out to both the wider Islamic community and even Muslim extremist groups. So far, it has not attempted to work with the huge Somali community that has moved into the Eastleigh section of Nairobi. The Somalis in Kenya tend to distrust both the Turks and the philosophy of Fethullah Gülen. One of the obstacles is Gülen's position on polygamy. He argues there is nothing in the Qur'an that requires a man to marry more than one woman and "no one can consider marrying four women a matter of fulfilling a *sunna.*"[29] While he says there are exceptional circumstances that make polygamy acceptable, Gülen is not enthusiastic about the practice.

---

26 Mehmet Kalyoncu, "Gülen-inspired Schools in the East Africa: Secular Alternative in Kenya and Pragmatist Approach to Development in Uganda," *Islam in the Age of Global Challenges: Alternative Perspectives of the Gülen Movement Conference Proceedings* (2008). http://medya.zaman.com.tr/2008/11/17/kalyoncu.pdf.

27 Author's meeting on 31 August 2012 in Nairobi, Kenya with Fatih Akdogan. www.respectfoundation.co.ke/.

28 Author's meeting on 31 August 2012 in Nairobi, Kenya with Sister Lilian.

29 Fethullah Gülen, "Polygamy," (1997). www.fethullahgulenchair.com/index.php?option=com_content&view=article&id=144:polygamy-&catid=41:gulen-thoughts&Itemid=186.

Gülen's view is contrary to a strongly held Somali position that favors polygamy. Muslims on Kenya's Swahili coast reportedly hold this belief less fervently; this is where the Respect Foundation will focus its effort. The Foundation has also concluded that there is not a common understanding in Kenya on the role of interfaith dialogue, which often becomes a debate where both sides agree to disagree.[30]

Ufuk Dialogue Foundation in Nigeria

Although only established in 2011, the Ufuk Dialogue Foundation has become one of the most active Gülen dialogue centers in Africa. It has a main office in Abuja and a branch office in Lagos. There are an estimated 1,000 Turks living in Nigeria and, according to one Gülen supporter, about 70 percent of them are affiliated in some way with the Gülen Movement.[31] The Foundation's stated purpose is to promote peace in the world and contribute to the peaceful coexistence of the followers of different faiths, cultures, ethnicities, and races. It uses the same tools as the other dialogue centers and promotes the Gülen-published *The Fountain*, a bimonthly periodical of science and spiritual thought. The Foundation says it is willing to work with anyone who is willing to work with it.[32]

The Foundation has close ties with the National Mosque in Abuja and cooperates with the Catholic and Anglican communities in Nigeria. It has much less contact with evangelical Protestant and other religious groups. Although the goal is to expand outreach to additional groups, it is limited by staffing. In 2012, the Foundation reportedly arranged for 1,000 Nigerians to visit Turkey. Participants included groups of Christian pastors, emirs, judges, university professors and vice chancellors, newspaper editors, journalists, and the Hausa Translation Committee. Important individuals included the Sultan of Sokoto, minister of education, and leaders of the Tijani Sufi movement. Unlike some dialogue centers in Africa, the Ufuk Dialogue Foundation hopes to separate the dialogue function from charity activity.[33]

Ibrahim A. Jega, Executive Secretary of the National Mosque in Abuja, the largest in Nigeria, and co-chair of the Abuja Interfaith Peacebuilding Forum, commended *Hizmet* for emphasizing dialogue and understanding in a country

---

30 Author's meeting on 31 August 2012 in Nairobi, Kenya with Fatih Akdogan.

31 Author's meeting on 31 December 2012 in Abuja, Nigeria with Hüseyin Sert, vice chancellor of Nigerian Turkish Nile University.

32 *www.ufukfoundation.org*.

33 Author's meeting on 31 December 2012 in Abuja, Nigeria with Oguzhan Dirican, president of the Ufuk Dialogue Foundation, and Suleiman Yahaya, in charge of corporate relations for the Foundation.

where Boko Haram is taking a very different and violent approach to religion. He praised Gülen's book *Love and Tolerance*, which he uses for educational purposes, and noted that Gülen's *Messenger of God* is being translated into Hausa, the principal language of northern Nigeria.[34]

One of the persons who took part in a visit to Turkey, a Catholic priest, described the trip as "eye opening." He first became acquainted with the Gülen Movement at an *Iftar* dinner in Kaduna, Nigeria. This led to the *Hizmet*-sponsored visit to Turkey. He then became interested in interfaith dialogue and improving relations between Muslims and Christians. Upon his return to Nigeria, he became vice chairman of the Justice Development and Peace Commission in Kaduna, a town in northern Nigeria that has 50 Catholic parishes and had experienced considerable violence between the Christian and Muslim communities. The crisis brought religious leaders together to encourage a campaign of peace. He said the situation in Kaduna subsequently improved.[35]

One of the biggest events hosted by the Ufuk Dialogue Foundation was a two-day conference in 2011 on "Establishing a Culture of Coexistence and Mutual Understanding: Exploring Fethullah Gülen's Thought and Action" in Abuja, Nigeria. The Foundation organized the conference in collaboration with the Gülen-produced *The Fountain* magazine, Nigeria's Ministry of Education, the National Universities Commission, and six federal universities in Nigeria. Some 1,250 persons attended from Nigeria and a number of other African countries. One purpose of the conference was to explore how media, education, and cultural activities could play a role in building the culture of coexistence, mutual respect, and hope as demonstrated by the ideas of Fethullah Gülen.[36]

Several of the author's Nigerian interlocutors more than a year after the conference commented favorably on it.[37] Hamid Bobboyi, director of the Center for Regional Integration and Development, was one of the speakers at the conference, a two-time visitor to Turkey, and strong proponent of *Hizmet* dialogue programs and schools.[38] According to Ibrahim A. Jega, the conference also helped solidify relations between the Foundation and Nigeria's National Mosque.[39] Fethullah Gülen sent a message to the conference expressing his regret that he could not attend for health reasons and noting that "I consider my humble

---

34 Author's meeting on 31 December 2012 in Abuja, Nigeria with Jega.

35 Author's meeting on 1 January 2013 in Kaduna, Nigeria with the Catholic priest.

36 "Report on the Nigeria Conference." *http://fgulen.com/en/press/news/27123-report-on-the-nigeria-conference*.

37 Author's meeting on 1 January 2013 in Kaduna, Nigeria with Catholic priest and Baptist pastor.

38 Author's meeting on 31 December 2012 in Abuja, Nigeria with Bobboyi.

39 Author's meeting on 31 December 2012 in Abuja, Nigeria with Jega.

name being used in the titles of conferences, such as this one, is an indication of their good faith and generosity."[40]

Events in 2013 included an afternoon invitation in Abuja to members of the Nigeria Association of Women Journalists, who received a briefing at the Foundation headquarters followed by field visits to three Gülen-affiliated institutions in the city: the Nigerian Turkish International College (a secondary school), the Nigerian Turkish Nile University, and a new Nizamiye Hospital project.[41] The Foundation and the Nigerian Turkish Nile University organized a media panel on "Reportism in Conflict" for 250 participants. The guest speaker was the general manager of the Istanbul-based Cihan News Agency, another Gülen-affiliated organization. Turkey's ambassador to Nigeria attended the event.[42]

The Foundation and Nizamiye Hospital collaborated in hosting a large *Iftar* at the Abuja Hilton, where the president of the Foundation detailed the goals and activities of the organization.[43] In 2013, the Foundation also arranged for two Nigerian academics and two journalists to join 160 participants in the Abant International Forum's three-day meeting in Turkey on "Africa: Between Experience and Inspiration." The Gülen-affiliated Journalists and Writers Foundation organized the session.[44]

The Ufuk Dialogue Foundation has a branch office in the commercial capital of Lagos on the Atlantic coast of Nigeria. Its director was previously the principal at a Gülen-affiliated school in Lagos and the office is located in one of the schools. The goal is to move to a new office and hire a Nigerian staffer. Because of limited staff and the high cost of operating in Nigeria, all of its activities are confined to Lagos, the most populous city in Africa. The office cooperates with local universities and identifies Nigerians for trips to Turkey. It plans to send Nigerian academics to universities in Turkey for doing research. It also distributes food packages during Ramadan. The director would like to expand operations into the Niger Delta, where there is a history of conflict but no Gülen presence.[45]

The Foundation has developed a good relationship with one of the local papers in Lagos, *The Nation*, a daily with a circulation of about 70,000. Most of the readers live in Lagos but the paper reaches Abuja and Port Harcourt. The

---

40 "M. Fethullah Gülen's Letter to the Conference." *www.ufukfoundation.org*.
41 Hajiya Bilkisu, "Nigeria" Ufuk Foundation – Investing in Peace and Development," *Daily Trust* (31 January 2013).
42 "Media Release Reportism in Conflict." *http://fgulen.com/en/press/news/34169-media-release-reportism-in-conflict*.
43 Hajiya Bilkisu, "Ufuk Foundation's Interfaith Iftar," *Daily Trust* (15 August 2013).
44 "Nigerian Delegation Attended Africa Meeting." *www.ufukfoundation.org*.
45 Author's meeting on 2 January 2013 in Lagos, Nigeria with Mehmet Sabapli, manager of Lagos branch office.

editor and managing director of the paper cooperated with the Foundation on the media panel cited earlier dealing with the reporting of conflict. The paper reaches militants in the Niger Delta but has no circulation in northern Nigeria, where Boko Haram is active. The paper's editor and managing director, both of whom have visited Turkey, say they agree with what the Foundation stands for. It is in discussion with *Today's Zaman* for information on Turkey and the Middle East in exchange for news about Nigeria.[46]

The activities of the Ukuk Dialogue Foundation in Nigeria underscore the degree to which *Hizmet* organizations are interrelated. They share space and draw on each other for staffing support. They exchange contact lists and publicize each other's events. The financial backers of these different programs are often the same Turkish business persons. There does not seem to be any controlling mechanism in place. Rather, the Gülen-affiliated community is small enough and believes in the same general principles. It would be surprising if the different parts did not cooperate in a significant manner.

Atlantique Turquie-Sénégal Association (ATSA) pour le Dialogue Culturel entre les Civilisations

Orhan Ipek, president of the Atlantic Turkish-Senegalese Association for Cultural Dialogue between Civilizations, known as ATSA, opened the office in 2009. He arrived directly from Turkey. Ipek has three assistants, but due to staffing and funding limitations their activities are confined to the capital of Dakar. ATSA emphasizes seminars and conferences. Working with other Gülen-affiliated organizations, ATSA helps with the distribution of food packages. The first panel discussion it organized occurred in 2010 and dealt with the family and poverty.[47]

The major ATSA event in 2013 was a conference in Dakar hosted jointly with the Gülen-published *Ebru Magazine* titled "Diversity and Cohesion in a Globalized World: Contributions of the Gülen Movement." The conference attracted 240 delegates from almost 40 countries. It examined topics such as transnational education as inspired by the ideas of Gülen, intercultural dialogue, social cohesion, integration, religion, and human rights. Senegal's Prime Minister Abdoul Mbaye opened the conference. He compared the work of Senegal's first president, Leopold Sedar Senghor, a Christian in an overwhelmingly Muslim country, to the efforts of Gülen to improve education for engagement in the modern world.[48]

---

46 Author's meeting on 2 January 2013 in Lagos, Nigeria with Gbenga Omotoso, editor, and Victor Ifijeh, managing director, of *The Nation*.

47 Author's meeting on 8 January 2013 in Dakar, Senegal with Orhan Ipek.

48 "Reflections on the Gülen Movement Conference in Senegal." *http://hizmetnews.com/801/reflections-on-the-gulen-movement-conference-in-senegal/*. "Discours de

ATSA has developed a good relationship with a major Senegalese daily paper, *Le Quotidien*, which circulates throughout the country. The paper has published some of Gülen's thinking and signed a contract in 2013 with ATSA to publish one page once a week on Gülen's philosophy. The chairman and managing director of the paper praised the approach of *Hizmet*, especially its efforts to modernize education in Senegal.[49]

Nilüfer: Centre de Langues et de Culture in Morocco

The Nilüfer (meaning water lily in Turkish) Center of Languages and Culture operates differently than the other dialogue centers discussed in this chapter. It does not have an interfaith focus because Morocco's population is overwhelmingly Muslim. There are tiny Christian and Jewish communities in Morocco. Nilüfer began as a holding company in 2011 and has three components today: the education and culture center, a student dormitory, and an educational company.[50]

The cultural director, a former *Hizmet* teacher in Senegal, explained that the center offers cultural programs and teaches Turkish to Moroccans and French and Arabic to Turks. Fees cover the cost of the language program and any loss is covered by the holding company. There is no charge for cultural programs such as a recent whirling dervish concert in Rabat, where all programing took place as of early 2013. The goal is to expand activities to Casablanca. Nilüfer is trying to change its status to a foundation and may separate the language program from the other activities.[51]

During the 2011–2012 academic year, the language program accommodated 80 students: 10 Turks studying French and 68 Moroccans and two foreigners studying Turkish. Most of the Moroccans wanted to learn Turkish for business reasons or to study in Turkey.[52]

The male student dormitory in Casablanca was established in 2012 and accommodates 50 Moroccan and Turkish university students. Fees are expected to cover the cost of the program and any profit is said to go for the construction

---

Monsieur le Premier Ministre Abdoul Mbaye." *www.gouv.sn/Colloque-international-de-la.html*.

49 Author's meeting on 7 January 2013 in Dakar, Senegal with Madiambal Diagne, chairman and managing director of *Le Quotidien*.

50 Author's meeting on 6 January 2013 in Casablanca, Morocco with Ibrahim Aktas, director general of Nilüfer.

51 Author's meeting on 5 January 2013 in Rabat, Morocco with Ismail Danyildizi, Nilüfer cultural director.

52 Author's meeting on 6 January 2013 in Casablanca, Morocco with Saim Guzel, Nilüfer language school in Rabat.

of additional dormitories. There is discussion of building a dormitory for girls in either Casablanca or Rabat. The dormitory includes a mentoring program that encourages Gülen's ideas as part of the teaching process. Some of the Moroccan students are interested in Gülen and others are not. If there is no interest, there reportedly is no pressure to join. Interestingly, Gülen's actual writings are rarely used in the teaching program because they are thought to be too dense.[53]

Egyptian-Turkish Friendship and Culture Association

There are six Gülen-affiliated cultural, friendship, and welfare associations in Egypt. The first one was established in 1997. There are three branches in Cairo and one each in Alexandria, Mansoura, and Tanta. They offer Turkish courses for Egyptians, Arabic lessons for Turks, high school-level courses, cultural activities, and concerts. In 2011, the branch in Alexandria distributed supplies to Egyptian citizens evacuated from Libya on a Turkish ship. In 2012, one of the centers in Cairo offered a seminar on the development of education.[54]

The branches of the Egyptian-Turkish Friendship and Culture Association do not appear to engage in the promotion of Gülen's ideas in the way described earlier at most other Gülen dialogue centers in Africa. The Movement promotes Gülen's philosophy in Egypt using a different approach. In 2009, for example, Cairo University and the Gülen-affiliated, Arabic-language magazine *Hira* held a three-day conference at the Arab League headquarters in Cairo titled "Future of Reform in the Muslim World: Comparative Experiences with Fethullah Gülen's Movement in Turkey."[55] The involvement, if any, in this event by the local Gülen-affiliated culture and friendship associations is not clear.

Concluding Thoughts

While there are many similarities in the organization and activities of the *Hizmet* dialogue and culture centers, there are some important differences. In order to become established in an African country, each center must follow local law. Consequently, they are variously founded as non-governmental organizations, foundations, or companies, depending on local legal requirements. The focus of activities also varies from country to country. Interfaith dialogue is important

---

53   Ibid.
54   Author's meeting on 5 January 2013 in Casablanca, Morocco with teachers from Gülen-affiliated schools in Egypt. "Turk Culture Center Opens in Cairo," *Daily News* (24 February 2012). "Turkish Ship Evacuates over 1,000 Egyptians from Libya," *Today's Zaman* (21 March 2011).
55   Hakan Yeşilova, "Social Reform and Fethullah Gülen: The Cairo Perspective," *The Fountain*, issue 72 (November–December 2009). www.fountainmagazine.com.

in countries that have sizeable communities from at least two different religious groups. Interfaith dialogue is largely absent in countries, especially Muslim countries, where there is effectively only one religion represented.

Based on limited research in North Africa's Arab countries, it appears that Gülen's philosophy has encountered less receptivity in the Arab world than in the non-Arab, Muslim world and especially in countries that have two or more important religious groups. This may be due to historical suspicion about Turkey and its traditionally secular approach to Islam. It may also be related to growing Salafist thinking in the Arab world and Salafi hostility towards Sufi theology. This is an area for further research.

The key question is the impact that these *Hizmet* dialogue and cultural centers have in Africa. They are thinly staffed and, in some cases, only offer programming in the capital city. Those centers with branch offices have greater geographic reach but funding is limited. These factors suggest that they have minimal impact, especially in the most populous African countries. On the other hand, they draw on volunteer help from the wider *Hizmet* community for special events such as conferences and *Iftars*. Anecdotal feedback from Africans who have participated in some of the *Hizmet* programs indicates they have a much wider and positive impact than their limited staffing and funding would suggest is possible.

CHAPTER 6

HIZMET HUMANITARIAN ACTIVITIES

Hizmet engages in a variety of humanitarian activities in Africa. The largest and most structured humanitarian organization is *Kimse Yok Mu* (Turkish for "Is Anybody There?"). Gülen supporters in Europe fund a much smaller organization, *Yardim Zamani Derneği* (Time to Help). In addition, individual groups of *Hizmet*-inspired doctors, dentists, and health professionals independently make periodic volunteer visits to African countries. Others are establishing fee-based medical facilities on the continent.

Kimse Yok Mu Structure and Organization

Kimse Yok Mu (KYM) is a Gülen-affiliated humanitarian organization implemented in Africa primarily through the efforts of volunteers. It developed in the aftermath of the 1999 earthquakes in Turkey. In 2002, it became an association based in Istanbul and in 2004 a non-governmental organization functioning as an international humanitarian aid association. In 2006, it obtained official status from Turkey's Council of Ministers as a public interest group. In 2010, the UN Economic and Social Council added KYM to its list of consultants. Unlike most other Gülen-affiliated organizations, KYM has a formal, hierarchical structure and well-organized procedures for fundraising. It operates in Turkey and 75 countries globally; it has been especially active in Africa. While its connection to the Gülen Movement is well known, you would not be aware of the link based on KYM's website and promotional literature.[1]

As of 2012, KYM had a staff of about 400 persons, including a president, two vice presidents, and five office directors. It operated four branches outside Turkey, including offices in Sudan and Somalia. It relies heavily on volunteer assistance in the field from teachers and staff at the Gülen-affiliated schools. In some cases, school alumni associations invite graduates to volunteer their time on behalf of

---

1   *www.kimseyokmu.org.tr*. Helen Rose Ebaugh, *The Gülen Movement: A Sociological Analysis of a Civic Movement Rooted in Moderate Islam* (Heidelberg: Springer, 2010), 101–103.

KYM projects. In fact, KYM faces significant challenges operating in countries where there are no schools. KYM funds a wide range of projects, including building construction, annual Ramadan and Eid al-Adha food donations, disaster relief, support for refugees and orphans, and development projects. It provides in-kind and cash support for food, clothing, medicine, fuel, rent, shelter, health care, scholarships, and employment assistance.[2]

KYM accepts donations for a specific campaign or purpose and unconditional donations that can be used to cover administrative costs. In 2011, KYM raised about $92 million for its global programs. About $43 million came from bank transfers, $21 million as in-kind contributions, $17 million as online donations, $4 million as in-person donations, and $7 million by text message. The number of persons making donations increased from almost 600,000 in 2008 to more than 3.6 million persons in 2011. Of the $92 million received in 2011, KYM spent $31.5 million or 34 percent outside Turkey. About half of KYM's 2012 $4.4 million Eid al-Adha donations went to Africa.[3] From 2010 through 2013, almost 68 percent of all KYM funding outside Turkey went to countries in Africa.[4]

KYM works with a number of organizations that have their own activities in Africa. For example, it is an associate member of the Aegean International Federation of Health (ESAFED) that conducts health-related activities in Somalia, Cameroon, Kenya, Nigeria, Tanzania, Guinea-Bissau, Sudan, and Egypt. ESAFED brought 42 Somali doctors and nurses to Turkey for specialized training. It provided cataract surgery training in Sudan, emergency medicine training in Tanzania, and emergency medical intervention training in Cameroon.[5]

KYM has partnerships with at least 21 Gülen-affiliated organizations in Africa. These include, for example, Horizon Education in Burkina Faso, the Nile Humanitarian Development Agency in Uganda, College La Lumiere Internationale in Madagascar, and Association Turco Gabonaise in Gabon.[6]

After the falling out between *Hizmet* and the Turkish government, KYM's President Ismail Cingöz described early in 2014 a defamation campaign by pro-government media.[7] By the end of the year, the government ordered the blocking

---

2   Oğuzhan Tekin, "The Role of '*Kimse Yok Mu*' in Humanitarian and Peace Activities in the Middle East and Africa," paper presented at Doshisha University in Kyoto, Japan, in November 2012, 2–4. Author's meeting on 1 September 2012 in Nairobi, Kenya with Ismail Küçük, head of Light Academy Schools Alumni Association.

3   Tekin, 3–4 and 7–11.

4   *KYM 2010–2013 Africa Report*, 3.

5   www.esafed.org.

6   *KYM 2010–2013 Africa Report*, 52.

7   "*Kimse Yok Mu* Chair: Everyone Feels Some Type of Oppression in Turkey," *Today's Zaman* (16 February 2014).

of KYM's bank accounts on grounds the organization violated Turkish charity regulations. KYM filed a legal complaint against this action and Cingöz charged it was a blatant effort to paralyze the aid organization.[8]

The government's campaign did not stop the African Union from signing a memorandum of understanding with KYM in April 2015 that marked a new phase in collaboration between the two organizations. The African Union Commissioner for Political Affairs described KYM as an important partner. KYM pledged to build 1,000 new schools in Africa by 2020 and noted that it had provided more than 500 scholarships already in 2015 to African students.[9]

Value of KYM Aid to Africa

KYM has only been providing assistance to African countries since 2006. The growth in its programs in terms of both dollar value and diversity of projects has been impressive, although contributions declined somewhat in 2012 and 2013. In 2006, KYM distributed $201,000 worth of food packages to 18 African countries. In 2007, it sent $517,000 worth of assistance, almost all of it food, to 20 countries. In 2008, it provided $593,000 to only six countries. Five countries received only food packages while Sudan's Darfur region received most of the annual donation for food, construction, and health care. In 2009, KYM allocated $834,000 to 14 countries. Most of it consisted of food, although Sudan again received significant help with building construction and health care. In 2010, KYM donations rose to $1.7 million, but all countries except Sudan received only food packages. Again, Sudan's Darfur region accounted for over half of the total African program, and received support for water wells, school construction, education, and food.[10]

In 2011, there was a dramatic increase in KYM's aid to Africa. It distributed $22.4 million to 31 countries. Most of the programs consisted only of food, but those in Sudan and Somalia were large and highly diversified. Uganda also became a major recipient of KYM assistance. In 2012, total aid to Africa decreased slightly to $21.7 million in 45 countries but KYM diversified its projects in many countries. Sudan, Somalia, and Uganda remained the largest recipients; they were joined by Ethiopia and Kenya.[11]

---

8   Sevgi Akarçeşme, "Government Blocks Bank Accounts of Aid Organization," *Today's Zaman* (27 October 2014).

9   "African Union and *Kimse Yok Mu* Sign Landmark Agreement to Further Aid Efforts in Africa," *Today's Zaman* (27 April 2015).

10 *Kimse Yok Mu Africa Report 2006–2012* attached to 3 April 2013 email to author from KYM headquarters. All calculations are in $US.

11 Ibid.

In 2013, KYM distributed about $17.5 million to 43 countries in Africa. Less than one-third was humanitarian assistance. Most of the aid went to development projects, health, education, water wells, and support for orphans. The principal recipients were Somalia ($3.8 million), Kenya ($2.8 million), Uganda ($2 million), Ethiopia ($1.9 million), Sudan ($1.8 million), and Niger ($1.7 million). While KYM kept its focus on East Africa and the Horn, there was also a shift of resources into the Sahel region.[12]

From the beginning of its assistance to Africa in 2006 through 2013, KYM has provided about $65.4 million to 45 countries. KYM assistance reached a high in 2011 and has been on the decline since then. Almost 48 percent of the total has gone to Somalia, although the percentage dropped significantly in 2013. KYM's total assistance to Africa is modest compared to major humanitarian, international non-governmental organizations. On the other hand, because it goes to so many countries and relies heavily on the volunteer efforts of the local Turkish communities, it probably has a greater impact than its dollar value suggests. Of all Turkish non-governmental organizations that send assistance outside Turkey, KYM in 2012 provided globally almost twice the amount of the next highest organization, the Humanitarian Relief Foundation.[13]

KYM in Sudan and Somalia

The KYM program in the Darfur region of Sudan was its largest in Africa from 2007 through 2010. In 2011, Somalia received more than half of all KYM aid to Africa and continued to be the largest program in 2012 and 2013. Sudan slipped to the fourth-largest program in 2012 after Somalia, Uganda, and Ethiopia and fell to fifth largest in 2013. As two of the most troubled and overwhelmingly Muslim regions in Africa, it is not surprising that KYM emphasized Sudan and Somalia. They are also geographically close to Turkey, which has had a strong relationship with both countries since they became independent.

KYM began operations in Darfur in 2007 by supplying clean water to internally displaced persons. KYM subsequently constructed three mills and three water wells and repaired an existing clinic, mosque, and police station at a village renamed Orhaniye after a historic village in Turkey's Bursa Province. In 2009, KYM announced more ambitious plans to rebuild the small town.[14] Hasan Öztürk, who did research for a PhD in Darfur, described the project as a success.[15]

---

12 *KYM 2010–2013 Africa Report.* All calculations are in Turkish Lira. For 2013, the $US figures used here were calculated on the basis of two Turkish Lira per one $US.

13 TIKA, *Turkish Development Assistance 2012.* http://store.tika.gov.tr.

14 "Orhaniye to Be Home for War-stricken Darfuris," *Today's Zaman* (5 July 2009).

15 Author's meeting on 12 January 2013 in Istanbul with Öztürk, research fellow at the

KYM subsequently reduced funding for the program in Darfur most probably because of the ongoing conflict and challenges of implementing development projects there.

In 2011, KYM laid the foundation for two primary and two secondary schools at Nyala in South Darfur.[16] It has maintained an extensive cataract surgery program. Between 2008 and 2013, 53 volunteer doctors performed 80,000 eye exams and conducted 12,000 cataract surgeries.[17] KYM has built facilities for orphans in South Darfur and has supported about 3,000 of them.[18] It continues to provide food parcels during Ramadan and Eid al-Adha and to build water wells. In 2011, the 300-person-capacity Ikbal Gürpinar Hospital opened in Darfur. Financed by well-known Turkish television host Ikbal Gürpinar, KYM will operate the facility until the Sudanese Ministry of Health is able to take responsibility for its operation.[19]

The decrease in KYM aid to Sudan's Darfur region became war-ravaged Somalia's gain. The government of Turkey began a major initiative in support of the Somali government. The Erdoğan government hosted two conferences in Istanbul focused on building donor support for Somalia and resolving differences between Somalia and Somaliland. In 2011, Turkey opened one of the few embassies in Mogadishu and Prime Minister Erdoğan led a large Turkish delegation to Somalia. Turkey established a major assistance program and Turkish Airlines even inaugurated regular air service to Mogadishu. KYM became an important part of this surprising Turkish initiative.[20] Even before the falling out between Fethullah Gülen and the ruling Justice and Development Party, the KYM program operated independently of the Turkish government and did not collaborate formally with the Turkish Cooperation and Coordination Agency (TIKA).[21]

For a relatively small humanitarian assistance organization, measured by global standards, KYM began in 2011 a massive effort in Somalia. The Gülen-affiliated Nile Organization, which operates four schools in Mogadishu, has worked closely with KYM. The program includes an extensive distribution of meat

---

Wise Men Center for Strategic Studies (BILGESAM).

16 "*Kimse Yok Mu* to Build 4 Schools in Sudan," *Today's Zaman* (2 May 2011).

17 "KYM Volunteer Physicians Bring Light to Eyes in Darfur," 5 April 2013. http://hizmetmovement.blogspot.com.

18 "Sudanese Orphans," *www.kimseyokmu.org.tr*. KYM 2010–2013 Africa Report, 33.

19 "Turkish Donors Set to Open Medical Facilities in Sudan." *Today's Zaman* (24 May 2011).

20 Julia Harte, "Turkey Shocks Africa," *World Policy Journal*, 29 (Winter 2012/2013), 27–38.

21 Author's meeting on 31 August 2012 in Nairobi, Kenya with Orhan Erdoğan, KYM coordinator for East Africa operations.

and food packages during Ramadan and Eid al-Adha and hot meals for children at internally displaced person (IDP) camps. At its peak, KYM provided daily food rations to almost 120,000 Somalis. It also takes care of about 1,400 orphans and constructed two parks for children. It built water delivery sources, shower stalls, and toilets in Mogadishu. KYM constructed a bazaar where some 100 Somalis opened small businesses and rehabilitated several mosques. It imported a loom for teaching weaving, pasta machines for teaching pasta making, sewing machines for teaching women to sew, and flour for a local business person to set up a bread-making business.[22]

KYM renovated Mogadishu's Benadir Hospital, established an operating room, installed medical equipment, and provided medicine for the pharmacy. Turkish doctors affiliated with an organization known as Doctors Worldwide, which is not associated with the Gülen Movement, staff the hospital. Dozens of Gülen-affiliated medical teams and hundreds of KYM-sponsored doctors have worked in Somalia since 2011. On any given day there are between 20 and 25 Turkish doctors in Somalia. KYM opened a clinic at the Seyidka IDP camp, where it treats 600 patients daily. KYM is also training Somali doctors and nurses.[23]

KYM constructed and furnished a non-Gülen school for 760 students. It provides scholarships for 500 Somali students, 220 of whom attend Gülen-affiliated high schools in Turkey, and 280 of whom are in both Gülen and non-Gülen universities in Turkey. KYM selected them solely on the basis of test results and not political connections.[24] This may account for the complaint from the Somali education ministry's director general, Muse Farah Hayd, that KYM bypassed the ministry when it implemented the scholarship program.[25] KYM renovated a 500-person school at the Seyidka IDP camp and provides vocational training for adults at IDP camps in an effort to ensure sustainable income.[26]

International and non-governmental organizations have routinely been subject to attack by the extremist al-Shabaab group in Somalia that is dedicated to toppling the government and creating an Islamic state. The Turkish presence and KYM were initially no exception. In 2011, an al-Shabaab suicide bomber attacked a large group of Somali students applying for KYM-sponsored scholarships to Turkey while assembled at the Ministry of Education. The bomber killed more

---

22 "East Africa Campaign" and "Africa." *www.kimseyokmu.org.tr*. Tekin, 5–6. Author's meeting with Orhan Erdoğan.
23 Author's meeting with Orhan Erdoğan. "East Africa Campaign." *www.kimseyokmu.org.tr*.
24 Author's meeting with Orhan Erdoğan.
25 International Crisis Group, "Assessing Turkey's Role in Somalia," *Policy Briefing*, No. 92 (8 October 2012), 8.
26 "East Africa Campaign."

than 100 persons, including many students. Al-Shabaab was certainly aware of the connection between KYM and the scholarship program. Speculation at the time indicated that al-Shabaab considered Turkey too western and its brand of religion as "Islam light."[27]

There was even an unsuccessful al-Shabaab attempt in Mogadishu to assassinate the KYM coordinator for East Africa operations. Turkey and KYM then provided assistance to about 950 prisoners being held in Mogadishu by the Somali government. It turned out that most of the prisoners were linked to al-Shabaab. Once this support for prisoners began, al-Shabaab attacks aimed at Turks and KYM temporarily ended.[28] Attacks on the extensive Turkish presence in Somalia resumed, however, early in 2013.[29] While the Turkish presence and KYM have been highly popular with Somalis, at least one area expert has concluded that Turkey's humanitarian effort in Somalia is "naïve" and appears as though it can be easily manipulated by Somalis.[30]

KYM in Uganda, Ethiopia and Kenya

In Uganda, the KYM effort focused initially on the distribution throughout the country of food packages during Ramadan and Eid al-Adha at mosques, churches, orphanages, military bases, hospitals, and other institutions. KYM constructed a 33-bed hospital staffed by 50 professionals at Jinja, about 75 kilometers east of Kampala. In addition, it is building in Jinja a school, dormitory, and soup kitchen. KYM medical teams have been active in central and western Uganda. For example, between October 2011 and July 2012, KYM doctors examined more than 9,000 patients in Uganda. Volunteer doctors provide medical services at Mulago Research Hospital. KYM also organizes scholarships for a modest number of students to study in Turkey and intends to open permanent food centers and vocational training programs.[31]

---

27 "Somali Bomber Who Killed 100 Slammed Education," *AP* (6 October 2011). Author's meeting on 31 December 2012 in Abuja, Nigeria, with a Turkish doctor who was in Mogadishu at the time of the bombing.

28 Author's meeting with Orhan Erdoğan. Author's meeting on 12 January 2013 in Istanbul with Metin Çetiner, KYM vice president.

29 Andrew McGregor, "Somalia's Al-Shabaab Targets Turkish Nationals in Mogadishu," *Terrorism Monitor* 11, issue 8 (19 April 2013): 2–4. "Suicide Attack on Mogadishu Turkish Compound Kills Two," *AFP* (27 July 2013).

30 Laura Heaton, "Saving Somalia," *Foreign Policy* (24 April 2012). www.foreignpolicy.com/articles/2012/04/24/saving_somalia.

31 Tekin, 6. "Africa." "East Africa Campaign." "Turkish NGOs-initiated Hospital Underway in Uganda," 18 March 2013. "Turkish Doctors Leave Country to Volunteer at Uganda's Nile Hospital," *Today's Zaman* (29 May 2014). www.hizmetmovement.com.

Hizmet-affiliated Turkish business persons residing in Ethiopia established in 2012 the Rainbow Charitable Association, which has effectively become the local arm of KYM. Although Gülen-affiliated schools in Ethiopia also support KYM activities, *Hizmet's* humanitarian model in the country is somewhat unusual and suggests an intention to develop an extensive program.

KYM has focused much of its effort on Ethiopia's Harari region, which was once under the loose administration of the Ottoman Empire. In 2012, KYM opened the Harar Medical Center with three Turkish doctors and the capacity to handle 90 patients daily. KYM and Turkey's Marmara Health Federation then expanded the medical center to a 40-bed hospital with 50 healthcare professionals from Turkey and Ethiopia. Five of the Turkish doctors remain on-site permanently while others rotate in and out of Harar every three to six months.[32]

As in other African countries, the distribution of food packages is a key part of the KYM program. The focus is on the cities of Addis Ababa, Harar, and Mekele, and Oromia and Afar regions. KYM medical volunteers offer health screenings and provide medicine in several regions, making a special effort to serve orphans. It has initiated a scholarship program for sending Ethiopian orphans to Turkey to study in high schools and universities. KYM is constructing a school, dormitory, and soup kitchen in Harar.[33]

KYM began its operations in Kenya with the distribution of food packages to Somali refugees at the huge Dadaab camp in the northeastern part of the country near the border with Somalia. It also focused its food distribution effort in the Muslim coastal cities of Mombasa, Malindi, and Lamu and the ethnic Somali town of Garissa in the northeast. In 2012, it constructed at Dadaab a health center that serves 250 patients daily and provides medicine. Ambitious future plans include the construction of water wells, offering vocational courses, opening cultural centers, building orphanages, teaching beekeeping, and rehabilitating government schools and hospitals.[34]

KYM has been especially active on the Kenyan coast. Business persons from Konya, Turkey, funded a 720-capacity school, 36-bed hospital, dormitory, and soup kitchen in Malindi, which opened in 2013. The soup kitchen is designed to serve 500 persons daily and the school includes underprivileged students on scholarships. Medical teams coordinated by Gülen-affiliated schools regularly visit the coast. KYM hosts medical camps, which are open to the public, once a year for two to three weeks at a time. KYM distributes

---

32 "Turkish Charitable Organizations to Open Hospital in Ethiopia," *Today's Zaman* (17 July 2013).

33 "East Africa Campaign." *KYM 2010–2013 Africa Report*, 18.

34 "East Africa Campaign." "Africa." Author's meeting with Orhan Erdoğan.

food packages throughout the year and meat, including to the coastal prison population, during Eid al-Adha.[35]

KYM has worked closely with the Kenya-based and Gülen-affiliated Omeriye Educational Foundation and Medical Charitable Trust. While the main focus of the Foundation is oversight of the Gülen-affiliated schools in Kenya, it also engages in distribution of food packages and sacrificial meat during Muslim holidays, provision of clothing, and organization of *Iftar* meals (see chapter 4 concerning the Omeriye Foundation's role with schools). In 2013, 160 KYM volunteers from Konya visited Mombasa and Malindi, where they joined representatives of the Omeriye Foundation to inaugurate the complex at Malindi.[36]

KYM Elsewhere in Africa

KYM's programs in other African countries are considerably smaller than those in Sudan, Somalia, Uganda, Ethiopia, and Kenya. In 2013, however, countries in the Sahel region, especially Niger, attracted greater KYM attention. Chad, Senegal, Mauritania, and Mali were among the larger recipients of KYM help.[37] While KYM offers most African countries at least modest donations of food packages and sacrificial meat on the occasion of Eid al-Adha and Ramadan, a few such as Botswana, Lesotho, Swaziland, and Seychelles have not yet received assistance from KYM. This is probably explained by the absence of a meaningful Turkish community in these countries and the very small percentage of local nationals who are Muslim.

As KYM expanded beyond the distribution of food packages and meat during Muslim religious periods, it began a program for increasing access to clean water by constructing water wells. One of its largest programs has been in Niger, where since 2010 it has sponsored more than 200 wells at a cost of $8,500 each.[38] KYM has opened more than 400 wells in Burkina Faso, Chad, Cameroon, Kenya, Niger, Central African Republic, Senegal, Somalia, and Sudan.[39] It has also extended its campaign of cataract surgeries to Chad, Cameroon, Central African Republic, and Niger. In 2013, it added Mali, Ghana, Togo, Benin, Sierra Leone, and Burkina Faso to the cataract campaign.[40]

---

35 Author's meeting on 2 September 2012 in Mombasa, Kenya, with Mustafa Genç, headmaster of the Light Academy primary school in Mombasa. "Bridges of Love Extending from Konya to Kenya," 30 October 2013. *http://hizmetnews.com.*
36 "Bridges of Love Extending from Konya to Kenya."
37 *KYM 2010–2013 Africa Report.*
38 "Turkish Schools in Niger," 23 October 2013. *http://hizmetmovement.blogspot.com.*
39 *KYM 2010–2013 Africa Report*, 14.
40 "Su Kuyuları." *http://global.kimseyokmu.org.tr.*

Burkina Faso is an example of KYM's program for delivering food packages and sacrificial meat. In 2013, KYM reportedly reached 60,000 families through aid deliveries at five different locations in the country. It also hosted 10,000 persons at *Iftar* dinners and delivered food to 2,800 orphans at seven orphanages.[41] After three consecutive years of providing food, meat, and clothing during Eid al-Adha to the village of Transalya in Burkina Faso, the residents renamed the village "Turkiye" in honor of their Turkish benefactors.[42]

Chad is another country where KYM has emphasized food packages during the Muslim holidays. In 2013, KYM delivered 1,600 aid packages and offered *Iftar* dinners for 5,400 persons working with the Gülen-affiliated school Complexe Scolaire International Tchado-Turc. There was a special effort to reach orphanages and foundations for the handicapped and widows.[43] Working with the Gülen-affiliated Ufuk (Horizon) schools in Mali, KYM has been hosting Eid al-Adha celebrations since 2004.[44] Three Malian ministers attended the festivities in 2013. Turkish volunteers from the Gülen-affiliated organization Time to Help in Germany and Belgium participated in the distribution of meat to 100,000 families in six cities across Mali.[45]

Since 2012, Sami Karasin has been the official representative in Senegal for KYM. He helps coordinate small KYM programs in nearby Mali, Mauritania, and Côte d'Ivoire. He receives no payment from KYM but also represents and receives a salary from the Gülen-affiliated Senegalese-Turkish Businessmen's Association (see chapter 3). In 2012, KYM distributed 4,400 food packages in Senegal, provided 100 tons of sacrificial meat for Eid al-Adha, and hosted *Iftar* dinners for about 1,000 poor and needy Senegalese. He also oversees the KYM well construction program, normally contracting with Senegalese companies, which are cheaper than Turkish companies.[46]

The Senegalese editor of a local paper explained that the Gülen Movement took root slowly in Senegal. Eventually the Senegalese, especially poor ones, saw the delivery of food packages and sacrificial meat as the face of Turkey in the

---

41 "Samples of *Kimse Yok Mu* Ramadan Aid Activities Worldwide," 20 July 2013. *www.hizmetmovement.com*.

42 "Locals Name African Village 'Turkey' to Show Thanks for Aid," *Today's Zaman* (31 October 2012).

43 "Turkish People's Aid Reaches Out to Chad through *Kimse Yok Mu*," 2 August 2013. *www.hizmetmovement.com*.

44 "Mali Minister of Education Visits *Kimse Yok Mu*," 2 November 2012. *www.hizmetnews.com*.

45 "Samples from *Kimse Yok Mu* Eid Al-Adha Efforts," 19 October 2013. *http://hizmetmovement.blogspot.com*.

46 Author's meeting on 8 January 2013 in Dakar, Senegal with Sami Karasin.

country. The editor suggested that the recipients do not associate KYM activities with the Gülen Movement, but they see the program as humanitarian and aimed at the common people. Gülen-affiliated schools, on the other hand, are aimed at Senegalese elites, as are most of the activities of the influential Catholic Church.[47]

A group of Turkish women composed of artists, doctors, and business leaders is building an orphanage in Burundi, where Turkey does not even have an embassy. The project is headed by the president of the Istanbul-based World Businesswomen's Association and a prominent gynecologist. KYM supports the project.[48]

KYM has been less engaged in North Africa in spite of the fact there are large Turkish communities there. Egypt, Libya, Tunisia, and Algeria have benefitted from small programs but KYM has been inactive in Morocco. While this may be due to less need in these countries, it may also have something to do with a greater reluctance by Arab countries to accept aid from Turkey and especially from an organization linked to Sufi beliefs. Since 2011, KYM has sent food packages to Libya and Egypt. In the case of Egypt, there was a sharp increase in the delivery of food packages in 2013. However, Egypt serves primarily as KYM's gateway to Palestine. KYM also supplied medicine and medical teams to Libya. In 2011, KYM provided food packages and medicine to Libyan refugees in Tunisia.[49]

Yardim Zamani Derneği (Time to Help)

The Time to Help organization is much smaller than KYM and draws its support primarily from Turkish business persons residing in Europe who are sympathetic with Gülen's philosophy. It is an affiliate of KYM and has independent branches in Germany, Austria, Belgium, Denmark, Netherlands, and Switzerland. In 2014, Time to Help opened an office in the United Kingdom. The branches have selected particular countries in which to concentrate their activities. For example, the branch in Denmark has focused its effort in Sudan, especially the Darfur region. In 2013, the German and Belgian branches, two of the most active in Africa, distributed food packages and sacrificial meat in Senegal, Mali, Burkina Faso, Guinea, Niger, Nigeria, Central African Republic, Uganda, Ethiopia, Somalia, Kenya, Tanzania, Malawi, Mozambique, and Madagascar.[50]

---

47 Author's meeting on 8 January 2013 in Dakar, Senegal with Papa Amadou Fall, editor of *La Gazette*.

48 Menekse Tokyay, "Turkish Women Make a Difference in Africa," 30 January 2014. *http://gulen101.org/turkish-women-make-a-difference-in-africa/*.

49 Author's meeting with Orhan Erdoğan. "*Kimse Yok Mu* to Build 4 Schools in Sudan," *Today's Zaman* (2 May 2011). *KYM 2010–2013 Africa Report*, 42.

50 *www.timetohelp.eu/*. "'Time to Help' Launched in England," 19 February 2014.

On some occasions, Time to Help operates its own programs in Africa and on others it collaborates with KYM. In 2013, for example, the branches from Germany and Belgium joined KYM in Mali during Eid al-Adha, when they distributed sacrificial meat across the country.[51]

The German affiliate of Time to Help on 12 different occasions between 2011 and 2012 sent teams of about 15 persons each to Kenya, where they distributed food packages and medicine to Somali refugees at the Dadaab camp near the Somali border and to poorer areas of Kenya. They renovated orphanages in Garissa in northeast Kenya and sponsor about 35 Somali orphans at one of the Gülen-affiliated secondary schools in Nairobi and Mombasa. The German affiliate has varied activities in Somalia, Ethiopia, Uganda, and Tanzania.[52]

Other *Hizmet* Humanitarian Activities

It is not always clear when persons engaged in humanitarian projects affiliated with the Gülen Movement, sometimes only loosely affiliated, are visiting under the aegis of KYM, Time to Help, some other Turkish organization, or acting independently. As of 2012, for example, five teams of approximately 20 doctors from Izmir visited Tanzania for two weeks each to perform checkups, perform operations, and leave behind medicine and medical supplies. In 2012, several of the doctors were on the island of Zanzibar, where the author met them at the residence of a Turkish teacher who taught in the Gülen-affiliated school on Zanzibar. The school supported the visit by the doctors, who also treated the school's students and their parents. This delegation was associated with the Aegean International Federation of Health (ESAFED) and all of the doctors were part of the Gülen Movement. On the other hand, not all ESAFED members are associated with *Hizmet*. ESAFED had also provided scholarships for 20 Tanzanian students to study health in the Izmir region. Separate Turkish health federations in Ankara, Erzurum, Istanbul, and Gaziantep have similar programs in Africa.[53]

In 2013, 47 doctors from the Ufuk Doctors Association, a branch of the Marmara Health Federation, with the support of TIKA, visited Tanzania for ten days. They examined patients and performed surgery in the coastal town of Bagamoyo just north of Dar es Salaam and on Zanzibar. This ongoing cooperative

---

http://hizmetnews.com.

51 "Samples from *Kimse Yok Mu* Eid al-Adha Aid Efforts," 19 October 2013. http://hizmetmovement.blogspot.com.

52 Author's meeting on 1 September 2012 in Nairobi, Kenya with Ahmet Ökmen, secretary general of the Turkish-Kenya Businessmen Association.

53 Author's meeting on 29 August 2012 on Zanzibar, Tanzania with visiting Turkish medical team.

program includes visits by Turkish doctors, dentists, pharmacists, and assistant medical personnel.[54] The Ishik Education and Medical Foundation, which is primarily responsible for managing the Feza Schools in Tanzania, brings two or three Turkish doctors to the country each year to perform free operations in government hospitals.[55]

In 2010, dozens of doctors with the Izmir-based Aegean Health Volunteers' Association (EGESADER) traveled to Cameroon to conduct health screenings and operations. TIKA coordinated the effort.[56] The following year, a delegation of 20 doctors and five students sponsored by EGESADER and supported by TIKA returned to Cameroon. They also received assistance from the Turkish embassy in Yaounde.[57]

Some of the more permanent Gülen-related activities, such as establishing an eye hospital or dental facility, may be designed as profit making, even if they are filling an important medical service that was not previously available. It is almost impossible to document these projects and their financial models without visiting each one.

The eye hospital in Dakar, Senegal, which is discussed in chapter 3, is an example of a business venture by a *Hizmet* doctor who was encouraged to come to Dakar by *Hizmet* supporters. His goal is to provide high-quality eye care that does not now exist in Senegal and to make a profit.[58]

In 2011, Turkish dentists with ties to *Hizmet* and EGESADER opened the Esnan Dental Center in Tanzania. It is equipped with state-of-the-art equipment and can provide dental implants and orthodontics treatment. While based on a profit-making model, it provides services that were not previously available in Tanzania.[59]

The most ambitious for-profit medical project so far in Africa associated with *Hizmet* is the Nizamiye (meaning large gate in Turkish) Hospital in Abuja, Nigeria that opened in 2013. *Hizmet* considered several countries for this project but decided upon Nigeria because the Nigerian authorities acted so

---

54 "Support in the Health Sector in Tanzania," 12 September 2013. *www.tika.gov.tr*.
55 Author's meeting on 28 August 2012 in Dar es Salaam, Tanzania with Ibrahim Bicakci, director of Feza Schools.
56 "African Experience Changes Turkish Doctors' Outlook," *Today's Zaman* (8 December 2010).
57 "Doctors from Turkey Undertake Health Check Ups in Cameroon," *Cameroon Today* (February 2011).
58 Author's meeting on 8 January 2013 in Dakar, Senegal with Cavit Kalkan, doctor in charge of new eye hospital.
59 "Africa's First Turkish Dental Hospital Opens," *Today's Zaman* (14 March 2011).

quickly. In fact, Nigerian President Goodluck Jonathan opened the completed structure, which began with 55 beds and is planned to increase to 80 beds. A Turkish company built the hospital, which started with 15 doctors from Turkey and seven from Nigeria. The numbers will increase as necessary. The supervisory staff will remain Turkish; nurses come primarily from Nigeria.[60]

Hizmet supporters provided funding for the hospital; it received no money from TIKA or the Turkish government. It is intended to become self-sustaining; any profit reportedly will be ploughed back into capital expenditures such as the provision of mobile hospitals. The Nigerian government went out of its way to support the project following a visit by key officials to hospitals in Turkey. Most supplies initially will come from Turkey, although the goal is to obtain 70 percent of all medicine from Nigeria. *Hizmet* followers believe this hospital serves as a model for others under consideration in Senegal and Somalia, and two that recently opened in Kenya and Uganda. The goal is to provide health services according to the values of the Gülen Movement. The Gülen name is not associated with the hospital. If Nigerians who work at or who use the hospital express an interest in the Movement, *Hizmet* representatives will provide information about it.[61]

Concluding Thoughts

KYM, Time to Help, and independent *Hizmet* humanitarian activities in Africa are notable not because of the large amount of money they spend each year but because of the degree to which they depend on small donations and volunteer support. Their annual budgets in Africa are modest by international standards. Most international, humanitarian, non-governmental organizations depend heavily on grants from governments and international organizations. KYM and Time to Help depend on donations, primarily from the Turkish business community. As a result, many similar international organizations have huge budgets as compared to those of *Hizmet* organizations. But the large international groups also have higher overhead costs and mobilize minimal volunteer help. The *Hizmet* model is different.

Much of the volunteer help comes from the staff of Gülen-affiliated schools discussed in chapter 4 and which now exist in all but a few African countries. But there is also close collaboration with *Hizmet* business associations in Africa (chapter 3) and *Hizmet* dialogue centers (chapter 5). The links are strong among all of these *Hizmet* organizations. Historically, there has been some cooperation between *Hizmet* humanitarian organizations, on the one hand, and Turkish

---

60 Author's meeting on 31 December 2012 in Abuja, Nigeria with Mustafa Ahsen, chief medical director of Nizamiye Hospital. *www.nizamiyehospital.com*.

61 Author's meeting with Mustafa Ahsen.

embassies in Africa and some government organizations such as TIKA, on the other hand. The falling out between the Gülen Movement and Turkey's ruling Justice and Development Party has ended, at least for the time being, any cooperation between *Hizmet* and the Turkish government and even threatens future KYM operations.

While there is at least a small *Hizmet* humanitarian program in almost every country in Africa, it is not surprising that the effort is concentrated in Muslim countries such as Sudan, Somalia, and Niger, or those that have a significant Muslim minority such as Ethiopia, Kenya, and Uganda. While *Hizmet* is careful to include non-Muslims in its programs, a large majority of its beneficiaries are Muslim, while less than 50 percent of Africa's total population is Muslim. One of *Hizmet's* most popular programs is designed primarily to reach Muslims through the delivery of food packages and sacrificial meat during Ramadan and Eid al-Adha. *Hizmet's* humanitarian programs are intended, however, to assist Africa's neediest populations, irrespective of religion.

CHAPTER 7

GÜLEN-AFFILIATED MEDIA AND OUTREACH PROGRAMS

The Gülen Movement has mastered the media. It has the second-largest media conglomeration in Turkey, which includes the two largest daily newspapers, six television channels, two radio stations, a global news agency, more than 20 publishing houses, and a variety of magazines and journals.[1] The two major components of the conglomerate are the Feza Media Group and Kaynak Publishing Group. Feza is connected to Samanyolu Broadcasting Company, which operates several television stations in Turkey. One Gülen organization describes Kaynak Holding and Feza Media Group as Gülen-inspired companies. The companies are not controlled by Gülen, nor do they have any direct link with him. Gülen provides the inspiration, motivation, vision, and some guiding and overarching principles.[2]

The Movement has a mass media empire that attracts more international attention than any other public opinion-making source in Turkey. Collectively, it acts as Turkey's primary international voice. In 2013, before the end of close relations between the Gülen Movement and Turkey's ruling Justice and Development Party, the AKP and the Movement operated as a mutually supportive, albeit tenuous coalition.[3] As discussed in chapter 8, their subsequent disagreements ended all cooperation, including through their respective media outlets.

The Gülen media and outreach effort is closely linked to the dialogue centers discussed in chapter 5 and other components of its presence in Africa. The outreach program openly propagates the writings, ideas, and teachings of

---

1   M. Hakan Yavuz, *Toward an Islamic Enlightenment: The Gülen Movement* (Oxford: Oxford University Press, 2013), 90. Graham E. Fuller, *The New Turkish Republic: Turkey as a Pivotal State in the Muslim World* (Washington: United States Institute of Peace Press, 2008), 58. Gülen Institute, *Fethullah Gülen: Biographical Album* (Houston, TX: University of Houston, no date), 35.

2   Cited in Suzy Hansen, "The Global Imam," *The New Republic* 241, issue 19 (2 December 2010): 11.

3   Joshua D. Hendrick, *Gülen: The Ambiguous Politics of Market Islam in Turkey and the World* (New York: New York University Press, 2013), 177–179.

Fethullah Gülen. Periodicals, books, a news service, websites, and television programming are designed to reach a much wider foreign audience than Africans. These media originate, therefore, in Turkey and some other locations selected because of technical, language and/or geographic advantages. The Istanbul-based Journalists and Writers Foundation is a key organization in the outreach effort, even if Africa is not a major focus of its activities. The U.S.-based Gülen Institute is also designed to advance Gülen's ideas and philosophy.

Hizmet dialogue centers in Africa distribute Gülen-linked magazines, journals, and books. They can also be found in Gülen-affiliated schools. The dialogue centers help organize Gülen-related seminars and conferences and usually run a feed from its television channel, as do many of the *Hizmet* schools. Several *Hizmet* magazines co-sponsor Gülen conferences. There is considerable interconnectivity among the various Movement components.

Magazines, Journals, Newspapers, News Agency, and the Internet

The Movement publishes a wide range of print material in a variety of formats and languages to spread the word and ideas of Fethullah Gülen. Many of these publications are in Turkish and, therefore, not relevant to Africa. A few others are in languages such as Russian or, although in English as in the case of the *Turkish Review* and the *Turkish Journal of Politics*, not intended for an African audience. There is, nevertheless, a rich selection of print media that is distributed in Africa, although circulation numbers appear to be small for a continent of more than one billion people. All of the publications are aimed at African elites, not the person in the street.

The English-language magazine *The Fountain* is published bimonthly in Clifton, New Jersey, by Tughra Books, a Gülen-affiliated company, and is available throughout the world by subscription. It has representatives in several countries, including South Africa and Nigeria. First published in 1993, it discusses Gülen themes on life, beliefs, knowledge, and the universe. Recent issues have included articles such as "Laborers of Thought, Building the Future" by Fethullah Gülen, "The Psychology of Morality," "Religion Is Not a Zero Sum Game," "Artificial Replacement of the Failing Heart," "Freedom from Cigarettes," and "Hui People: Chinese Speaking Muslims."[4]

One of the most ambitious publishing projects is the Istanbul-based and Arabic-language *Hira* magazine, which was launched in 2005. Appearing every two months, it is the first Arabic-language magazine with Turkish writers. Each issue begins with an article by Gülen, who provides original material for this magazine. *Hira* follows the same general principles as *The Fountain*. It deals with

---

4   *www.fountainmagazine.com*.

education, religion, art and culture, philosophy, civilization, history, poetry, and the spiritual formation of the human soul through a Sufi lens of Islam. The goal is to teach religiosity that can interact confidently with modernity.[5]

Hira tries to attract contributions by intellectuals from throughout the Islamic world where Arabic is understood, not just the Arab world. It has published articles by authors from Yemen, Sudan, South Africa, Kuwait, United Arab Emirates, Syria, Iraq, Morocco, Malaysia, Algeria, Libya, and Tunisia, in addition to Turkey. Arabic is the principal language in North Africa and Sudan and spoken as a second language in a number of Sub-Saharan countries. Each edition of *Hira* is printed in 60,000 copies, with about 60 percent of the circulation devoted to North Africa, Sudan, and the Sahel region. It is printed primarily in Cairo and has a small printing in Istanbul for distribution in Turkey. There is a print run of about 9,000 in Rabat, all of which circulates in Morocco, with 20 percent provided free of charge and 80 percent by paid subscription. In Morocco, *Hira* breaks even financially.[6]

Hira also organizes meetings and conferences concerning Gülen's philosophy. It has done so in a number of countries, including Egypt, Morocco, Tunisia, Algeria, Sudan, Mauritania, Kenya, Tanzania, Uganda, Senegal, and the Democratic Republic of the Congo.[7] In 2009, *Hira* and Cairo University hosted a three-day conference for some 400 participants titled "Future of Reform in the Muslim World: Comparative Experiences with Fethullah Gülen's Movement in Turkey" at the Arab League headquarters in Cairo.[8] In 2012, *Hira* hosted in Istanbul a conference called "According to Gülen, the Basic Dynamics of the Resurrection" for scholars from Egyptian universities.[9] In 2013, *Hira* collaborated with the Fadil bin Asur Research Center in Tunisia on a symposium called "Tunisia and Turkey: Concepts of Culture and Reform in the Cases of Tahir ben Asur and Fethullah Gülen." Organized at the request of the Tunisian Ministry of Culture, the minister said Tunisia needs the example of Gülen and *Hizmet*.[10]

In 2013, *Hira* and the Gülen Turkish-language *Yeni Ümit* magazines held a two-day international symposium in Istanbul called "A Shared Road Map: Ijma'

---

5 Paul L. Heck, "Turkish in the Language of the Qur'an: *Hira* Magazine," in *The Muslim World and Politics in Transition: Creative Contributions of the Gülen Movement*, ed. Greg Barton, Paul Weller and Ihsan Yilmaz (London: Bloomsbury, 2013), pp. 143–153.

6 Author's meeting on 5 January 2013 in Rabat, Morocco with Orhan Caskun, *Hira* office.

7 "*Hira* Magazine Changes Perception of Turkey in Arab World," *Today's Zaman* (12 June 2012).

8 Hakan Yeşilova, "Social Reform and Fethullah Gülen: The Cairo Perspective," *The Fountain*, issue 72 (November–December 2009): 18.

9 "*Hira* Magazine Brings Together Arab Scholars in Istanbul," Cihan News Agency (5 October 2012).

10 "We Need the *Hizmet* Movement in Tunisia," Cihan News Agency (10 May 2013).

and Collective Consciousness" for nearly 3,000 participants from 80 countries. African countries were well represented; key speakers came from Nigeria, Egypt, Sudan, and Tunisia.[11] The head of Tunisia's largest opposition group, Rachid Ghannouchi, was invited to participate but could not for health reasons. He commented, however, that Tunisians value Gülen's contemporary Islamic activities, adding that Gülen's views combine the nobility of Islam with the modernism of our era. Ghannouchi praised the timing and purpose of the symposium.[12]

The French-language *Ebru Magazine* is similar to *The Fountain* and *Hira* but with articles designed for the francophone world and especially intellectuals. Originating in Istanbul in 2012, it is published four times a year. In addition to Belgium and France, it has representatives in Senegal, Morocco, Cameroon, Mali, Niger, and the Central African Republic. It tends to put a stronger emphasis on culture than science. Recent articles include "L'amour" by Fethullah Gülen, "Quand le desert redevient vert!" "La pollution sonore," and "Dialogue interculturel: vivre son identité et ses convictions religieuses en paix."[13]

There is a Spanish-language magazine with independent content called *Revista Cascada* that is published four times a year in Istanbul. It has no offices in Africa. The first issue came out in 2012. It is similar to *The Fountain* and *Ebru Magazine*, adapting the same themes to a Spanish-speaking audience. While designed for Latin America and Spain, it is relevant for Spanish speakers in Equatorial Guinea and the Western Sahara.[14]

The Movement is making some effort to place Gülen's writings in local media. *Le Quotidien*, a national paper in Senegal, signed, for example, a contract with the Gülen dialogue center in Dakar to publish one page each Monday. The first page appeared at the beginning of 2013. The chairman and managing director of *Le Quotidien* explained that Gülen's Sufi philosophy is similar to prevailing Islamic beliefs in Senegal and it helps offset a growing Salafist movement.[15]

The Gülen paper *Today's Zaman* is Turkey's leading English-language daily. Although it has a daily circulation in Turkey of only about 10,000 copies, it is available on the Internet, where it often serves as the leading source of news about Turkey in English.[16] The goal of *Today's Zaman* is to reach a global audience, the

---

11 "Sultan of Sokoto Spoke in Istanbul Conference," *www.ufukfoundation.org*.

12 "Tunisian Scholar Ghannouchi: Gülen Promotes 'Noble Islam,'" *Today's Zaman* (25 April 2013).

13 *www.ebrumagazine.com*.

14 *www.revistacascada.com*.

15 Author's meeting on 7 January 2013 in Dakar, Senegal with Madiambal Diagne, chairman and managing director of *Le Quotidien*.

16 *www.todayszaman.com*.

foreign press, business people in Turkey, and anyone doing research about Turkey on the Internet.[17] The paper provides extensive coverage of Gülen-affiliated schools, Gülen conferences, and TUSKON activities in Africa.

The Turkish-language *Zaman* has the highest circulation of any paper in Turkey, with about 1.1 million copies daily. *Today's Zaman* is not a translation of *Zaman*; their content is quite different. *Zaman* contains almost twice as many pages as *Today's Zaman*. A few of their stories are the same and both draw on the Cihan News Agency, another *Hizmet* institution. Each Friday, *Today's Zaman* devotes one page to the views of Gülen. Although *Today's Zaman* has one Nigerian on its staff, its coverage of Africa, other than non-Gülen-affiliated activity, is limited.[18]

The Cihan News Agency is a Gülen-affiliated organization and a sister agency of the Zaman Media Group. The Istanbul-based service has 600 personnel and a full-time staff in Cairo and Johannesburg, South Africa. It has part-time reporters in 65 countries overseas, including Nigeria, Senegal, Kenya, Algeria, and Mauritania. It provides articles in Turkish, English, Arabic, Kurdish, and Russian and reportedly makes enough money to cover its costs. It pays special attention to *Hizmet* activities globally and cooperates with Ebru TV.[19]

In 2012, Cihan's website added English, Arabic, and Russian. The English version of the website offers news in video, text, and photos, while the Arabic and Russian versions provide news stories and photos. Subscribers in the foreign languages are able to download photos and videos and search the archive. Non-subscribers can read the main stories, watch lower resolution videos, and search the archive.[20]

There are many websites, most of them sponsored by the Gülen Movement, that deal with *Hizmet*. Gülen's personal websites include *www.fgulen.com* and *www.fethullah-gulen.org*. The Gülen Institute in Houston, Texas, uses *www.guleninstitute.org*. The Fethullah Gülen Forum uses *www.fethullahgulenforum.org*. The Institute of Interfaith Dialog is *www.interfaithdialog.org*. The Istanbul-based Journalists and Writers Foundation is at *www.gyv.org.tr*. Conferences on the Gülen Movement are available at *www.fethullahgulenconference.org*. The *Hizmet* Movement News Portal is at *http://hizmetnews.com*. There are also many foreign language websites.[21]

---

17 Hendrick, 187.

18 Author's meeting on 13 January 2013 in Istanbul with Abdülhamit Bilici, columnist at *Today's Zaman*.

19 Ibid. *http://en.cihan.com.tr*.

20 "Cihan News Agency's New Website Welcomes 2012 with Four Languages," *Today's Zaman* (2 January 2012).

21 For a partial listing of foreign language sites, see Journalists and Writers Foundation, *Understanding Fethullah Gülen* (Istanbul: no date): 103.

There is a wealth of material on the Internet that is critical of the Gülen Movement. While most of it has little or no convincing documentation and falls in the rumor category, one useful site that raises some serious questions is "A Guide to the Gülen Movement's Activities in the US," which can be found at *http://turkishinvitations.weebly.com*. There is a longer list of Gülen-related links at *www.gulenmovement.us/links*.

Book Publishing

The Gülen Movement attaches a high priority to book publishing. While most of the titles are in Turkish, a surprising number are available in English, Arabic, and French, all of which are important in Africa. The largest Gulen-affiliated publisher is the Kaynak Publishing Group, first established in 1979. It includes some 20 different companies that have about 7,000 employees. The companies have published some 200 titles in English, 50 in Arabic, and about ten in French. They include translations of Gülen's works and books on Sufism, Mohammed's life, Islamic civilization, and Ottoman history. Some of the books reach the Gülen-affiliated schools and dialogue centers in Africa.[22]

Two of the publishing houses are located in the United States and publish in English. Tughra Books in New York City publishes books on Islam, Islamic history and art, and Islamic spirituality and traditions. It has offices in Istanbul, Cairo, and Moscow. Tughra Books emphasizes subjects that foster common understanding and mutual respect.[23] Blue Dome Press is located in Clifton, New Jersey, and publishes works primarily in the areas of interfaith dialogue, intercultural studies, art, and history. Its goal is to promote and encourage books that contribute to common understanding and dialogue among different cultures, religions, and communities of the world.[24]

Dar al-Nile Publishing is the Arabic-language affiliate of Kaynak. It exhibited, for example, books at the 20th Casablanca International Book Fair in Morocco, where Gülen's *The Messenger of God: Muhammad* drew the most interest.[25] Editions du Nil is the French-language publishing house under Kaynak.

In addition, there are informal arrangements to translate some of Gülen's books into more esoteric languages. The Hausa Translation Committee in Nigeria is translating Gülen's *The Messenger of God: Muhammad* from English to

---

22 Author's meeting on 12 January 2013 in Istanbul with Hakan Yeşilova, editor of *The Fountain*.
23 *www.tughrabooks.com*.
24 *www.bluedomepress.com*.
25 "Gülen Named Author of the Month in Casablanca," *Zaman* (12 March 2014).

Hausa.²⁶ Islamic studies scholar Hassan Tajir is translating the book from Arabic to Amharic.

Kaynak publishes a number of periodicals, including the Turkish-language *Sizinti*, a monthly magazine of popular science and culture, *Yeni Ümit*, on religious thought, *Yağmur*, on arts and literature, and *Gonca*, a monthly for children. While these are not relevant in Africa, Kaynak also has editorial responsibility for *The Fountain*, *Ebru Magazine*, *Hira*, and *Revista Cascada*.²⁷

Television Channels

Television is a relatively new effort by the Gülen Movement to reach an African audience. The Turkish-based Samanyolu Broadcasting Company (SBC), founded in 1993, now reaches viewers in more than 80 countries through several television and radio stations. Ebru (Turkish for the art of water marbling) TV, a majority-owned subsidiary of SBC, began operations in the United States in 2006, operating out of Somerset, New Jersey. It broadcasts 24 hours a day, seven days a week in English. Ebru TV only began to make a serious effort to attract viewers in Africa in 2012, when it opened an office in Nairobi, Kenya.²⁸

Ebru TV in Somerset provides a 24/7 feed in English to Africa, where it can be accessed only by satellite dish. It bills the programming as "clean, family fun." It includes news and sports, children's programs, family movies such as "Robin Hood" and "Call of the Wild," dramas, lifestyle and culture, and documentaries. There tends to be considerable program repetition. Ebru has a travel series called Ayna (mirror) for countries around the world. Kenya, Tunisia, Uganda, Guinea, Togo, Ethiopia, Benin, Mauritania, Morocco, Cote d'Ivoire, Burkina Faso, Cameroon, Liberia, and Tanzania have been featured in the series.²⁹

Programming in Africa is still a work in progress. Ebru has learned that you cannot just run programs and assume there will be interest. Reaching audiences in 54 different countries is a challenge. Establishment of the office in Kenya, which includes a production company and studios, has been a major improvement, but it has only about ten full-time Kenyan and Turkish staff. Editorial decisions are made in Kenya and not New Jersey. Ebru has begun production of a drama series in Kenya. The goal eventually is to open offices in Nigeria, South Africa, and Senegal.³⁰

---

26 Author's meeting on 31 December 2012 in Abuja, Nigeria with Oguzhan Dirican, president of the Ufuk Dialogue Foundation.

27 *www.kaynakpublishing.com/en/index/*.

28 *www.ebruafrica.tv*.

29 Ibid.

30 Author's meeting on 23 April 2014 in Somerset, New Jersey with Sertac Pehlivan,

Ebru TV has a memorandum of understanding with Inciproduction in Abuja, Nigeria. The company, which is affiliated with the Gülen Movement, produces programs for Ebru and other channels. The managing director, Imran Aydogdu, was previously a teacher in a Gülen-affiliated school in Nigeria. He works directly with the Ebru office in Kenya on all programming concerning Nigeria.[31]

Some of Ebru's programming is done by volunteers. Mesut Göcan Ateş is an example of a volunteer for Ebru TV. He works in Dakar, Senegal for Turkish Radio and Television Corporation but helps Ebru TV four or five times a week on his own time. He avoids controversial political issues and focuses on culture and special events. He also volunteers for the Gülen-affiliated schools in Senegal.[32]

For the time being, Ebru TV Africa broadcasts only in English. There is no immediate plan to increase the number of languages. Most programming comes from Somerset, but the news is produced in Nairobi. The goal is to move all operations to Africa. Ebru has no idea how many viewers it has in Africa or where they are concentrated. It is available in Gülen-affiliated schools and dialogue centers.[33] At least in Liberia, Ebru programs occasionally are rebroadcast over private and government channels.[34] The challenge is to match content with African interest in an economical way. Ebru can't afford recent Hollywood movies or major soccer matches. It must produce much of its own content. It is still trying to master the business model. SBC provided the capital investment. Ebru does not accept direct donations but relies on ad-based income. Advertising from Kenya is very new and limited. Funding is a major issue.[35]

Ebru TV programming is consistent with the main principles of Gülen, but does not explicitly advocate his philosophy. It does cover Gülen conferences in Africa, activities of Gülen-affiliated schools, *Kimse Yok Mu* projects, and success stories related to Gülen organizations. It avoids sex, profanity, and violence. In the case of news coverage of sensitive situations, such as religious violence in the Central African Republic, it tries just to report the facts. As for the future of Ebru TV in Africa, management takes as an article of faith that it will work out.[36]

The newest *Hizmet* television initiative is the Arabic language Hira TV.[37] It

---

Ebru TV vice president for programming.
31 Author's meeting on 31 December 2012 in Abuja, Nigeria with Aydogdu.
32 Author's meeting on 8 January 2013 in Dakar, Senegal with Ateş.
33 Author's meeting with Pehlivan.
34 Author's meeting on 3 January 2013 in Casablanca, Morocco with Ramazan Burak, general manager, Liberian-Turkish Light International School.
35 Author's meeting with Pehlivan.
36 Ibid.
37 *www.hira.tv*.

began operation in May 2014 as an Internet-only broadcast. Preparations are being made for satellite broadcasting. The goal is to build stronger ties between Turkey and the Arab world. Its first program was the live broadcast of an international symposium titled "Wealth of Islam: Islamic Opinion and Comparison." Hira TV features programming from Samanyolu, which has been broadcasting in Arabic for almost 20 years. Programs include lectures by Fethullah Gülen.[38]

Journalists and Writers Foundation and Gülen Conferences

A major participant in the *Hizmet* outreach effort is the Istanbul-based Journalists and Writers Foundation (JWF). Founded in 1994, its stated purpose is to bring together all segments of society from different ideological and religious backgrounds to debate issues pertaining to the nation and society. Gülen is the honorary chairman. Six units report to the JWF: the Abant Platform, the Intercultural Dialogue Platform, the Dialogue Eurasia Platform, the Medialog Platform, the Women's Platform, and the Research Center. The Abant Platform is the most relevant for Africa. It deals with issues such as democracy, human rights, laicism, globalization, and Islam in Turkey.[39]

The JWF is part think tank and part publishing house. It receives donations from Gülen-affiliated Bank Asya and *Hizmet*-related businesses to produce books by or about Gülen, Turkish Islam, and interfaith dialogue. It has become one of the Movement's most visible institutions. In 1994, it held its first forum, which dealt with fissures in Turkish society in the western Turkish mountain resort town of Abant, hence the Abant Platform. This event served as a "coming out" for the Movement and positioned it as one of Turkey's most important policy style think tanks. Today, the JWF and the Abant Platform host conferences in Istanbul and around the world, most of which specifically promote the ideas of Gülen. While the JWF claims to be "nonpolitical," it clearly tries to influence public policy, raising questions about its nonpolitical nature.[40]

The JWF is a standard stop for visits to Turkey organized by the Movement. In 2009, for example, six Nigerian journalists met with the JWF in Istanbul as part of a broader program. An assistant to the president of Senegal made a similar stop when he praised the quality of education at Gülen-affiliated schools

---

38 "Turkey's First Private Arabic Station Starts to Broadcast," *Today's Zaman* (11 May 2014).

39 *http://gyv.org.tr*. For background and an explanation of the dialogue platforms, see: Muhammed Çetin, *Hizmet: Questions and Answers on the Gülen Movement* (New York: Blue Dome Press, 2012), 30–34.

40 Hendrick, 200-203.

in Senegal.[41] President Ahmed Abdullah Mohammad Sambi of the Comoro Islands visited the JWF while attending a standing committee meeting of the Organization of Islamic Cooperation. On the occasion, he commented that "God willing Fethullah Gülen's ideas will bring relief to the world again."[42]

The major event in Africa organized by the Abant Platform of the JWF in cooperation with the Gülen-affiliated Nejashi Ethio-Turkish International Schools, the African Union Commission, and the Inter-Religious Council of Ethiopia was the "Africa Dialogue Forum" at the African Union in Addis Ababa in May 2012. Some 2,500 persons from 40 countries attended. Gülen sent a message to the delegates underscoring that mutual tolerance and maintenance of cultures is the focus of the conference, which also reviewed *Hizmet*'s contributions on the continent. In his remarks to the delegates, Ethiopian Federal Affairs Minister Shiferaw Teklemariam praised the *Hizmet* schools in Ethiopia.[43]

Mahdi Ahmed Ali, special advisor to the Ethiopian deputy prime minister and foreign minister, commented that the conference was both timely and the biggest in memory. The Ethiopian government was surprised by the number of participants. An interfaith event, it was especially well attended by Ethiopian Muslims. There were 15 participants from the Ministry of Education alone.[44] The person in charge of the human rights department of the African Union described the dialogue during the conference as a real success. The African Union has a mandate to promote interfaith dialogue and there is a widely held belief that *Hizmet* can help with this process. The next step is to create an appropriate structure for pursuing interfaith dialogue in the context of the African Union.[45]

The Abant Platform and African Union held a joint follow-up meeting in Addis Ababa in March 2014 for 155 participants from 15 countries. It emphasized respect for sacred values and the encouragement of freedom of religion by international and regional organizations.[46]

In June 2013, the Abant Platform organized a meeting titled "Africa: Between Experience and Inspiration" on Lake Abant in Turkey's Bolu Province.

---

41 Journalist and Writers Foundation, *Towards Universal Peace* (Istanbul: no date): 32–33 and 59–60.

42 "The President of Comoros Islands Sambi: 'Gülen's Ideas Will Give Relief to World'," 11 November 2009, *http://gyv.org.tr*.

43 "Hizmet Movement Discussed in Heart of African Union," *Today's Zaman* (30 May 2012).

44 Author's meeting on 4 September 2012 in Addis Ababa with Mahdi Ahmed Ali.

45 Author's meeting on 4 September 2012 in Addis Ababa with Saleh Ahmed.

46 "Abant Platform Calls for 'Respect for Sacred' in Africa Meeting," *Today's Zaman* (10 March 2014).

Approximately 80 participants each from Africa and Turkey participated. The Ufuk Dialogue Foundation organized the travel for the Nigerian delegation, which consisted of two academics and two journalists. The panel discussion on education included the ministers of education from Mali and the Democratic Republic of the Congo, and a professor from Chad. Other panels included the former foreign minister from Mauritania and the Anglican bishop from South Africa.[47]

The symposium was divided into five sessions: (1) Africa: Images and Realities; (2) Contribution of African Values to Universal Coexistence; (3) Education in Africa: Challenges and Opportunities; (4) Health in Africa: Challenges and Opportunities; and (5) Economic Development of Africa: Different Approaches to Sustainable Growth. The final communique was, however, anodyne and offered little to solve practically the problems discussed at the conference.[48]

The JWF outreach effort concerning Africa extends to the United States. In 2014, JWF and the Gülen-affiliated Peace Islands Institute in New York organized four panel discussions primarily for African permanent representatives to the United Nations as part of its Ambassadors Series. Called "African Solutions to African Problems," the first one took place in February with the permanent representatives to the UN from Uganda and Gambia and the counselor from the Nigerian mission. The principal issues were the significance of natural resources in African conflicts, the place of culture in finding African solutions to African problems, and the role of women in conflict.[49]

The second panel took place in April with the permanent representatives from Equatorial Guinea and South Africa and the deputy permanent representative from Egypt.[50] The third panel in May attracted the permanent representatives of Botswana, Chad, and Burundi. The theme was peace and security in Africa.[51] The fourth and final panel in June featured the permanent representatives of Senegal, Gambia, and Montenegro. Senegal's Ambassador Abdou Salam Diallo used the occasion to praise the *Hizmet* schools in Senegal.[52]

---

47 "Abant Platform on Africa to Convene on Friday," *Today's Zaman* (26 June 2013). "Turkey: A Forum on Africa," *Daily Trust* (Nigeria), (11 July 2013).

48 "Abant Platform on Africa," *Today's Zaman* (28 June 2013). "29th Abant Platform 'Africa: Between Experience and Inspiration' Final Declaration, 30 June 2013, Abant, Bolu," *www.abantplatform.org*.

49 "Ambassadors Series Panel Seeks African Solutions to African Problems," 12 February 2014, *http://jwfglobal.org*.

50 PR Newswire (25 April 2014).

51 "JWF and PIINY Hosted Third Panel on African Solutions to African Problems," 14 May 2014, *http://jwfglobal.org*.

52 "African Solutions to African Problems—Africa Panel 4," 18 June 2014, *www.peaceislands.org*.

Occasionally there are conferences devoted to the teachings of Gülen organized by groups not directly affiliated with Gülen. In 2012, for example, the Faculty of Islamic Sciences at the University of Algiers organized a conference called "Perception of Civilization in the Light of Teachings of Fethullah Gülen and Algerian Scholar Malik bin Nabi." It attracted academics, journalists, and writers from 18 countries. Algerian presidential adviser Mohammed Ali Boughazi cited both Gülen and Nabi for their efforts in promoting peace and tolerance. Conference participants included the editor-in-chief of *Hira* magazine and the president of the Board of Trustees of Fatih University, a Gülen-affiliated university in Turkey.[53]

One other institution that has the potential for outreach concerning Africa is the Gülen Institute at the University of Houston in Texas. Established in 2007, it is a non-profit research organization dedicated to the promotion of peace and civic welfare and the philosophy of Gülen. It offers research grants and scholarships, organizes lectures at the University of Houston, and facilitates workshops and panel discussions. It is a joint initiative of the Graduate College of Social Work at the University of Houston and the Institute of Interfaith Dialog. The only visible connection it has had so far with Africa is the fact that Ghanaian-born Kofi Annan, Secretary-General of the United Nations from 1997 to 2006, spoke at an Institute event in 2010.[54]

Hizmet Discussion Groups

Where there is a critical mass in Africa or other countries of persons who are interested in the teachings of Gülen, there will likely be an informal group that meets regularly to discuss his views. These evening discussions often focus on a particular *Hizmet* theme or Gülen writing. Most of the participants, at least in Africa, appear to be from the Turkish business community and the discussion tends to be in Turkish. While non-Turkish nationals are welcome, the language issue limits participation.

In the case of Casablanca, Morocco, the group meets weekly. Normally seven or eight persons attend. The goal is to keep the number at about ten and when it passes 15, a new group will be formed. The session is also used to raise money for local *Hizmet* projects. Although not a stated purpose of the meetings, they offer an excellent opportunity for the Turkish business community to share information and ideas on expanding their commercial contacts and even developing their business.[55]

---

53 "Gülen's Teachings Discussed at Conference in Algeria," *Today's Zaman* (22 November 2012).

54 *www.guleninstitute.org*.

55 Author's attendance on 3 January 2013 at a discussion group meeting in Casablanca.

Concluding Thoughts

For a small movement in terms of the likely number of financial contributors, the *Hizmet* media and outreach effort is large and impressive in Turkey and, increasingly, beyond. In the case of Africa, the dialogue centers discussed in chapter 5 are a modest, but essential, part of the outreach activities. Although thinly staffed and absent from most African countries, they offer an on-the-ground presence in key countries that facilitate the distribution of *Hizmet* publications, increase the awareness of Ebru and Hira TV, and assist with the organization of meetings and conferences about Gülen.

It is much too soon to assess the impact of Ebru TV and especially Hira TV, which was launched in 2014 and initially was only available online. The challenges will be great for both because of the high cost of accessing television audiences in Africa, well-established competition, programs only in English and Arabic, and the importance of providing appropriate program content to a diverse African audience.

It is hard to judge the impact of the periodical and book distribution programs. The periodicals are professionally prepared and available in the major *lingua franca* used in Africa. Nevertheless, only modest numbers are distributed on the continent. While the books are not expensive and sometimes are provided free of charge, they are not widely available in Africa. In any event, they are designed for elite audiences and not the general public. On the other hand, the Movement's goal is to bring Gülen's ideas to the attention of opinion leaders in the political, journalistic, and religious communities and hope they take root and are passed on to others. There is some evidence this is occurring, but there is no way to measure the actual impact.

The Movement seems to have had considerable success with its symposia and conferences on Gülen themes, especially from those held in Africa, rather than in Turkey or elsewhere. An event that occurs in Africa is guaranteed to attract more publicity than one held in Turkey. There was widespread praise from African participants at the two large conferences in Abuja, Nigeria, in 2011, and Addis Ababa, Ethiopia, in 2012. The Movement has also established a solid link with the African Union.

There is no evidence as of this writing that the dispute between the Gülen Movement and Turkey's ruling Justice and Development Party has impacted negatively the *Hizmet* media or outreach efforts in Africa.

CHAPTER 8

HIZMET, THE AKP, AND TURKEY-AFRICA RELATIONS

Hizmet activities in Africa are only a small part of the broader relationship involving the Gülen Movement, the Justice and Development Party (AKP), and the government of Turkey. *Hizmet*'s role in Turkey and even certain other parts of the world is much more important. Nevertheless, how these relations play out in Africa sheds light on the wider *Hizmet*-AKP-government relationship. In addition, the 54 countries in Africa represent more than one-quarter of the membership of the United Nations and in recent years Turkey has made a major effort to expand its presence on the continent. *Hizmet* schools preceded Turkish embassies in most African countries and they are still seen as the face of Turkey in a few of them. Consequently, the relationship between *Hizmet* and the Turkish government in Africa is especially important.

AKP and *Hizmet*: The Early Years

The AKP has Islamic roots but has moved to the center-right in order to avoid the fate of its defunct predecessors. All previous Islamist parties—National Order Party, National Salvation Party, Welfare Party, and Virtue Party—were shut down by military intervention or rulings by the constitutional court. Recep Tayyip Erdoğan and Abdullah Gül were young leaders in the Welfare Party. In 2001, Erdoğan created the AKP from the remains of the dissolved Welfare Party and Virtue Party. He put democratic reforms at the top of the AKP agenda. The AKP won the election in 2002 with 34 percent of the vote. Initially Gül was prime minister, the more important position in the Turkish system, but was replaced by Erdoğan in 2003.[1]

The early AKP leaders—Erdoğan, Gül, and Bülent Arinç—had reasonably good personal relations with the Gülen Movement. Erdoğan had attended dialogue meetings of the Gülen-affiliated Journalists and Writers Foundation and even gave a keynote address at one of them. Arinç was the first politician to defend Gülen when elements of the media launched a campaign against him in 1999. The

---

1   Ömer Taşpinar, "Turkey: The New Model?" Brookings (April 2012), *www.brookings.edu*.

domestic and foreign policy views of the young AKP leaders were similar to those of the Gülen Movement. On domestic issues they both emphasized democracy, passive secularism, and the importance of interfaith dialogue. On foreign policy they supported efforts to take advantage of globalization's opportunities, rather than pursuing an isolationist policy to avoid its challenges.[2]

The Gülen Movement and the AKP emerged from different Islamic traditions. Perhaps oversimplifying, the Gülen Movement represents "civil Islamic" tradition while the AKP reflects political Islam. The two groups formed a tactical alliance to curb the military's role in politics and to rebuild the state and Turkish society. The Gülen-affiliated media and supporters within the Turkish bureaucracy, especially those in the police and judiciary, gave their support to the AKP. The Gülen Movement then benefited from the AKP's proactive policies outside the country, including those in Africa.[3]

In a study of Gülen, Joshua Hendrick concluded that the Gülen Movement was the most influential player in the AKP-led passive revolution. He described the AKP as the political mechanism, which operated through parliament, the presidency, and the state apparatus. The Gülen Movement was the civilian arm, which used education, business, and the media.[4] Put another way by a Turkish scholar, "the period of the rise of the AKP to power in Turkey was also the time of growing significance for the Gülen movement."[5] The Movement saw itself "as *the* motivating factor behind the AKP's political success, and as *the* primary agent in the transformation of Turkish Islamic activism in general."[6] Mustafa Yesil, president of the Journalist and Writers Foundation, said that the Movement supported the AKP based on the premise it would fight against military tutelage, democratize, pursue admission to the European Union, and create a new civilian constitution.[7]

---

2   Ahmet T. Kuru, "Changing Perspectives on Islamism and Secularism in Turkey: The Gülen Movement and the AK Party," in *Muslim World in Transition: Contributions of the Gülen Movement*, ed. Ihsan Yilmaz (London: Leeds Metropolitan University Press, 2007), 145–147.

3   Gönül Tol, "The Clash of Former Allies: The AKP versus the Gülen Movement," Middle East Institute (7 March 2014), *www.mei.edu*.

4   Joshua D. Hendrick, *Gülen: The Ambiguous Politics of Market Islam in Turkey and the World* (New York: New York University Press, 2013), 25.

5   İştar B. Gözaydin, "The Fethullah Gülen Movement and Politics in Turkey: A Chance for Democratization or a Trojan Horse?" *Democratization* 16, no. 6 (December 2009), 1217.

6   Ibid., 238. See also Graham E. Fuller, *The New Turkish Republic: Turkey as a Pivotal State in the Muslim World* (Washington: US Institute of Peace Press, 2008), 58–59.

7   Cited in Suzy Hansen, "Whose Turkey Is It?" *New York Times Magazine* (5 February 2014), 37.

The *Hizmet*-AKP Relationship Matures

In 2007, Turkish police began arresting more than 200 nationalist and secularist members of an organization known as Ergenekon, whose goal allegedly was to create chaos and to bring down the AKP government. The AKP, Gülen-affiliated media, and some liberals welcomed the trials against the plotters. By this time, significant numbers of Gülen Movement supporters had moved into positions in the police and judicial system. The Ergenekon affair led to charges in Turkey that the Gülen Movement had set up parallel structures within government institutions that could bypass the official structures of which they were a part. Some Turks equated the arrests with growing power of the Gülen Movement inside the governmental system. The Movement responded that the arrests took place for the sake of democracy and that there is nothing unusual with its followers being employed as police and in the judiciary.[8]

Never a transparent movement, in part because it is so loosely organized, the Ergenekon affair only underscored concerns about *Hizmet* transparency. Suzy Hansen, a journalist living in Turkey, wrote that "what the Gülenists have yet to reckon with, however, is that when a relatively non-transparent movement starts asserting itself politically, it is going to make people nervous—even some inside the government."[9]

The Gülen Movement has traditionally eschewed supporting any political party, although mainstream conservative parties have been close to both Gülen and the Movement.[10] Y. Alp Aslandoğan, president of the Gülen-affiliated Alliance for Shared Values, explained that the Movement is engaged in politics not by aligning with a particular party but by supporting common issues, values, and attitudes. Today, one party may reflect common values and garner Movement support but tomorrow it might be a totally different party. Aslandoğan added that anyone closely identified with the Movement is discouraged from running for political office.[11]

In the July 2007 parliamentary elections and especially the contest for president, the Gülen-affiliated press opposed the assertive secular groups that tried to prevent the election of the AKP presidential candidate—Abdullah Gül.

---

8   Suzy Hansen, "The Global Imam," *The New Republic* 241, issue 10 (2 December 2010), 14–15.

9   Ibid., 15.

10 Ihsan Yilmaz, "*Ijtihad* and *Tajdid* by Conduct: The Gülen Movement," in *Turkish Islam and the Secular State: The Gülen Movement*, ed. M. Hakan Yavuz and John L. Esposito (Syracuse, NY: Syracuse University Press, 2003), 226.

11 Responding to questions during a meeting on the Gülen Movement at the Center for Strategic and International Studies in Washington on 17 June 2009. Aslandoğan is also a board member of the Gülen Institute.

The AKP and Gül won handily, aided by support from the Gülen Movement. The AKP increased its share of the vote to almost 47 percent. Erdoğan remained as prime minister and Gül became president. The AKP and the Gülen Movement demonstrated their joint belief in passive secularism.[12]

Mehmet Kalyoncu, author of a book on the Gülen Movement, explained in 2008 that there are similarities and differences between the Movement and AKP positions on social, economic, and political issues. As a result, there are different ways to interpret the relationship between the Movement and the AKP. He argued the Movement and the AKP seem to share a similar vision for Turkey in promoting participatory democracy and civil liberties at all levels. They also share Mustafa Kemal Atatürk's vision of bringing Turkey up to the level of modern civilizations by creating a Turkey that can compete politically and economically in the global arena. He then cited the role played in this mutual vision by the *Hizmet* schools and TUSKON.[13]

The close links between the AKP/Turkish government and *Hizmet* played out in Africa in the form of visits to Gülen-affiliated schools by senior members of the Turkish government as they travelled around the continent (see chapter 4). The visits began at least as early as 2008 when then Foreign Minister Ali Babacan visited a school in Senegal and continued until early in 2013 when the wife of Prime Minister Erdoğan visited one in Niger. President Gül seems to have made more visits to *Hizmet* schools than any other senior official. There was also collaboration until 2013 involving senior Turkish government officials and TUSKON concerning trade and investment-related events in Africa and Turkey (see chapter 3). In some countries there is even a widespread misunderstanding that *Hizmet* projects are supported by the Turkish government. This is reportedly the case in Nigeria, for example, where *Hizmet* has been especially active and its efforts have overshadowed those of the government.[14]

The degree to which Turkish embassies in Africa interact with *Hizmet* schools and other activities seemed to vary significantly. Whenever senior Turkish officials visited a *Hizmet* school in Africa, the local Turkish embassy became involved. There are also numerous cases where Turkish embassy officials attended *Hizmet* school openings and graduation ceremonies. The personal position of Turkish ambassadors in Africa on the Gülen Movement also impacted the relationship. During the author's visit to seven African countries, all of which had a Turkish embassy at the time, the *Hizmet* personnel who arranged the schedule never included a stop at a Turkish embassy.

---

12 Kuru, 148–150.
13 Mehmet Kalyoncu, "Gülen and the AK Party," *Sunday's Zaman* (2 July 2008).
14 Author's meeting on 31 December 2012 in Abuja, Nigeria with Mustafa Ahsen, chief medical director of Nizamiye Hospital.

A former South African ambassador to Turkey, who continues to follow Turkey-Africa relations, explained that in South Africa the Turkish embassy tended to keep its distance from Gülen activities. He said the relationship between the Turkish government and the Gülen Movement has varied over time. To the best of his knowledge, there was as of 2012 no written guidance from the Turkish Ministry of Foreign Affairs concerning interaction with Gülen-affiliated organizations.[15]

There were also occasions when the government's international aid organization, the Turkish Cooperation and Coordination Agency, collaborated in Africa with *Hizmet*'s counterpart organization, *Kimse Yok Mu* (see chapter 6). The goals of the two organizations are similar, but *Kimse Yok Mu* travels through Islam while the Turkish Cooperation and Coordination Agency operates strictly as a governmental institution.[16]

Cracks Develop in the Relationship

The AKP and the Gülen Movement never marched in lockstep. Although they shared some important general principles, they also occasionally disagreed on policies and tactics. And then there was always the intangible factor concerning a desire for influence and power by both the AKP and the Movement. One of the first open disagreements occurred in 2010 when the *Mavi Marmara*, the Turkish ship carrying supplies to Palestinians in Gaza, triggered a crisis. Before the ship reached Gaza, Israeli commandos boarded and killed nine Turkish activists. Gülen argued that Turkish authorities should have prevented the ship from sailing in the first place. The AKP supported the venture and reacted angrily to Gülen's rebuke. The following year, Gülen-affiliated media criticized Erdoğan for reducing sentences given to football officials who were charged and convicted of rigging matches. The Gülen media also spoke out against some AKP officials' concerns about the length of pretrial detentions for persons accused of involvement in the Ergenekon affair.[17]

In the middle of these disagreements, both Gülen and Gülen-affiliated media endorsed an AKP-backed constitutional referendum. Erdoğan acknowledged the

---

15 Author's meeting on 26 August 2012 in Johannesburg, South Africa.

16 Author's meeting on 7 January 2013 in Dakar, Senegal with Mesut Gökcan Ateş.

17 Thomas Seibert, "Tensions between Turkey's Ruling AKP and Gulenics Fester," *The National* (26 December 2011). Alexander Brock, "What is the Gülen Movement?" Appendix B of the Council on Foreign Relations Independent Task Force Report No. 69 on *U.S.-Turkey Relations: A New Partnership*, May 2012, 59. Hansen, "The Global Imam," 15. Notes taken by author during remarks at Georgetown University by Thomas Michael on 6 February 2013. Bayram Balci, "Turkey's Gülen Movement: Between Social Activism and Politics," 24 October 2013, *http:// carnegieendowment.org*.

support he received from "friends across the ocean," an obvious reference to Gülen, who lived in Pennsylvania.[18] In June 2011, the AKP won its third electoral victory with almost 50 percent of the vote. The top AKP leadership remained in place.

The Economist was among the first international publications to pick up on the growing schism between the Gülen Movement and the AKP. A story early in 2012 referred to "a nasty power struggle" between Erdoğan and Gülen. It suggested that the Movement might withdraw its support of the AKP.[19] Later in the year, Ihsan Yilmaz, a professor at Gülen-affiliated Fatih University and columnist for *Today's Zaman*, agreed with some critics of *Hizmet* that Gülen-affiliated media had been too pro-AKP and did not give sufficient space to opposition parties. He then lashed out at the AKP for promising to democratize Turkey but failing to tackle military tutelage since the 2011 elections.[20]

By the end of 2012, others were focusing on the Gülen-AKP rivalry. Claire Berlinski, the Istanbul-based senior fellow for Turkey at the American Foreign Policy Council, commented on Erdoğan's increasing discomfort with "Gülen's control over the judiciary and police" and the political cost of investigations launched by the special authority courts. She wrote that the final straw was Erdoğan's attempt to abolish the special authority courts; the divide between Gülen and the AKP was now impossible to ignore.[21] Dorian Jones, a freelance reporter based in Istanbul, added a few weeks later that the tactical alliance between Erdoğan and Gülen is unraveling and "the breakup is threatening to turn acrimonious."[22] It took several more months, however, for the split to take hold. Early in 2013, for example, AKP deputy chairman Hüseyin Çelik expressed appreciation for Gülen's support for ongoing talks with the Kurdistan Workers' Party, likening Gülen's remarks to those of South Africa's Nelson Mandela.[23] This compliment came in spite of differences Gülen had on the way Erdoğan was handling the Kurdish question in Turkey.[24]

---

18 Hansen, "The Global Imam," 15.
19 "Turkey's Political In-fighting: Erdoğan at Bay," *The Economist* (25 February 2012).
20 "Criticizing Hizmet," *Today's Zaman* (15 September 2012).
21 Claire Berlinski, "Anatomy of a Power Struggle," *The Journal of International Security Affairs* (19 December 2012), www.afpc.org.
22 "Showdown Looms between Erdoğan and Gülen Movement," *Inter Press Service* (8 January 2013).
23 "Çelik Likens Gülen's Stance on Peace Talks to that of Mandela," *Today's Zaman* (11 January 2013).
24 Bayram Balci.

The Crack Splits Wide Open

By mid-2013, the disagreements between the Gülen Movement and the AKP reached the point where they became more important than the areas of agreement. A peaceful protest against plans to replace Gezi Park, the last green space in central Istanbul, with a replica of an Ottoman-era barracks that once stood on the site, resulted in a police crackdown in late May and demonstrations that spread across Turkey. Gülen and the Gülen-affiliated press expressed disapproval of the manner in which the government dealt with the protestors.[25] Columnists who support the AKP began attacking the Gülen Movement, alleging that it was plotting against Erdoğan. The Gülen-affiliated Journalists and Writers Association issued an 11-point manifesto rebutting the claims.[26] Deputy Prime Minister Bülent Arınç commented that the fight between the AKP and *Hizmet* "is very ugly" and the government never wanted it to reach such a point. He urged discussions take place.[27]

As the Gülen-affiliated media attacked the government's restrictions on press freedom, policies in the Middle East and especially those dealing with Syria, and the post-Gezi crackdown, Erdoğan announced the closure of the country's private exam prep schools. About a quarter of these schools were run by followers of Gülen. Not only were they an important source of revenue, they were used to attract young followers to the Movement. The government argued they perpetuate social inequalities between those who can and cannot afford them, creating a parallel system of education. The government subsequently agreed to allow them to operate until 2015 when they would become private schools.[28]

In mid-December 2013, following police raids and an investigation by a prosecutor in Istanbul believed to be sympathetic to Gülen, authorities brought charges against Erdoğan's son, the sons of three AKP ministers, and several business persons linked to Erdoğan. They were alleged to have engaged in shady deals with Iran and bribery for winning construction projects. Erdoğan charged that followers of Gülen were engaged in a conspiracy against him as part of a "parallel

---

25 Michael Birnbaum, "In Turkey Protests, Splits in Erdoğan's Base," *The Washington Post* (14 June 2013). Hansen, "Whose Turkey Is It?" 39. Yüksel Sezgin, "Erdoğan-Gülen-Gül Rivalry: All the Sultan's Men," *Aljazeera* (1 January 2014). Bayram Balci.

26 "*Hizmet* Movement and the AK Party," *Today's Zaman* (16 August 2013). "Turkish Politics: Lonely Command," *The Economist* (24 August 2013).

27 "Deputy PM Says Image of Gov't-Hizmet Fight Ugly," *Today's Zaman* (27 August 2013).

28 Piotr Zalewski, "Turkey's Erdoğan Battles Country's Most Powerful Religious Movement," *Time* (4 December 2013). Hansen, "Whose Turkey Is It?" 39. Ayla Jean Yackley, "Turkish Parliament Votes to Shut Schools Run by Erdoğan Rival," *Reuters* (1 March 2014).

state." One Turkish columnist concluded that the Erdoğan-Gülen dispute is "a divorce proceeding that is getting uglier by the day."[29]

The relationship deteriorated quickly from this point. Deputy Prime Minister Bülent Arinç said the corruption charges amounted to a plot within the state and suggested the government would purge those responsible for the investigation. Marking the beginning of a wide-scale purge, five senior police officials believed to be linked to the Gülen Movement were removed from their jobs.[30] Friends of Gülen responded that government supporters were engaged in a "smear campaign" against Hizmet.[31] Gülen's lawyer wrote that Erdoğan had become too powerful, too authoritarian, and had abandoned his democratic policies. He also denied that Gülen had any involvement in the corruption investigations.[32]

As the purge expanded and began to snare government journalists, Gülen personally lashed out publicly against those who act contrary to the teachings of the Prophet Mohammed. He said "those who don't see the thief but go after those trying to catch the thief, who don't see the murder but try to defame others by accusing innocent people—let God bring fire to their houses, ruin their homes, break their unities..."[33] Curiously, pro-government newspapers then charged that the American ambassador to Turkey was behind the corruption investigation. The Turkish Foreign Ministry quickly accepted the embassy's denial of any involvement in the investigation.[34]

The scandal forced Erdoğan to call for the resignation of three of his ministers whose sons had been accused of corruption, fired a fourth, and realigned his cabinet. The resigning minister of environment and urban planning did not leave quietly. He suggested that Erdoğan also resign because he had approved most of the construction projects involved in the corruption scandal.[35] By the end of 2013, the crisis had destabilized the Turkish economy and led to efforts by

---

29 Hansen, "Whose Turkey Is It?" 39. Tim Arango and Sebnem Arsu, "Graft Inquiry Intensifies Turkish Political Rivalry," *The New York Times* (17 December 2013). "Turkish Politics: Erdoğan v Gülen," *The Economist* (14 December 2013), 60–61.

30 Tim Arango, "Raids and Graft Inquiry in Turkey Are Seen by Some as Muslim Cleric's Plot," *The New York Times* (18 December 2013).

31 Kerim Balci, "The Dangers of Demonization," *Today's Zaman* (18 December 2013).

32 Tim Arango, Sebnem Arsu and Ceylan Yeginsu, "Growing Corruption Inquiry Hits Close to Turkish Leader," *The New York Times* (19 December 2013).

33 "For First Time, Fethullah Gülen Curses Purge of Police Officials in Emotional Speech," 21 December 2013, *http://hizmetnews.com*.

34 Tim Arango, "Turkish Premier Blames Foreign Envoys for Turmoil," *The New York Times* (21 December 2013).

35 Emre Peker, "Turkish Leader Pressed to Quit," *The Wall Street Journal* (26 December 2013). Hansen, "Whose Turkey Is It?" 39.

Erdoğan to improve relations with his former nemesis, the military. Irrespective of the final outcome of the dispute, some commentators suggested it will leave Erdoğan with permanent political scars.[36]

Early in 2014, a *Hizmet* spokesperson claimed the government had changed all prosecutors that opened the original corruption cases, removed 3,000 police officers including 20 police chiefs in major cities, and removed 5,000 bureaucrats. The government also drafted a bill to limit freedom of the Internet.[37] Osman Can, a member of the AKP's Central Executive Committee, argued these purges should continue because *Hizmet* members "do not conform with the state hierarchy but take orders from the movement. They run their own political system inside the institutions within the state."[38]

The Wall Street Journal in a late January interview pressed Gülen whether his "alliance" with the AKP had come to an end. Gülen responded that any alliance was based solely on shared democratic values; *Hizmet* has never formed an alliance with a political party or candidate. He then identified principles where the AKP and *Hizmet* had separated company.[39]

A few days later in an interview with the *BBC*, Gülen's first televised interview in 16 years, he said it is certain there is corruption in Turkey but emphasized he has no connection to the investigations. He said it is wrong to think that all of the people being purged are sympathetic to *Hizmet*. Some are social democrats, nationalists, and ultranationalists. He insisted he did not even know 0.1 percent of the persons running the corruption investigations. Gülen added that those behind the defamation campaign are trying to scare people by exaggerating *Hizmet*'s size and influence. As for upcoming Turkish elections, Gülen did not endorse any party but urged people to vote for whoever stands for the rule of law and is respectful of democracy.[40]

---

36 Seda Sezer and Dan Williams, "Erdoğan Vows Graft Scandal in Turkey Won't Topple Him," *The Washington Post* (29 December 2013). Frida Ghitis, "World Citizen: How Erdoğan Is Losing Turkey," *World Politics Review* (9 January 2014).

37 Oğuzhan Tekin, "Beginning of the End for Erdoğan," *Today's Zaman* (20 January 2014).

38 Joe Parkinson and Ayla Albayrak, "From His Refuge in the Poconos, Reclusive Imam Fethullah Gülen Roils Turkey," *The Wall Street Journal* (20 January 2014).

39 *The Wall Street Journal* interview with Gülen posted on 21 January 2014. Others, for example Gönül Tol, director of the Center for Turkish Studies at the Washington-based Middle East Institute, described the Gülen-AKP relationship as a "decade-long alliance."

40 "Islamic Scholar Gülen Says Turkey's Graft Scandal Can't Be Covered Up," *Today's Zaman* (27 January 2014). Tim Franks, "Fethullah Gülen: Powerful but Reclusive Turkish Cleric" and Guney Yildiz, "Analysis: Power of Turkey's Fethullah Gülen," *BBC* (27 January 2014), *www.bbc.co.uk*.

While Gülen was careful in his choice of words during interviews with *The Wall Street Journal* and *BBC*, that was not the case with all persons speaking on behalf of *Hizmet*. One analyst wrote in *Today's Zaman*: "No government can survive these allegations and scandals. Like leaders of opposition parties and many commentators, I think Erdoğan has come to the end of his power. He should resign or flee for the sake of the country."[41]

By mid-March, Gülen became more outspoken about the situation faced by *Hizmet* at the hands of the AKP. In a five-part interview with *Today's Zaman*, he said the pressure and slander against *Hizmet* was worse than that seen during military regimes in Turkey, although he urged his supporters to remain patient and not despair. The government's goal seems to be to attribute every inexplicable event to *Hizmet* and use it as a scapegoat. He criticized the Erdoğan government for failing to combat corruption but then cracking down on those who investigated the charges. Concerning allegations that *Hizmet* is a "parallel state," he said if this is true "then may God curse us; but if not, may He curse those who attribute this slander to this innocent movement!" He reiterated that *Hizmet* is not and will not be a political party and lamented the fact that Turkish officials have been asked to denounce *Hizmet* schools outside the country. Concerning upcoming local elections at the end of March 2014, he urged his followers to support deserving candidates rather than parties. He even suggested some AKP candidates may deserve support.[42]

Several weeks later, Orhan Erdemli, a lawyer for Gülen, wrote that Erdoğan is bringing all kinds of pressure against Gülen-affiliated institutions and business persons, including an order to Turkish ambassadors to ask foreign governments to close *Hizmet* schools (see chapter 4). Erdemli argued that the AKP has declared war on *Hizmet*. He quoted a pro-government columnist who wrote at the end of 2013 that he knew an operation against the Gülen Movement had been under way for about a year.[43]

The AKP won 45 percent of the vote in the March 2014 local elections. Most observers considered this a significant victory for Erdoğan, although he faced setbacks in the courts as he tried to consolidate his control.[44] On the foreign front, as noted in chapter 4, Turkey convinced the president of Gambia to close the single *Hizmet* school in the country. More significantly, the government of Azerbaijan agreed to close the Gülen-affiliated Caucasus University, 13 high schools, and 13 university exam preparation centers. There had been some

---

41 Oğuzhan Tekin, "Resign or Flee," *Today's Zaman* (3 March 2014).
42 Fethullah Gülen, 5-part interview with *Today's Zaman* on 16, 17, 18, 19, 20 March 2014.
43 Orhan Erdemli, "Is *Hizmet* Being Subjected to Genocide?" Journalists and Writers Foundation (18 April 2014), *http://gyv.org.tr*.
44 "Turkey's Prime Minister: Erdoğan v Judges, Again," *The Economist* (19 April 2014).

concern within the Azerbaijan government about the schools, but pressure from the Turkish government almost certainly led to the closures.[45]

Near the end of 2014, the government initiated a new round of arrests, which included senior Gülen-affiliated journalists, including key personnel at the Samanyolu Broadcasting Group and *Zaman* newspaper. This attack on press freedom resulted in a rebuke from the European Union and a warning from the U.S. Department of State.[46] A Turkish court subsequently issued an arrest warrant for Gülen. Prosecutors told the court that Gülen "has committed crimes within the scope of the indictment" but that he could not be compelled to answer the charges "because of his long-term residence abroad."[47]

Erdoğan was not permitted by the constitution to serve again as prime minister. He decided, therefore, to seek the presidency with the goal of making constitutional changes that would give the position more power. He won the August election impressively in the first round with 51.7 percent of the vote. He does not have, however, a sufficient majority in Parliament to change the constitution and must wait until elections in 2015, when he hopes to obtain a constitutional majority to make these changes.

In the meantime, he will operate as a de facto executive president. Gül, who historically had cordial relations with the Gülen Movement, wanted to shift from the presidency to the position of prime minister, but Erdoğan opposed this move and selected his foreign minister, Ahmet Davutoğlu, to replace Gül. While Davutoğlu is loyal to Erdoğan, he has his own ideas and will not serve as a puppet. As president, Erdoğan must sever all relations with his party and cannot campaign for the AKP. The period until the parliamentary elections will be delicate for both Erdoğan and the Gülen Movement.[48]

When asked if he could imagine reconciling with Erdoğan, Gülen responded that *Hizmet* did not start the fight. The AKP would have to make the first move toward reconciliation. In addition, Erdoğan would need to confess that his comments about *Hizmet* "were nothing more than lies and slander."[49]

---

45 Shahla Sultanova, "Azerbaijan Backing Turkey's Crackdown on Gülen Movement," *EurasiaNet* (15 April 2014), www.eurasianet.org. "Azerbaijan Shuts Down 'Gülen-linked' Schools," *Daily News* (8 July 2014).

46 Sebnew Arsu, "In Push against Muslim Cleric, Turkey Detains Police Officers and Journalists," *New York Times* (14 December 2014).

47 Ceylan Yeginsu, "Turkey Issues Arrest Warrant for a Rival of Its President," *New York Times* (19 December 2014).

48 Sinan Ülgen, "Erdoğan Is the Victor But He Is Not Yet Almighty," *Financial Times* (11 August 2014). Henri J. Barkey, "Turkey after Erdoğan's Non-Victory," Wilson Center Viewpoints no. 59 (August 2014). Yüksel Sezgin.

49 Fethullah Gülen interview with German newspaper *Süddeutsche Zeitung* on 13

Impact of Split on *Hizmet* in Africa

The breakup of the relationship between the Gülen Movement and the AKP has had important implications for Turkish domestic politics. So far, the impact on *Hizmet* in Africa has been minimal. The only tangible result has been the closure of one *Hizmet* school in Gambia. As noted in chapter 4, a few African leaders have been vocal in their praise of *Hizmet* schools after the Gülen-AKP split became widely known. Although there was an instruction from Turkey's Foreign Ministry to its ambassadors around the world to curb *Hizmet* activities, especially schools, it is not clear exactly what that guidance hopes to achieve. Nor is it clear what Turkish embassies are willing to do about it.

Since 2005, Turkey has expanded significantly its presence and activities in Sub-Saharan Africa; it always had a strong presence in the five North African countries. Except for Morocco, however, the *Hizmet* presence is generally weak in North Africa. The battleground, if there is to be one, will likely occur in Sub-Saharan Africa, where *Hizmet* is more firmly established in many countries than is the Turkish government. *Hizmet* has another advantage in that no government, including those in Africa, likes to be threatened by another. If the Turkish government uses heavy-handed tactics in Africa to shut down *Hizmet* activities, it will almost certainly encounter resistance.

In any event, with the exception of a few Sub-Saharan African countries, Turkey does not have that much leverage. Turkey has developed a strong political and aid relationship with Somalia and Sudan. In 2012, Somalia was the largest recipient of Turkish aid at $87 million and Sudan was second at $62 million. The next largest recipients in Sub-Saharan Africa were the Comoro Islands and Ethiopia ($4 million each) and Niger ($3 million). With the exception of Somalia, Sudan, and the tiny Comoro Islands, where there is no *Hizmet* presence anyway, Turkish aid just does not provide meaningful leverage unless Turkey plans to give substantially more money.[50]

Turkish trade with Sub-Saharan Africa also offers little prospect to put pressure on *Hizmet*. First, the government does not control trade. Most of it depends on the role of the private sector, including organizations such as the Gülen-affiliated TUSKON. Second, Turkey's trade with Sub-Saharan Africa is not very important. In 2012, only 1.7 percent of Turkey's global trade was with Sub-Saharan Africa—2.6 percent of global Turkish exports and 1.1 percent of global Turkish imports. Of the 53 countries in all of Africa for which there were trade figures in 2012, Turkey was not a huge buyer of products from any of them. In fact, Turkey had a trade surplus with 32 African countries and a trade deficit

---

December 2014.

50. "Turkish Development Assistance 2012." *http://store.tika.gov.tr*.

with only 10 of them. For the remaining 11, Turkey had virtually no trade or it was in balance.[51]

Turkish companies do have important investments in several African countries, mostly in North Africa, but also a few Sub-Saharan African countries, such as Ethiopia and Sudan. Turkey's control over these companies is, however, tenuous and a few of them are sympathetic to the Gülen Movement. TUSKON is also the most active organization that is trying to increase Turkish investment in Africa. State-owned Turkish Airways has expanded its routes impressively throughout Africa, but it is difficult to see how this serves as leverage for the Turkish government. Cancellation of routes would inflict more damage on Turkey than on the African country currently served by the flights.

Concluding Thoughts

The informal alliance between the Gülen Movement and the AKP that developed after the AKP's electoral victory in 2002 began to show serious divisions 10 years later and had completely disintegrated after 12 years. Soner Cagaptay, director of the Turkish Research Program at the Washington Institute for Near East Policy, commented that the AKP "was never completely comfortable with the Gülen movement."[52]

During the first 10 years, *Hizmet* and the AKP contributed to each other's successes in Africa. It remains to be seen how much pressure the government of Turkey will put on African governments to reign in or even close down *Hizmet* activities in Africa. Strong-arm tactics by the Turkish government will almost certainly fail. On the other hand, outspoken opposition to the Gülen Movement by President Erdoğan and the Turkish government may cause some African governments to pull back support for new *Hizmet* initiatives. Because funding for these activities is dependent on Turkish business persons, government pressure against them may result in decreased financial support. In the end, everyone may be a loser in this saga—*Hizmet*, the government of Turkey, and the Africans.

---

51 International Monetary Fund, *Direction of Trade Statistics Yearbook 2013*, 553–554.

52 Quoted in Holly Yeager and Lyndsey Layton, "Turkish Prime Minister Recep Tayyip Erdoğan's Turmoil May Stem from a Former Ally," *Washington Post* (28 December 2013).

CHAPTER 9

CONCLUSION

Results of the Gülen Movement in Africa

Hizmet has a disproportionately significant impact in Africa, especially Sub-Saharan Africa, compared to the modest human and financial resources that its supporters invest there. The impact is not so much in propagating the writings and beliefs of Fethullah Gülen but rather the goodwill the Movement generates for Turkey while, at the same time, increasing opportunities for the Turkish business community. The ties between *Hizmet* and business are symbiotic, but in a positive way. They support each other. TUSKON, in particular, has helped to expand Turkish trade and investment throughout Africa.

It is impossible to measure the degree to which Fethullah Gülen's values, such as tolerance and avoidance of drugs and alcohol that are taught in *Hizmet* schools and practiced by *Hizmet* business persons, are internalized by African students, parents, and business persons. But in their limited way, they probably have an effect. What has not occurred in the 20 years since *Hizmet* has been active in Africa is the transformation of Gülen into a household word. The vast majority of Africans have never heard of him. Anecdotal evidence suggests that even most of those who have benefitted from *Hizmet* programs have not made a connection with Fethullah Gülen, the Sufi Islamic philosopher living in the United States. On the other hand, they have made a connection with Turkey.

Africans who are familiar with Gülen commented to me on numerous occasions that the name is unknown to all but small numbers of their colleagues. A senior Ethiopian official said, for example, that the impact of the Gülen Movement is not visible in the country. Ethiopians don't know what Gülen is and what he is not.[53] A South African professor commented that *Hizmet* tends not to blow its own horn. As a result, most educated South Africans have no

---

53 Author's meeting on 21 May 2014 in Addis Ababa, Ethiopia with Ethiopian official.

idea what is the Gülen Movement. He added, however, that its *Iftar* dinners bring together an extraordinary group of people and *Hizmet* makes an effort to remain in contact with these persons.[54]

This conclusion was surprising given the fact that Gülen himself is the most important single factor in *Hizmet*'s success. He is a transformational leader who motivates his followers, provides the vision, and defines the values of the Movement.[55] His Turkish followers have migrated to many parts of the world as educators and business persons. While a small number of African elites have taken an interest in Gülen's writings, his philosophy has had little obvious impact on the African public.

This can be explained in part by the fact that *Hizmet* is a recent arrival in Africa. It probably has more to do, however, with the "business model" of the Movement. TUSKON, *Hizmet* schools, and *Kimse Yok Mu* eschew any visible link to Gülen. Only the small *Hizmet* dialogue centers and more extensive media outreach programs make an effort openly to propagate the ideas and values of Gülen.

Hizmet, Africa, and Islam

Islam underpins all of Gülen's thinking and all *Hizmet* activities in Africa. Most *Hizmet* activity takes place in the Muslim-inhabited parts of Africa, which constitute less than half of the total population of the continent. Yet the Movement goes out of its way to accommodate and interact with persons representing other religions. Unlike most Islamic schools in Africa, *Hizmet* schools accept Muslims, Christians, and students from other faiths. A few of the schools actually have a majority Christian student population. Some African Muslims do not believe the *Hizmet* schools are sufficiently Islamic and send their children to all-Islamic schools. Even *Hizmet* compromised in South Africa, where it has two educational trusts—one for schools that accept students from all religions and the other strictly for Muslims.

There are many different reactions to *Hizmet* by African Muslims. A Kenyan business person, for example, who contributed construction equipment for building *Hizmet* schools, sent his children to the schools, and has served since 2007 as a trustee of the school's governing board, offered an interesting analysis. He said when the Turkish community began to set up schools in Kenya, it knew nothing about Muslim-Christian relations in the country. Kenyan Muslims saw

---

54 Author's meeting on 25 August 2012 in Cape Town, South Africa with Professor Stanley Ridge, University of the Western Cape.

55 Michael J. and Karen A. Fontenot, "The Characteristics and Appeal of the *Hizmet* Movement," in *The Gülen Hizmet Movement and its Transnational Activities*, ed. Sophia Pandya and Nancy Gallagher (Boca Raton, FL: BrownWalker Press, 2012), 24.

the Turks not as Muslims but foreigners who could offer something, in this case high-quality education. The Kenyan business person is now sending his children who have graduated from *Hizmet* schools to universities in Turkey.[56]

Hizmet's humanitarian arm, *Kimse Yok Mu*, devotes most of its assistance to Muslim communities in Africa. In fact, its most extensive program—the distribution of food packages and meat on the occasion of Ramadan and Eid al-Adha—is intended almost exclusively for Muslims. On the other hand, when *Kimse Yok Mu* offers assistance in communities where the religions are mixed, it makes no distinction between Muslim and non-Muslim recipients.

A number of countries, especially Saudi Arabia and several Gulf States, have provided substantial funding for building mosques in Africa. *Hizmet* has rarely used its resources for this purpose. One important exception is the Nizamiye Mosque Complex at Midrand, between Johannesburg and Pretoria, in South Africa. South African President Jacob Zuma opened the complex in 2012. The largest mosque in the southern hemisphere, it includes a *Hizmet* school, dormitory, Turkish bazaar, shopping center, restaurant, bakery, and clinic to serve the local community. Modelled after the Selimiye Camii mosque in Edirne, Turkey, it can accommodate 3,000 worshippers. A Turkish business person, Ali Katircioğlu, who is known locally as "Uncle Ali," financed the entire complex. He is a friend of Gülen. The resident imam, who served for eight years as an imam in the United States, is trained in Gülen principles.[57]

Hizmet and the Arab Countries

Of Africa's 54 countries, only Sudan and the five countries in North Africa are considered as Arab. My research for this project permitted a visit to only one of the six—Morocco. In any event, most Arab countries are located outside Africa. The comments in this section are intended to raise more questions than answers, although available evidence suggests that *Hizmet* encounters more resistance in Muslim Arab countries in Africa than in predominantly Muslim non-Arab countries or those that have a Muslim minority.

The fact that there are no *Hizmet* schools in Algeria and Tunisia and only one in Libya that opened in 2012 suggests those countries, at least until recently, have not been especially accommodating. Sudan has a single school and populous Egypt just three. Morocco is the exception, with both the first Gülen-affiliated school and a strong *Hizmet* school program. But *Hizmet* faces special restrictions

---

56 Author's meeting on 1 September 2012 in Nairobi, Kenya with Hilal Salim Abdalla.

57 Author's visit on 26 August 2012 to the Nizamiye Mosque Complex and meeting with Imam Ibrahim Atasoy. Muhammad Shaahid Abdool, "Zuma Opens Nizamiye Mosque in Johannesburg," Cihan News Agency (6 October 2012).

even in Morocco, which only allows the teaching of Arabic, French, and English, thus excluding Turkish.

Part of the problem may be ideological. Unlike Arab leaders, Gülen sees Turkey at the center of the Muslim world, with Arab and Muslim African countries to the south and Muslims in the Balkans, Caucasus, and Central Asia to the north. While he is careful to avoid the idea of Turkish political leadership in the region, he distances himself from the Arab world and Iran. He has concluded that Islam as practiced in Turkey is culturally different from that practiced in the Arab world. The strong element of Turkish nationalism in Gülen's writings and in the Movement also raises questions in Arab countries. Gülen attributes the lack of *Hizmet* schools in the Arab world to the difficulties presented by Arab governments.[58]

The Gülen Movement faces some practical hurdles as it tries to expand in the Arab world. Language is one of them. The Arab countries put a premium on the use of Arabic, although there is a strong history of French or English as a second language in all six Arab countries in Africa. In the rest of Africa, there are usually so many languages in play that the addition of Turkish in the school system does not pose a problem. In addition, Fethullah Gülen and Turkey have tended to look to the West in the past couple decades. This too, may raise suspicions in some Arab countries.[59]

Although the situation for *Hizmet* in Arab Morocco may be unique, it merits special attention. Two Moroccan professors who are knowledgeable with Gülen's works said his writing is perceived in the Arab world as a Turkish model. Gülen modernized Islam in a practical way but did not take Arab history into account. As a result, his work is not seen as relevant to the Arab world.[60] This view was in sharp contrast to those of a number of Muslim scholars in Sub-Saharan Africa where an Arab background is rarely a factor.

There are, not surprisingly, different opinions on Gülen's philosophy even in Morocco. A professor of Islamic studies at Ibn Tofail University in Kinitra argued that Gülen's emphasis on shared human values is an important contribution. Differences in religious beliefs allow followers to learn from each other. The professor added that Arab Islamic thinkers react differently to Gülen depending

---

58 Hasan Kösebalaban, "The Making of Enemy and Friend: Fethullah Gülen's National-Security Identity," in *Turkish Islam and the Secular State: The Gülen Movement*, ed. M. Hakan Yavuz and John L. Esposito (Syracuse, NY: Syracuse University Press, 2003), 173–174.

59 Author's notes on remarks made 6 February 2013 at Georgetown University in Washington by Reverend Thomas Michel, Department of Theology at Marquette University.

60 Author's meeting on 4 January 2013 in Marrakech, Morocco with Rida Brahim and Abdeljalil Hanouche.

on whether their background is Sufi, Salafi, or modern Islamic. Gülen is 180 degrees from the Salafists and most of them oppose his Sufi background. But a few Salafists see value in his approach.[61]

A Moroccan professor who teaches reform thought in the Islamic and Arab world at El Jadida University and recently wrote a book in Arabic on Gülen said that four to five years earlier, few Moroccans had heard of Gülen. Moroccan intellectuals now are aware of him and some Moroccan institutions teach his ideas. He said Moroccans are not easily swayed by anti-Gülen material on the Internet. The old way of thinking is that Turks and Arabs were enemies from the demise of the Ottoman Empire until 20 or 30 years ago. This has begun to change and there is now a positive view of Turkey in Morocco. The anti-Gülen views of most Salafists represent only a small segment of Islamic thought.[62]

Hizmet and African Extremist Movements

I discussed in chapter 4 the ability of *Hizmet* schools to continue operations in Mali during the height of attacks against the government of Mali by extremist groups, including al-Qaeda in the Islamic Maghreb. In this case, the schools were not located in areas where fighting was taking place but, unlike *Hizmet*, many foreign organizations shut down during this period. The fact that the *Hizmet* schools remained open sent a strong, positive message to Malian officials.

Chapter 6 recounted the ups and downs of the *Hizmet* presence in Somalia, where the extremist organization al-Shabaab is active in south/central Somalia and periodically carries out terrorist attacks in the capital, Mogadishu, where Turkey has a significant presence. Al-Shabaab has links with al-Qaeda. In this case, Turkish interests, including *Hizmet* personnel, have come under attack. Nevertheless, the *Hizmet* schools remain open and *Kimse Yok Mu* continues with its humanitarian program in Somalia. The Somali government appreciates the entire Turkish program there.

Hizmet has schools in northern Nigeria, where the extremist group Boko Haram is active (see chapter 4). While Boko Haram has attacked a number of schools in the country, it has not targeted *Hizmet* schools, which maintain a low profile. As of 2015, Boko Haram has made no public comment about *Hizmet* or the Gülen Movement. The Abuja-based newspaper *Leadership* periodically carries material written by Gülen. A *Hizmet* representative explained that care is taken not to publish anything that would offend Boko Haram or any other group.[63]

---

61 Author's meeting on 5 January 2013 in Rabat, Morocco with Ahmed Bukeyle.

62 Author's meeting on 5 January 2013 in Rabat, Morocco with a Moroccan professor.

63 Author's meeting on 31 December 2012 in Abuja, Nigeria with *Hizmet* representative.

In 2014, Fethullah Gülen strongly condemned the beheadings of American and British nationals in Syria by the Islamic State of Iraq and the Levant (ISIL). The Gülen-affiliated Alliance for Shared Values sent the statement as an advertisement to major American papers. The condemnation included a reference to Boko Haram, noting that both organizations have in common "a totalitarian mentality that denies human beings their dignity."[64]

Ethiopia's Minister of Federal Affairs, Shiferaw Teklemariam, argued that poverty and ignorance are the root causes of extremism. Following a trip organized by *Hizmet* to Turkey, he concluded that the Gülen Movement has a similar understanding. He said the *Hizmet* schools in Ethiopia reflect tolerance, living together, and respect for others in their instruction. Shiferaw suggested this approach to education complemented what Ethiopia is trying to do as a government in its effort to counter extremism.[65]

As extremist Muslim groups expand their areas of operation in Africa, this will present a growing challenge for *Hizmet*. Al-Shabaab predated *Hizmet*'s arrival in Somalia and the Movement should have known the risk that it was taking. On the other hand, *Hizmet* was active in northern Nigeria and Mali before Boko Haram and al-Qaeda in the Islamic Maghreb posed a threat in those two areas. *Hizmet* was also established on the Kenya coast before al-Shabaab expanded its attacks there. *Hizmet* schools and other activities make every effort to avoid antagonizing extremist groups, but as they discovered in Somalia, there are limits to their ability to prevent hostile targeting.

Hizmet after the Break with Erdoğan

Writing before the split between the Gülen Movement and the ruling Justice and Development Party, author Joshua Hendrick said that the rise of the Movement is tied to the rise of Turkey. He added that "its future is dependent on Turkey's continued emergence as a regional and world power."[66] While Hendrick overstates the link between the future success of the Gülen Movement and the rise of Turkey, there is some validity to the argument. Because some components of *Hizmet* offer tangible benefits, however, the Movement can continue successfully in places like Africa, even if Turkey falters.

---

64 "Gülen Condemns ISIL Atrocities in Ads in Leading Newspapers," *Today's Zaman* (17 September 2014). The advertisement went to *The New York Times*, *The Wall Street Journal*, the *Chicago Tribune*, and the *Los Angeles Times*.

65 Author's meeting on 5 September 2012 in Addis Ababa, Ethiopia with Shiferaw Teklemariam.

66 Joshua D. Hendrick, *Gülen: The Ambiguous Politics of Market Islam in Turkey and the World* (New York: New York University Press, 2013), 241.

The break between *Hizmet* and the Justice and Development Party described in chapter 8 continues to play out. The impact of this situation has complicated *Hizmet*'s future globally. Gülen has expressed both outrage and philosophical acceptance at this turn of events. He commented in March 2014 that "I have spent the past 15 years in spiritual retreat and, irrespective of what happens in Turkey, I intend to continue to do so."[67] He added that *Hizmet* is not a political organization and has no interest in the privileges of power. Its personal and financial commitment is to humanitarian aid, education, and dialogue, as well as remaining absent from political office.[68]

If Erdoğan and the Justice and Development Party continue to pressure African countries to sever ties with *Hizmet*, it will likely result in little or no success, especially in Sub-Saharan Africa. Turkey has minimal leverage in Sub-Saharan Africa unless it offers huge amounts of new funding. This tactic would quickly become an expensive proposition for Turkey. In any event, the *Hizmet* schools and other programs have too much local support in most African countries. Such a policy by Turkey would almost certainly become self-defeating.

Hizmet after Gülen

Fethullah Gülen is in his seventies and is not in good health. During his interview with the BBC in January 2014, the BBC team concluded that his physical capabilities appeared to be ebbing and he seemed to be a man in discomfort.[69] It is not surprising that the followers of Gülen and outsiders wonder what will happen to the Movement when Gülen is no longer able to lead it. At least publicly, Gülen seems to have removed himself from the speculation.

Persons closely associated with the Gülen Movement tend to finesse the question of succession. They emphasize that decision-making in *Hizmet* is not concentrated at the top or held by a small number of individuals. There is constant turnover of leadership. Decision-making resides with those who participate in network meetings.[70] In 2008, a sociologist conducted interviews with 106 members of the Movement and asked what will happen after the death of Gülen. The near unanimous response was that *Hizmet* is not about an individual. They expected the Movement to thrive after Gülen. They cited the growing influence

---

67 Fethullah Gülen, "Turkey Needs a New Constitution To Save Its Democracy," *Financial Times* (10 March 2014).

68 Ibid.

69 Tim Franks, "Fethullah Gülen: Powerful but Reclusive Turkish Cleric," *BBC News* (27 January 2014).

70 Muhammed Çetin, *Hizmet: Questions and Answers on the Gülen Movement* (New York: Blue Dome Press, 2012), 97.

of Jalaluddin Rumi, 13th century Persian poet, jurist, theologian, and Sufi mystic, following his death.[71]

When Gülen was asked by a German newspaper if the Movement will exist after he is gone, he replied that persons who do not necessarily share his worldview have supported the Movement and that *Hizmet* has always been based on universal values. He noted that Africans whom he has never met and expected nothing from, co-financed schools and hospitals there. Gülen concluded: "Every night when I go to bed I doubt whether I might wake up again. But I do not have the least amount of doubt about the future of the movement."[72]

Following the departure of Gülen, the impact on the Movement may vary from region to region. The one issue that will affect the Movement in all regions is the level of continuing financial contributions from supporters in Turkey and the Turkish diaspora. Should funding decline significantly, all regions will face a decline in *Hizmet* programs. In the event that funding continues at the same or even higher levels, *Hizmet* will be unaffected or even expand in Africa. Unlike the situation in Turkey and some other geographic regions, Gülen is not well known in Africa and *Hizmet* is not dependent on his name or the fact that he is heading the Movement. Most *Hizmet* activities in Africa are seen as Turkish programs. They are welcomed and there is no reason to believe this will change after the death of Gülen.

---

71 Y. Alp Aslandoğan, Q and A at the Center for Strategic and International Studies in Washington on 17 June 2009. *www.csis.org/event/gulen-movement*.

72 Fethullah Gülen interview with German newspaper *Süddeutsche Zeitung* on 13 December 2014.

APPENDIX

GÜLEN-AFFILIATED SCHOOLS IN AFRICA

ALGERIA
None

ANGOLA

City	School Name	Level	Date Est.
Luanda	Colégio Esperança International[1]	Pre-school through 12	2009

BENIN

City	School Name	Level	Date Est.
Cotonou	L'École Internationale Ufuk-Benin[2]	Pre-school through secondary	2006

BOTSWANA
None

BURKINA FASO

City	School Name	Level	Date Est.
Ouagadougou	Le Collège Horizon International[3]	Pre-school through secondary	2003

BURUNDI
None

---

1 www.coespi.org.

2 "Une Délégation Turque au Cabinet Présidentiel," *www.gouv.bj*. Saim Orhan, "The Former Kingdom of Dahomey: Benin," *Today's Zaman* (29 October 2010).

3 Issoufou Maiga, "Ekrem Oksar, Directeur du Collège Horizon International," *L'opinion* (Ouagadougou), (30 July – 5 August 2008). Relwendé Auguste Sawadogo, "Collège Horizon International," *Le Pays* (Ouagadougou), (29 June 2013).

CAMEROON

City	School Name	Level	Date Est.
Yaounde	Amity International College[4]	Primary	2003
Yaounde	Amity International College	Secondary	2003
Ngaoundere	Amity International College[5]	Primary	2005
Ngaoundere	Amity International College	Secondary	2005
Douala	Amity International College	Primary and secondary	Unknown

CAPE VERDE

In 2014, Ancela Silva, a business person from Cape Verde, said "we have Turkish schools in our country." The author has not been able to obtain the names or any information on the schools.[6]

CENTRAL AFRICAN REPUBLIC

City	School Name	Level	Date Est.
Bangui	L'École Internationale Centrafricano-turque[7]	Primary and secondary	2004

CHAD

City	School Name	Level	Date Est.
N'djamena	Complexe Scolaire International Tchado-Turc (CSITT)[8]	Primary	2001
N'djamena	CSITT	Boys secondary	Unknown
N'djamena	CSITT	Girls secondary	Unknown

COMORO ISLANDS

None, but land has been donated for construction of a Hizmet school.[9]

---

4   http://amity.cm/.

5   Rodrique Tapeo, "Pour Omer Faruk Dogan: Ngaoundéré Sera la Turquie du Cameroun," *www.integrationafrica.org*.

6   "Turkish Schools Help to Enhance Trade Relations with Africa," *Today's Zaman* (15 April 2014).

7   Sylvestre Krock, "La Turquie 'Mise' sur l'Education pour des Lendemains Meilleurs en RCA," Anadolu Agency (27 June 2014). Taha Akyor, "Turkish Schools in Africa," *Hurriyet* (2 May 2012).

8   *www.ecoletchadoturc.com*. "New Turkish School Launched in Chad," *Timeturk* (17 May 2013).

9   "A Prayer to the Volunteers of *Kimse Yok Mu* from the Islands of the Comoros," *http://hizmetmovement.blogspot.com* (12 April 2013).

CÔTE D'IVOIRE

City	School Name	Level	Date Est.
Abdijan	Groupe Scolaire Şafak[10]	Pre-school through Secondary	2006

DEMOCRATIC REPUBLIC OF THE CONGO

City	School Name	Level	Date Est.
Kinshasa	Şafak École Internationale Turco-Congolaise[11]	Pre-school through secondary	2006

DJIBOUTI

None

EGYPT

City	School Name	Level	Date Est.
Cairo	Salahaldin International School[12]	Kindergarten through 12	2009
Beni Suef	Salahaldin International School[13]	Kindergarten through 12	2011
Alexandria	Salahaldin International School[14]	Kindergarten through 12	2014

EQUATORIAL GUINEA

City	School Name	Level	Date Est.
Malabo	Turkish Equatorial Guinea International School[15]	Unknown; information sketchy	2014

ERITREA

None

---

10 www.ecolci.net/.

11 Trésor Kibangula, "RDC: École SAFAK, Bienvenue à Kinshasa-sur-Bosphore," *Jeune Afrique* (29 January 2014).

12 http://cairo.salahaldinschool.com.

13 Author's meeting on 5 January 2013 in Casablanca, Morocco, with teachers from Salahaldin International School. "Turkish School to Open Many New Branches in Egypt," *World Bulletin*, www.worldbulletin.net.

14 http://cairo.salahaldinschool.com.

15 See artist mock up at: http://gq.geoview.info/turkish_equatorial_guinea_international_school,80660093p.

ETHIOPIA

City	School Name	Level	Date Est.
Addis Ababa	Nejashi Ethio-Turkish International Schools—African Union Branch[16]	Grades 1 through 8	2004
Addis Ababa	Nejashi Ethio-Turkish International Schools—Alemgena Branch	Kindergarten through 12	2007
Addis Ababa	Nejashi Ethio-Turkish International Schools—Sarbet Branch	Kindergarten	2008
Addis Ababa	Nejashi Ethio-Turkish International Schools—CMC Branch	Kindergarten	2009
Mekelle	Nejashi Ethio-Turkish International Schools	Kindergarten through 12	2011
Harar	Nejashi Ethio-Turkish International Schools	Kindergarten through 12	2014

GABON

City	School Name	Level	Date Est.
Libreville	École Internationale Turco Gabonaise[17]	Pre-kindergarten through secondary	2008

GAMBIA

City	School Name	Level	Date Est.
Banjul	Yavuz Selim Anatolian School[18]	Kindergarten through 12	2010

GHANA

City	School Name	Level	Date Est.
Accra	Galaxy International School[19]	Preschool	2001
Accra	Galaxy International School	Primary	2001
Accra	Galaxy International School	Secondary	2001

---

16 *www.nejashiturkishschools.com*.

17 Abdullah Bozkurt, "OIC Head Says He Has Always Endorsed Turkish Schools Abroad," *Today's Zaman* (20 April 2012).

18 *www.ysaschool.com*. The school was forced to close in March 2014 by the government of Gambia, allegedly under pressure from the government of Turkey following the split between Gülen and Prime Minister Erdoğan. See Ralph Boulton and Orhan Coskun, "Erdoğan Takes Battle with Enemies beyond Turkish Frontiers," *Reuters* (3 April 2014) and Fehim Taştekin, "Turkish Schools Abroad Victims of AKP-Gülen Conflict," *al-monitor.com* (11 April 2014).

19 *www.galaxyschool.net*. William Yaw Owusu, "Ghana-Turkey Friendship Deepens," *Daily Guide* (Ghana), (16 December 2013). The preschool, primary, and secondary schools have separate principals.

GUINEA

City	School Name	Level	Date Est.
Conakry	Collège de la Citadelle[20]	4 schools: 2 primary, 1 middle, 1 high school	1st school in 2003

GUINEA-BISSAU

City	School Name	Level	Date Est.
Bissau	Ufuk International School[21]	Began with 1–3; add grade each year to 8	2012

KENYA

City	School Name	Level	Date Est.
Nairobi	Light Academy[22]	Boys secondary	1998
Nairobi	Light Academy	Girls secondary	2007
Nairobi	Light Academy	Primary—Cambridge system	2002
Nairobi	Light Academy	Primary—Kenya system	2003
Nairobi	Light Academy	Kindergarten	2012
Mombasa	Light Academy	Boys secondary	2001
Mombasa	Light Academy	Mixed primary and girls secondary	2001
Malindi	Light Academy	Primary through secondary	2014

LESOTHO

None

LIBERIA

City	School Name	Level	Date Est.
Monrovia	Light International School[23]	Pre-school through high school	2006

---

20 Mamadou Baldé, "Le Proviseur du Collège des Filles de la Citadelle: 'La Guinée Dispose d'un Potentiel Énorme' a Dit Ferhat AVCU," *Guinée Culture* (19 December 2012). Author's meeting on 7 January 2013 in Dakar, Senegal, with Mesut Gökcan Ateş, active in *Hizmet*.

21 "Guinea-Bissau Minister Pay Visit to Turkish School," (24 February 2014), http://hizmetnews.com. Author's meeting on 7 January 2013 in Dakar, Senegal, with sponsor of Ufuk International School.

22 *www.lightacademy.ac.ke*. Author's meeting on 30 August 2012 in Nairobi, Kenya, with Bilal Karaduman, chairman of the Omeriye Educational Foundation and Medical Charitable Trust, and Osman Özpinar, Light Academies director general.

23 *www.lightschool.net*. Author's meeting on 3 January 2013 in Casablanca, Morocco, with Ramazan Burak, general manager of Light International School.

LIBYA

City	School Name	Level	Date Est.
Tripoli	International Libyan Turkish School[24]	Kindergarten through grade 3 but adding grades	2012

MADAGASCAR

City	School Name	Level	Date Est.
Antananarivo	International Light College[25]	Boys secondary and high school/dormitory	2002
Antananarivo	International Light College	Girls secondary and high school/dormitory	2002
Antananarivo	International Light College	Primary	2002

MALAWI

City	School Name	Level	Date Est.
Blantyre	Bedir International[26]	Primary and secondary	2000
Lilongwe	Bedir International	Primary and secondary	2012

MALI

Hizmet has a major presence in Mali that began in 2002, although information on the number of schools, known as Ufuk or Horizon Schools, is conflicting. According to information obtained in January 2013, there were two primary, two secondary, and two high schools, all in Bamako, the capital.[27] However, the principal of a school in Segou, 130 kilometers northeast of Bamako, said his school opened late in 2012.[28] In mid-2013, Mali's minister of higher education and research said Hizmet had four kindergartens, four primary schools, five secondary schools, three high schools, one reading hall, and two dormitories.[29]

MAURITANIA

City	School Name	Level	Date Est.
Nouakchott	Bourge-el Ilm[30]	Kindergarten	2005
Nouakchott	Bourge-el Ilm	Primary	2005
Nouakchott	Bourge-el Ilm	Boys high school	2005
Nouakchott	Bourge-el Ilm	Girls high school	2005

---

24 http://muhtar-ilts.com.

25 www.collegelalumiere.com.

26 http://bedirschools.com.

27 Author's meeting on 7 January 2013 with Mesut Gökcan Ateş.

28 "Turkish Schools in Mali Stay Open despite Conflict," *Today's Zaman* (6 February 2013).

29 "Mali Education Minister Lauds Teachers in Nation's Turkish Schools," *Sunday's Zaman* (28 July 2013).

30 http://bourge-el-ilm.zic.fr.

MAURITIUS

None

MOROCCO

City	School Name	Level	Date Est.
Tangier	Mohammed Al Fatih (MAF)[31]	Kindergarten through 12	1994
Casablanca	MAF	Grades 7–9	2000
Fes	MAF	Grades 7–12	2003
Tetouan	MAF	Grades 7–12	2004
El Jadida	MAF	K through 12	2010
Casablanca	MAF International[32]	K through 12	2013

MOZAMBIQUE

City	School Name	Level	Date Est.
Maputo	Willow International School[33]	Primary	2003
Matola	Willow International School	Primary, girls/boys secondary	2003

NAMIBIA

None

NIGER

City	School Name	Level	Date Est.
Niamey	Complexe Scolaire Bedir[34]	K through 12	2003

NIGERIA

City	School Name	Level	Date Est.
Abuja	Nigerian Turkish International College (NTIC)[35]	Girls secondary	1998
Abuja	NTIC	Boys secondary	1998
Abuja	NTIC	Coed secondary	1998
Abuja	NTIC	Nursery and primary	1998

---

31 Author's meeting on 3 and 4 January 2013 in Casablanca and Marrakech with Mehmet Bozoğlan, assistant director general of Groupe Scolaire Mohammed Al Fatih.

32 Ibid. According to one counting of *Hizmet* schools in Morocco, there are two primary, five middle, three high schools, and a language school. See "Two Additional Turkish Schools to Open in Casablanca," *Today's Zaman* (9 October 2013).

33 http://willow.org.mz.

34 "Complexe Scolaire Bedir de Niamey: Symbole d'une Presence Turque Reussie au Niger," http://lesahel.org.

35 Author's meeting on 30 December 2012 in Abuja, Nigeria with Hikmet Coban, general manager of all *Hizmet*-related institutions in Nigeria. www.nticnigeria.com.

City	School Name	Level	Date Est.
Kaduna	NTIC[36]	Boys secondary	2007
Kaduna	NTIC	Girls secondary	2007
Kaduna	NTIC[37]	Coed nursery/primary	2007
Lagos	NTIC[38]	Nursery and primary	2008
Lagos	NTIC[39]	Boys secondary/ boarding	2000
Lagos	NTIC	Girls secondary/ boarding	2000
Kano	NTIC	Boys secondary	Unknown
Kano	NTIC	Girls secondary	Unknown
Kano	NTIC	Nursery/primary	Unknown
Yobe State	NTIC	Boys secondary/ boarding	Unknown
Yobe State	NTIC	Girls secondary/ boarding	Unknown
Yobe State	NTIC	Boys secondary/day only	Unknown
Ogun State	NTIC[40]	Secondary	2006
Abuja	Nigerian Turkish Nile University[41]	BA/BSc degree	2009

REPUBLIC OF CONGO

None

RWANDA

City	School Name	Level	Date Est.
Kigali	Hope Kids Academy[42]	Nursery and primary	2013

SÃO TOMÉ AND PRINCIPE

None

SENEGAL

City	School Name	Level	Date Est.
Dakar	Yavuz Selim-Bosphore[43]	Boys secondary	1997

---

36 Author's meeting on 1 January 2013 in Kaduna, Nigeria with Mahmut Fesli, principal NTIC.

37 Author's meeting on 1 January 2013 in Kaduna, Nigeria with Sinan Metin, principal of NTIC nursery/primary school.

38 Author's meeting on 2 January 2013 in Lagos, Nigeria with Yunus Emre Dogan, principal of NTIC nursery/primary school.

39 Author's meeting on 2 January 2013 in Lagos, Nigeria with Fatih Keskin, principal of NTIC secondary school.

40 Uchechukwu Nnaike, "Nigerian Turkish College Graduates 48," *This Daily Live* (6 July 2010).

41 Author's meeting on 31 December 2012 in Abuja, Nigeria with Hüseyin Sert, vice chancellor, NTNU. *www.ntnu.edu.ng*.

42 Frank Kanyesigye, "Rwanda: Turkish School Officially Opens," *The New Times* (24 February 2013).

43 *www.gsyavuzselim.edu.sn*. Author's meeting on 8 January 2013 in Dakar, Senegal

Dakar	Yavuz Selim-Sultan[44]	Girls secondary	1997
Dakar	Yavuz Selim-Ciel	Primary	2002
Dakar	Yavuz Selim-Bourgeons	Nursery	2005
Dakar	Yavuz Selim-Cascades	Primary	2008
Thies	Yavuz Selim-Printemps	Primary/middle	2009 and 2011
Thies	Yavuz Selim-Printemps	Nursery	2009

SEYCHELLES
None

SIERRA LEONE
None

SOMALIA

City	School Name	Level	Date Est.
Mogadishu	Bedir Turkish High School[45]	Boys high school	2011
Mogadishu	Kiblenuma	Primary	2012
Mogadishu	Kiblenuma Girl's School	Girls high school/boarding	2013
Hargeisa	Vifak Turkish-Somali School[46]	Boys high school/boarding	2012

SOUTH AFRICA

City	School Name	Level	Date Est.
Cape Town	Star International[47]	Primary through high school	1999

---

  with Adnan Demir, general manager of the Yavuz Selim schools.

44 Author's visit to Yavuz Selim-Sultan on 7 January 2013.

45 Yasin Kiliç, "Turkish Schools for a Brighter Future in Somalia," Cihan News Agency (22 February 2013). "Turkish Schools in Somalia Won 22 Medals in 2 Years," *Today's Zaman* (17 February 2014).

46 Author's meeting on 22 April 2013 in Washington, D.C. with Amina Haji Muhammad Jirde, wife of the president of Somaliland, which declared unilateral independence from Somalia in 1991.

47 Two separate Gülen-affiliated educational trusts have schools in South Africa. Horizon Educational Trust operates Star International in Cape Town, Horizon International in Johannesburg, Cemal Karacan Star College in Durban, and Moonlight primary school in Pretoria. See *http://myhorizon.org*; *www.starcollege.co.za*; and *www.horizoninternationalhigh.co.za*. The Fountain Educational Trust operates the Nizamiye schools in Johannesburg, Port Elizabeth, and Midrand. The schools in both trusts follow the national curriculum but the three Nizamiye schools also offer Islamic studies and Arabic. See *www.fountainet.org* and *www.nizamiyeschool.co.za*. Author's meeting on 24 August 2012 in Cape Town, South Africa, with Mahmut Ozer, deputy principal of Star International; on 26 August 2012 with Yavuz Aydin, educational director for Horizon Educational Trust, and Isak Turan, teacher at Nizamiye School Midrand.

City	School Name	Level	Date Est.
Johannesburg	Horizon International	High school	2000
Johannesburg	Nizamiye School (formerly Sama School)	Primary through high school	2003
Durban	Cemal Karacan Star College	Boys high school	2002
Durban	Cemal Karacan Star College	Primary/girls high school	2009
Port Elizabeth	Nizamiye School (formerly Al-Azhar Institute, founded in 1996)[48]	Primary through high school	2009
Pretoria	Moonlight	Primary	2012
Midrand	Nizamiye School	Primary through high school	2012

SOUTH SUDAN

None

SUDAN

City	School Name	Level	Date Est.
Khartoum	Sudanese-Turkish School[49]	Boys K through 12	1999
Khartoum	Sudanese-Turkish School	Girls K through 12	1999
Nyala	Sudanese-Turkish School	High school	2012

SWAZILAND

None

TANZANIA

City	School Name	Level	Date Est.
Dar es Salaam	Feza Boys School[50]	Secondary and high school	1998
Dar es Salaam	Feza Girls School	Secondary and high school	2005
Dar es Salaam	Feza Nursery School	Nursery	2001
Dar es Salaam	Feza Primary School	Primary	2001
Dar es Salaam	Feza International School	Grades 1 through 13	2011
Zanzibar	Feza School[51]	Nursery and primary	2005
Zanzibar	Feza Secondary School	Secondary	2012
Arusha	Feza International Junior Academy	Unknown	2014

48 http://nizamiyeschool-pe.co.za.

49 Information provided on 24 September 2014 by Marie Besancon who visited the schools in Khartoum. www.st-schools.com. "Turkish Experience in Sudan: Making a Difference," *Today's Zaman* (8 February 2011).

50 http://fezaschools.org. Author's meetings on 28 August 2012 in Dar es Salaam with Ibrahim Bicakci, director of Feza Schools, and Isa Otcu, headmaster of Feza Boys Secondary School.

51 Author's visit on 30 August 2012 to Feza Nursery and Primary School on Zanzibar.

TOGO

City	School Name	Level	Date Est.
Lome	École Internationale Togo-Turquie[52]	Nursery through secondary	2006

TUNISIA

None

UGANDA

City	School Name	Level	Date Est.
Kampala	Turkish Light Academy[53]	Nursery and primary	1999
Kampala	Turkish Light Academy	Secondary	1999
Lubowa	Galaxy International School[54]	Nursery through 13	2012
Jinja	Galaxy International School	Nursery through 13	2013

ZAMBIA

City	School Name	Level	Date Est.
Lusaka	Horizon School[55]	Primary through high school	2011

ZIMBABWE

None

---

52 Formerly known as École Internationale Zodiaque. "École Internationale Togo-Turquie," *www.goafricaonline.com*. Saim Orhan, "Africa's Silent Child—Togo," *Today's Zaman* (20 November 2009).

53 *www.lightacademy.ac.ug*.

54 *http://gisu.ac.ug*.

55 Patson Chilemba, "Rupiah Helps Turks Acquire Lusaka Land," *The Post Newspapers* (Zambia), (24 May 2011). The Horizon Education Trust broke ground in 2014 for a girls secondary school: "Turkish NGO Construct Girls' Secondary School," *Lusaka Voice* (9 May 2014).

SELECTED BIBLIOGRAPHY

Agai, Bekim. "Fethullah Gülen and His Movement's Islamic Ethic of Education." *Critique: Critical Middle Eastern Studies* 11, no. 1 (Spring 2002): 27–47.

Akdogan, Fatih. "Gülen-inspired Schools and Their Contribution to Christian-Muslim Relations in Nairobi, Kenya." MA thesis, St. Paul's University, 2012.

Angey, Gabrielle. "Turkish Islam in Africa: A Study of the Gülen Movement in Kenya," French Institute for Research in Africa, *Mambo!* 10, no. 3 (May 2012): 1–4.

Aslandoğan, Yüksel A. "The Gülen Movement," Center for Strategic and International Studies (17 June 2009). www.csis.org/event/gulen-movement.

Aydin, Hasan. "Educational Reform in Nigeria: The Case of Multicultural Education for Peace, Love, and Tolerance," *South African Journal of Education* 33, no. 1 (2013): 1–19. www.sajournaleducation.co.za.

_____. "Four Stakeholder's Perception on Educational Effectiveness of Nigerian Turkish International Colleges: A Qualitative Case Study," *Sage Open* (April–June 2013): 1–14. http://sgo.sagepub.com/content/spsgo/3/2/2158244013489693.full.pdf.

Balci, Bayram. "The Gülen Movement and Turkish Soft Power," Carnegie Endowment for International Peace (4 February 2014). http://carnegieendowment.org.

Barton, Greg, Paul Weller, and Ihsan Yilmaz, eds. *The Muslim World and Politics in Transition: Creative Contributions of the Gülen Movement*. London: Bloomsbury, 2013.

Berlinski, Claire. "Anatomy of a Power Struggle," *The Journal of International Security Affairs* (Fall/Winter 2012): 125–128.

Carroll, B. Jill. *A Dialogue of Civilizations: Gülen's Islamic Ideals and Humanistic Discourse*. Somerset, NJ: The Light, Inc., 2007.

Çelik, Gürkan. *The Gülen Movement: Building Social Cohesion through Dialogue and Education*. Delft: Eburon, 2010.

Çetin, Muhammed. *The Gülen Movement: Civic Service without Borders*. New York: Blue Dome Press, 2010.

_____. *Hizmet: Questions and Answers on the Gülen Movement.* New York: Blue Dome Press, 2012.

Conway, Trudy D. *Cross-cultural Dialogue on the Virtues: The Contribution of Fethullah Gülen.* Heidelberg: Springer, 2014.

Ebaugh, Rose Helen. *The Gülen Movement: A Sociological Analysis of a Civic Movement Rooted in Moderate Islam.* Heidelberg: Springer, 2010.

Ergene, Mehmet Enes. *Tradition Witnessing the Modern Age: An Analysis of the Gülen Movement.* Somerset, NJ: Tughra Books, 2008.

Esposito, John L., and Ihsan Yilmaz, eds. *Islam and Peacebuilding: Gülen Movement Initiatives.* New York: Blue Dome Press, 2010.

Fuller, Graham E. *The New Turkish Republic: Turkey as a Pivotal State in the Muslim World.* Washington: United States Institute of Peace, 2008.

Gözaydin, İştar B. "The Fethullah Gülen Movement and Politics in Turkey: A Chance for Democratization or a Trojan Horse?" *Democratization* 16, no. 6 (December 2009): 1214–1236.

Gülen, Fethullah M. *The Essentials of the Islamic Faith.* Somerset, NJ: The Light, Inc., 2005.

_____. *The Messenger of God—Muhammad—An Analysis of the Prophet's Life.* Somerset, NJ: The Light, Inc., 2005.

_____. *Pearls of Wisdom.* Somerset, NJ: The Light, Inc., 2005.

_____. *Toward a Global Civilization of Love and Tolerance.* Somerset, NJ: The Light, Inc., 2004.

Gülen Institute. *Fethullah Gülen: Biographical Album.* Houston, TX: Gülen Institute, n.d.

Gülen Movement Conference Papers. Contains full text of numerous papers presented at eight international conferences concerning the Gülen Movement. *http://en.fgulen.com/conference-papers.*

Hansen, Suzy. "The Global Imam," *The New Republic* 241, no. 19 (2 December 2010): 10–15.

_____. "A Megalomaniacal Prime Minister, a Cultish Leader: Whose Turkey Is It?" *New York Times Magazine,* (5 February 2014): 33–39.

Harrington, James C. *Wrestling with Free Speech, Religious Freedom, and Democracy in Turkey: The Political Trials and Times of Fethullah Gülen.* Lanham, MD: University Press of America, 2011.

Harte, Julia. "Turkey Shocks Africa," *World Policy Journal* 29 (Winter 2012/2013): 27–38.

Hendrick, Joshua D. *Gülen: The Ambiguous Politics of Market Islam in Turkey and the World*. New York: New York University Press, 2013.

Hunt, Robert A., and Yüksel A. Aslandoğan, eds. *Muslim Citizens of the Globalized World: Contributions of the Gülen Movement*. Somerset, NJ: The Light, Inc., 2006.

Journalists and Writers Foundation. *Towards Universal Peace*. Istanbul: Journalists and Writers Foundation, n.d.

_____. *Understanding Fethullah Gülen*. Istanbul: Journalists and Writers Foundation, n.d.

Kimse Yok Mu. *KYM 2010–2013 Africa Report*. Istanbul: *Kimse Yok Mu*, 2014.

Kim, Heon, and John Raines, eds. *Making Peace in and with the World: The Gülen Movement and Eco-Justice*. Newcastle upon Tyne, UK: Cambridge Scholars Publishing, 2012.

Koç, Doğan. *Strategic Defamation of Fethullah Gülen: English vs. Turkish*. Lanham, MD: University Press of America, 2012.

Pandya, Sophia, and Nancy Gallagher, eds. *The Gülen Movement and its Transnational Activities: Case Studies of Altruistic Activism in Contemporary Islam*. Boca Raton, FL: BrownWalker Press, 2012.

Saritoprak, Zeki, ed. "Islam in Contemporary Turkey: The Contributions of Fethullah Gülen," Special issue, *The Muslim World* 95, no. 5 (2005).

Soltes, Ori Z. *Embracing the World: Fethullah Gülen's Thought and Its Relationship to Jalaluddin Rumi and Others*. Clifton, NJ: Tughra Books, 2013.

Tekin, Oğuzhan. "The Role of '*Kimse Yok Mu*' in Humanitarian and Peace Activities in the Middle East and Africa." Unpublished paper prepared for the International Conference on Conflict Prevention in the Middle East at Doshisha University in Kyoto, Japan on 8–9 November 2012.

_____. "Turkish Foreign Policy towards Africa: Motivations and Interests 2001–2010." MA thesis, Fatih University, 2012.

Tittensor, David. "The Gülen Movement and the Case of a Secret Agenda: Putting the Debate in Perspective," *Islam and Christian-Muslim Relations* 23, no. 2 (April 2012): 163–179.

_____. *The House of Service: The Gülen Movement and Islam's Third Way*. New York: Oxford University Press, 2014.

Turquoise Harmony Institute. *Gülen Movement: It's Essentials in Thought and Practice and Potential Contributions to Reconciliation in South African Society*. Cape Town, South Africa: Turquoise Harmony Institute, 2010.

Wagner, Walter. *Beginnings and Endings: Fethullah Gülen's Vision for Today's World.* New York: Blue Dome Press, 2013.

White, Jenny. *Muslim Nationalism and the New Turks.* Princeton: Princeton University Press, 2013.

Yavuz, Hakan M. *Toward an Islamic Enlightenment: The Gülen Movement.* Oxford: Oxford University Press, 2013.

Yavuz, Hakan M., and John L. Esposito, eds. *Turkish Islam and the Secular State: The Gülen Movement.* Syracuse, NY: Syracuse University Press, 2003.

Yilmaz, Ihsan. "Civil Society and Islamic NGOs in Secular Turkey and Their Nationwide and Global Initiatives: The Case of the Gülen Movement," *Journal of Development Studies*, (2010): 115–130.

_____ ed. *Muslim World in Transition: Contributions of the Gülen Movement.* International Conference Proceedings, London 25–27 October 2007. London: Leeds Metropolitan University Press, 2007.

INDEX

Abant Platform, 80, 109–11
Abuja Interfaith Peacebuilding Forum (Nigeria), 78–79
Aegean Health Volunteers' Association (EGESADER), 97
Aegean International Federation of Health (ESAFED), 86, 96
African Union Commission: Africa Dialogue Forum on religious tolerance in Addis Ababa (May 2012), 71, 73, 110, 113; memorandum of understanding with KYM, 87; TUSKON and, 31
Aga Khan Foundation, 23–24
Agai, Bekim, 48
Akdogan, Fatih, 5, 77
AKP-led Turkish government, 115–27, 134–35; collaborations with TUSKON, 28–29, 118; creation and rise to power, 115–16; early alliances with *Hizmet*, 54–55, 115–19, 127, 134; Erdoğan and AKP victories in the March 2014 elections, 124; Erdoğan corruption scandal and purges, 121–23; Ergenekon affair, 117; Gülen-affiliated media endorsement of Erdoğan's constitutional referendum, 119–20; handling of Gezi Park protesters, 121; and KYM humanitarian activities, 89, 99, 119; leaders' visits to *Hizmet* schools in Africa, 54–55, 118; the maturing relationship with *Hizmet* (2007–10), 117–19; the *Mavi Marmara* crisis (2010), 119; political Islam, 116; the 2007 parliamentary elections, 117–18. *See also* AKP-led Turkish government's split with *Hizmet;* Erdoğan, Recep Tayyip
AKP-led Turkish government's split with *Hizmet*, 1, 10–11, 29, 40, 119–25, 134–35; cracks develop (by end of 2012), iv, 119–20; cracks split wide open (by mid-2013), 121–25; early international media stories on, 120; effects on Gülen-affiliated media and outreach programs, 101, 113; effects on KYM humanitarian activities in Africa, 86–87, 89, 99; the Erdoğan corruption scandal and purges, 121–23; government campaign to shut down Bank Asya, 40; government closures of *Hizmet* schools, 55–56, 121, 124–25, 126; government restrictions on press freedom, 121, 125; Gülen-affiliated media speaking out against AKP and Erdoğan, 119, 121, 124; Gülen's public interviews and statements on, 122, 123–24, 135; impact in Africa, 126–27, 134–35; and Turkey's trade and aid activities in Sub-Saharan Africa, 126–27, 135

Algeria: as Arab country without a *Hizmet* school, 46, 131; conferences devoted to teachings of Gülen, 112; KYM programs, 95
Ali, Mahdi Ahmed, 51, 110
Alliance for Shared Values, 117, 134
alumni networks and associations in Africa, 61–62, 64, 67, 85–86
American Foreign Policy Council, 120
Amity International College (Cameroon), 45, 53, 54
Anadolu Center (Dakar, Senegal), 66
Angola: *Hizmet* schools, 45, 46; TUSKON in, 33
Annan, Kofi, 112
Arab countries of Africa, 46, 131–33; Arabic language issues, 103, 132; awareness of/familiarity with Gülen, 133; Dar al-Nile Publishing, 3, 106; Gülen's attitudes toward the Arab Muslim world, 132; *Hira* magazine, 83, 102–4, 107, 112; Hira TV, 108–9, 113; *Hizmet* dialogue centers, 84; and *Hizmet* schools, 46, 67,

131–32; KYM humanitarian activities in, 95; Morocco, 131–33; Salafist Islam, 84, 133
Arinç, Bülent, 33, 54, 55, 115–16, 121, 122
Aslandoğan, Yüksel Alp, 1, 4, 20, 117
Association Nigéro-Turque d'Entrepreneurs (ANTE), 39
Association of Businessmen and Industrialists of Tanzania and Turkey (ABITAT), 35
Association of Businessmen and Investors of Nigeria and Turkey (ABINAT), 36–37
Association of Mozambican and Turkish Merchants (MOZTÜRK), 39
Association Turco Gabonaise (Gabon), 86
Atatürk, Mustafa Kemal, 44, 118
Ateş, Mesut Göcan, 108
The Atlantic, 10
Atlantique Turquie-Sénégal Association (ATSA) pour le Dialogue Culturel entre les Civilisations, 81–82
Aydin, Hasan, 64
Aydogdu, Imran, 108
Azerbaijan, 124–25

Babacan, Ali, 54, 118
Balci, Bayram, 1
Banda, Rupiah, 50
Bank Asya, 39–41
Baskent Educational Association, 65–67
Bedir International High School (Malawi), 52–53
Bedir School (Niger), 54
Beginnings and Endings: Fethullah Gülen's Vision for Today's World (Wagner), 3
Benadir Hospital (Mogadishu, Somalia), 90
Benin: *Hizmet* schools, 45; KYM activities, 93; TUSKON and, 32
Berlinski, Claire, 25, 120
Biya, Paul, 33
Blue Dome Press (Clifton, New Jersey), 3, 106
Bobboyi, Hamid, 79
Boko Haram in Nigeria, 63, 65, 70, 79, 81, 133–34
Boni, Thomas Yayi, 32
Botswana, 46, 93
Boughazi, Mohammed Ali, 112
Brislin, Stephen, 75
British Broadcasting Corporation (BBC), ʹ23–24, 135
Buddhism: Gülen on, 71; organizations, 23

Burkina Faso: *Hizmet* schools, 45, 51, 81, 86; KYM partnerships and activities, 86, 93–94
Burundi, 95
business community. *See* Islamic banking; Turkish business community in Africa; TUSKON (Confederation of Businessmen and Industrialists of Turkey)

Cagaptay, Soner, 127
Çağlayan, Zafer, 54
Cairo University, 83, 103
Cameroon: Cameroon-Turkey Economic Forum, 33; *Hizmet* humanitarian activities, 93, 97; *Hizmet* schools, 45, 53, 54; *Hizmet*-related local Turkish business association, 39; KYM activities, 93; TUSKON's bilateral activity in, 32–33, 39
Can, Osman, 123
Çankiri Karatekin University (Turkey), 65
Cape Verde: *Hizmet* dialogue center, 72, 73; *Hizmet* schools, 46
Carroll, B. Jill, 3
Cascade Primary School (Senegal), 66
Catholic Bishop's Council (South Africa), 74
Caucasus University (Azerbaijan), 124–25
Cebelitarik (Moroccan travel agency), 38
Celik, Emre, iii
Çelik, Gürkan, 4
Çelik, Hüseyin, 120
Central African Republic, 93
Çetin, Muhammed, 3, 20, 48
Chad: *Hizmet* school, 94; KYM activities, 93, 94
Chatham House (London), 30
Christianity, 17, 71
Çiçek, Cemil, 32
Ciel Primary School (Senegal), 66
Cihan News Agency, 50, 72, 80, 105
Cingöz, Ismail, 86–87
Citizens against Special Interest Lobbying in Public Schools, 25
Colégio Esperança International (Angola), 45
Collège de la Citadelle (Guinea), 45
Le Collège Horizon International (Burkina Faso), 45
College La Lumiere Internationale (Madagascar), 86
Comoro Islands, 110, 126
Complexe Scolaire International Tchado-Turc

(Chad), 94
conferences, Gülen Movement, 4–5, 18, 79–80, 103–4, 109–12, 113; Abant Platform, 80, 109–11; According to Gülen, the Basic Dynamics of the Resurrection (Istanbul) (2012), 103; Africa: Between Experience and Inspiration (Lake Abant) (2013), 80, 110–11; Africa Dialogue Forum on religious tolerance at the African Union in Addis Ababa (May 2012), 71, 73, 110, 113; collections of papers presented at, 4–5, 18–19; devoted to Gülen's teachings, 18, 103, 112; and dialogue centers in Africa, 18, 74, 79–80; Diversity and Cohesion in a Globalized World (ATSA conference in Dakar) (2013), 81; Establishing a Culture of Coexistence and Mutual Understanding (Abuja, Nigeria) (2011), 79, 113; Future of Reform in the Muslim World (Cairo) (2009), 83, 103; and *Hira* magazine, 83, 103–4; International Conference on Peaceful Coexistence (Erasmus University, The Netherlands) (2007), 4; Islam in the Age of Global Challenges: Alternative Perspectives of the Gülen Movement (Georgetown University) (2008), 4; the JWF, 18–19, 80, 109–12; panel discussions at the UN, 111; A Shared Road Map: Ijma' and Collective Consciousness (Istanbul) (2013), 103–4; South Africa's Turquoise Harmony Institute (2010 panel), 4–5, 74; Tunisia and Turkey (Tunisia) (2013), 103; Ufuk Dialogue Foundation in Nigeria, 79–80; websites, 105
Congo, Republic of the, 46
Conway, Trudy D., 3
Coşkun, Ali, 55
Côte d'Ivoire: *Hizmet* school, 45; KYM programs, 94
Cross-cultural Dialogue on the Virtues: The Contribution of Fethullah Gülen (Conway), 3
Curaming, Sister Lilian M., 77

Dar al-Nile Publishing, 3, 106
Davutoğlu, Ahmet, 54, 55, 125
De Lange, Johnny H., 74
Demirel, Süleyman, 10

Democratic Republic of the Congo (DRC): *Hizmet* schools, 32–33, 45, 54; Turkish embassy, 48; TUSKON's bilateral activity in, 32–33
Desalegn, Hailemariam, 33
Diallo, Abdou Salam, 111
dialogue centers. See *Hizmet* dialogue centers in Africa
A Dialogue of Civilizations: Gülen's Islamic Ideals and Humanistic Discourse (Carroll), 3
Dinçerler, Vehbi, 55
Diop, Adama, 67
Doctors Worldwide, 90

Ebaugh, Helen Rose, 4, 22
Ebru Magazine, 81, 104, 107
Ebru TV, 105, 107–8, 113; African programming, 107–8; Nairobi office, 107
Ecevit, Bülent, 10
École Internationale Turco Gabonaise (Gabon), 45
L'École Internationale Ufuk-Benin (Benin), 45
Economic Community of West Africa States' Summit (Lagos, Nigeria), 32
Economic Community of West Africa States-Turkish Exports Products Fair (Lagos, Nigeria), 37
Economic Community of West African States (ECOWAS)-Turkish Export Expo (2014), 30–31
The Economist, 120
Ecumenism and Interreligious Dialogue Committee of the Catholic Church of South Africa, 74
Editions du Nil, 3, 107
EGESADER. See Aegean Health Volunteers' Association (EGESADER)
Egypt: *Hizmet* dialogue center, 83; *Hizmet* schools, 49, 131; *Hizmet*-related local business association, 38; KYM programs, 95
Egyptian-Turkish Friendship and Culture Association, 83
El Jadida University (Morocco), 133
embassies, Turkish: and the AKP-led Turkish government, 48, 54, 89, 118–19; and *Hizmet* schools, 48, 54, 118
Embracing the World: Fethullah Gülen's Thought and Its Relationship to Jalaluddin Rumi and Others (Soltes), 3

Equatorial Guinea, 46
Erdemli, Orhan, 124
Erdoğan, Recep Tayyip: AKP victories in the March 2014 elections, 124; the AKP's rise to power and alliance with Gülen Movement, 115–16; campaign to close Bank Asya, 40; campaign to close *Hizmet* schools, 55–56, 121, 124–25; corruption scandal and purges, 121–23; as de facto executive president, 125; the falling out with Gülen, 1, 10–11, 29, 40, 119–25, 135; Gülen-affiliated media speaking out against, 121, 124; visits to *Hizmet* schools in Africa, 54–55, 118. *See also* AKP-led Turkish government; AKP-led Turkish government's split with *Hizmet*
Ergene, Mehmet Enes, 3, 19
Ergenekon affair, 117
Ertas, Gökmen, 38
ESAFED. *See* Aegean International Federation of Health (ESAFED)
Esnan Dental Center (Tanzania), 97
Esposito, John L., 4
Ethiopia: absence of a *Hizmet* dialogue center, 73; conference on religious tolerance at AU headquarters in Addis Ababa (2012), 71, 73, 110, 113; Ethiopia Chamber of Commerce, 33; *Hizmet* schools, 27, 36, 45, 48, 50, 51, 110, 134; *Hizmet*-related local Turkish business associations, 36; and Islamic extremists, 134; KYM humanitarian activities, 73, 87–88, 92; lack of awareness of/familiarity with Gülen, 129; Rainbow Charitable Association and the Turkish business community, 36, 73, 92; Turkish embassy, 48; Turkish government's political and aid relationship with, 126; TUSKON's bilateral activity in, 27, 33
Ethiopia-Turkey Trade and Investment Forum, 33
Ethio-Turkish Entrepreneur Association, 36
European Union, 116, 125
extremists. *See* Islamic extremist movements

Fadil bin Asur Research Center (Tunisia), 103
Fatih University (Turkey), 112, 120
Fegessa, Siraj, 51
Fethullah Gülen Forum, 105
Feza Media Group, 101
Feza Schools (Tanzania), 45, 76, 97
Foreign Policy, 11
The Fountain (bimonthly periodical), 78, 79, 102, 107
Fountain Educational Trust (South Africa), 45, 48, 49, 56, 58
Francis of Assisi, St., 77
Franciscan Family Association (Kenya), 77
Fuller, Graham E., 4, 20

Gabon: *Hizmet* schools, 28–29, 45, 50, 54; KYM partnerships in, 86; TUSKON's bilateral activity in, 28–29, 32
Galaxy Dialogue and Cultural Center (Mali), 72
Galaxy International School (Ghana), 37, 45, 54
Gallagher, Nancy, 5
Gambia, *Hizmet* schools in, 55, 56, 124
Georgetown University (Washington, D. C.), 4, 71; The Center for Muslim-Christian Understanding at, 4
Ghana: *Hizmet* schools, 37, 45, 50, 54; *Hizmet*-related local Turkish business associations, 37; KYM activities in, 93; TUSKON's bilateral activity in, 28–29, 32, 37
Ghana-Turkey Cooperation and Development Association (TUDEC), 37
Ghannouchi, Rachid, 104
Groupe Scolaire Şafak (Côte d'Ivoire), 45
Guinea: *Hizmet* schools, 45, 50–51; Islamic Bank, 41
Gül, Abdullah: and AKP government, 125; and early *Hizmet*-AKP relationship, 115, 117–18; and *Hizmet* schools in Africa, 50, 54–55, 118; and TUSKON in Africa, 28–29, 32–33, 39
Gülen, Fethullah, 1, 3, 9–12, 26, 129–30; Africans' awareness of/familiarity with, 6, 60–61, 66, 67, 129–30, 133; attitudes toward the Arab Muslim world, 132; biography, 9–12; books by, 3, 12, 79, 106–7; condemnations of ISIL beheadings, 134; critics, 3, 11, 14, 24–25; educational philosophy, 12–14, 43–45; falling out with the AKP-led Turkish government, 1, 10–11, 29, 40, 119–25, 135; future of *Hizmet* after death of, 135–36; health, 1, 135; as influential public intellectual, 11–12, 130; Islamic

philosophy of, 3, 12–17, 25, 130; Kemalist and secular critics of, 10–11, 14; *madrasa* education, 9, 14; personal websites, 105; public statements against Erdoğan and government corruption, 122, 123–24; Sufism, 3, 9, 10, 12, 84, 104, 133; and Turkey's military coups, 10; Turkish court arrest warrant (2014), 125; and Turkish nationalism, 1, 10, 132; U.S. residence, 1, 11, 125; views of the Abrahamic religions, 17, 71; views on conversion, 16–17; views on education, 12–14, 15–16; views on girls' education, 15–16; views on interfaith dialogue, 16–17, 71; views on polygamy, 77–78; views on science, 14–15, 44; views on tolerance, 15–16, 44. See also *Hizmet* (Gülen Movement)

The Gülen Hizmet Movement and its Transnational Activities: Case Studies of Altruistic Activism in Contemporary Islam (Pandya and Gallagher, eds.), 5

Gülen Institute at the University of Houston, 1, 18, 102, 112; website, 105

The Gülen Movement: A Sociological Analysis of a Civic Movement Rooted in Moderate Islam (Ebaugh), 4

The Gülen Movement: Building Social Cohesion through Dialogue and Education (Çelik), 4

The Gülen Movement: Civic Service without Borders (Çetin), 3

Gülen Movement: Its Essentials in Thought and Practice Hizmet in Africa and Potential Contributions to Reconciliation in South African Society (Turquoise Harmony Institute), 4–5

Gülen: The Ambiguous Politics of Market Islam in Turkey and the World (Hendrick), 5

"Gülen-inspired Schools and Their Contribution to Christian-Muslim Relations in Nairobi, Kenya" (Akdogan), 5

Gülerce, Hüseyin, 20
Günay, Mustafa, 29, 31
Gürpinar, Ikbal, 89

Hansen, Suzy, 117
Harar Medical Center (Ethiopia), 92
Harrington, James C., 3–4
Hausa Translation Committee, 78
Hayd, Muse Farah, 90

Hendrick, Joshua D., 5, 21, 24, 116, 134
Hinduism, 71
Hira (Arabic-language magazine), 83, 102–4, 107, 112
Hira TV (Arabic-language network), 108–9, 113
Hizmet (Gülen Movement), 1–8, 9–26; Africans' awareness of/familiarity with, 6, 60–61, 66, 67, 129–30, 133; authority and local leaders, 22; comparisons to/differences with other groups, 23–24; core believers, 21–22; critics, iv, 3, 5, 10–11, 14, 24–25, 26, 52–53, 74, 106; defining, 19–24; donors and funding, 22–23, 27, 47, 72–73; followers and membership, 1–2, 19, 21–22; for-profit projects, 23, 38, 47, 66, 69, 97–98; future of (after Gülen's death), 135–36; as lacking transparency, iii, 3, 26, 29, 117; literature on, 2–5; the name, 1, 9, 17–19, 26; organizational structure and financial resources, 20–21; political components, 20–21; results and impact in Africa, 129–30; service activities outside Turkey, 21; sympathetic book length accounts of, 3–4, 9n; and Turkish nationalism, 1, 10, 132. See also AKP-led Turkish government's split with *Hizmet*; conferences, Gülen Movement; Gülen, Fethullah; humanitarian activities of *Hizmet* in Africa; media and outreach programs, Gülen-affiliated; schools in Africa, Gülen-affiliated

Hizmet dialogue centers in Africa, 16, 71–84; activities, 71–73, 74–75; and Arab North Africa, 84; conferences, 18, 74, 79–80; conflicting information on existence and status of, 72; Egypt, 83; funding from the Turkish business community, 72–73; and Gülen-affiliated media, 71, 72, 102, 109; and Gülen's views on interfaith dialogue, 16–17, 71; Kenya, 76–78; Morocco, 82–83; Nigeria, 78–81, 111; professional staff and volunteers, 73, 84; question of impact, 75–76, 84; and seasonal *Iftar* dinners, 74, 75, 79, 80, 84; Senegal, 81–82; South Africa, 73–76; Tanzania, 76

Hizmet Movement News Portal, 72
Hizmet: Questions and Answers on the Gülen Movement (Çetin), 3

Hoca, Tuğrul, 9n
Hope Kids Academy (Rwanda), 45
Horizon Education (Burkina Faso), 86
Horizon Educational Trust (South Africa), 56–58
Horizon International High School (Johannesburg, South Africa), 57
Horizon School (Zambia), 45, 50, 58
humanitarian activities of *Hizmet* in Africa, 85–99; Arab countries, 95; cataract surgery programs, 89, 93; donations, 86, 87, 98; effects of the falling between *Hizmet* and the Turkish government, 86–87, 89, 99; Ethiopia, 73, 87–88, 92; food packages, 74–75, 87, 89, 90, 92–93, 94, 95, 96; for-profit projects, 97–98; and *Hizmet* schools, 59, 70, 85–86, 93, 94; hosting *Iftar* dinners, 93, 94; and Islamic extremists, 90–91, 133; Kenya, 59, 70, 87–88, 92–93, 96; *Kimse Yok Mu* (KYM), 73, 85–95, 98–99, 131; medical teams and hospitals, 89, 90, 91, 92–93; North Africa, 95; Ramadan and Eid al-Adha food donations, 86, 89, 90, 91, 93, 96, 99, 130; to refugees and IDPs, 90, 92, 96; Senegal, 37, 93, 94–95; Somalia, 87–88, 89–91, 93; student scholarships, 90–91, 92; Sudan's Darfur region, 87, 88–89, 93, 95; and TIKA, 89, 99, 119; Time to Help (*Yardim Zamani Derneği*), 85, 94, 95–96, 98; and the Turkish business community, 36, 73, 92, 94, 98; Uganda, 87–88, 91; water wells, 93. See also *Kimse Yok Mu* (KYM)
Humanitarian Relief Foundation, 88
Hunt, Robert A., 4

Ibn Tofail University (Kinitra, Morocco), 132
Iftar dinners, 130; *Hizmet* dialogue centers and, 74, 75, 79, 80, 84; hosted by KYM, 93, 94
Ikbal Gürpinar Hospital (Darfur, Sudan), 89
Inciproduction (Abuja, Nigeria), 108
Independent Industrialists' and Businessmen's Association (MÜSIAD), 31
Institute of Interfaith Dialog, 105, 112
International Libyan Turkish School, 45
International Light College (Madagascar), 45
International Peace College of South Africa (Cape Town), 76
International Trade Fair of Luanda (2012), 33
International Trade Fair of Maputo (2012), 33
Internet: critics of *Hizmet*, 3, 25, 52, 53, 106; Gülen-affiliated media, 105–6, 108–9, 113; Hira TV and Arabic-language broadcasts, 108–9, 113. *See also* media and outreach programs, Gülen-affiliated
Inter-Religious Council of Ethiopia, 110
Ipek, Orhan, 81
Ishik Education and Medical Foundation, 97
Islam, 130–31; African Muslims' reactions to *Hizmet*, 130–31; and the AKP-led Turkish government, 116; Gülen's Islamic philosophy, 3, 12–17, 25, 130; and *Hizmet* schools in Africa, 13, 43–44, 48–49, 53, 61, 130; *Iftar* dinners, 74, 75, 79, 80, 84, 93, 94, 130; Islamic banking, 39–41, 42; Kemalist and secular critics of *Hizmet*'s Islamist intentions, 10–11, 14; *madrasas*, 9, 14, 43–44, 48; mosque-building, 130; Ramadan and Eid al-Adha food donations by KYM, 86, 89, 90, 91, 93, 96, 99, 130; sacrifice and service as religious virtues, 12; Salafism, 3, 84, 104, 133; and science, 14–15, 44; Shia Ismaili, 24. *See also* Islamic extremist movements; Sufism
Islam and Peacebuilding: Gülen: Movement Initiatives (Esposito and Yilmaz, eds.), 4
Islamic Bank of Guinea, 41
Islamic Bank of Mauritania, 41
Islamic Bank of Niger, 41
Islamic Bank of Senegal, 41
Islamic banking, 39–41, 42; AKP-led Turkish government campaign to shut down, 40; Bank Asya, 39–41; Senegal-based Tamweel Africa Holding (TAH), 40–41
Islamic Corporation for the Development of the Private Sector (ICD), 40–41
Islamic Development Bank (IDB), 40–41
Islamic extremist movements in Africa, 133–34; attacks on KYM, 90–91, 133; Boko Haram in Nigeria, 63, 65, 70, 79, 81, 133–34; and *Hizmet* schools, 63, 65, 70, 133, 134; ISIL, 134; in Mali, 133, 134; PAGAD in South Africa, 75–76; al-Qaeda in Malawi, 52–53; al-Qaeda in the Islamic Maghreb, 133, 134; al-Shabaab in Somalia, 90–91, 133, 134; and Somali refugees in Kenya, 77

Islamic State of Iraq and the Levant (ISIL), 134
Itabaci, Ibrahim, 52–53
Izmir Businessmen's Association, 37

Jega, Ibrahim A., 51–52, 78–79
Jewish Board of Deputies (South Africa), 74
John Paul II, Pope, 16
Jomo Kenyatta University (Kenya), 77
Jonathan, Goodluck, 32, 98
Jones, Dorian, 120
Journalists and Writers Foundation (JWF), 102, 109–12; the Abant Platform, 80, 109–11; Bank Asya underwriting, 40, 109; early relations with the AKP government, 115, 116; and *Hizmet* dialogue centers, 71, 109; hosting Gülen conferences, 18–19, 80, 109–12; June 2013 meeting on Lake Abant, 80, 110–11; manifesto rebutting the AKP government attacks on the Gülen Movement, 121; panel discussions at the UN, 111; *Understanding Fethullah Gülen*, 3, 18; visits from African leaders in Turkey, 109–10; website, 105
Judaism, 17, 71
Justice and Development Party. *See* AKP-led Turkish government
Justice Development and Peace Commission in Kaduna (Nigeria), 79
JWF. *See* Journalists and Writers Foundation (JWF)

Kagame, Paul, 33
Kalkan, Cavit, 38
Kalyoncu, Mehmet, 118
Karasin, Sami, 37, 94
Katircioğlu, Ali, 131
Kaynak Publishing Group, 2–3, 101, 106–7
Keita, Ibrahim Boubacar, 56
Kemalist Republican People's Party (Turkey), 10
Kenya: Cambridge system primary schools, 59, 60; coastal cities, 92–93; Ebru TV (Nairobi office), 107; *Hizmet* dialogue center, 76–78; *Hizmet* schools, 45, 46, 48, 50, 53, 54, 58–62, 70, 93, 130–31; *Hizmet*-related local Turkish business association, 35–36; Kenya system schools, 59–60; KYM humanitarian activities, 59, 70, 87–88, 92–93; Muslim extremist groups, 77; Muslims' reactions to *Hizmet*, 130–31; Somali refugee community, 77–78, 92, 96; Time to Help humanitarian activities, 95, 96; Turkish embassy, 48
Kenyatta, Uhuru, 50
Kilimanjaro Dialogue Center (Tanzania), 76
Kim, Heon, 5
Kimse Yok Mu (KYM), 85–95, 98–99, 131; in Arab countries, 95; collaborations with Time to Help, 96; donations, 86, 87, 98; effects of the falling out between *Hizmet* and the Turkish government, 86–87, 89, 99; Ethiopia, 73, 87–88, 92; food packages, 74–75, 87, 89, 90, 92–93, 94, 95; and *Hizmet* alumni associations, 85–86; and *Hizmet* schools, 59, 70, 85–86, 93, 94; hosting *Iftar* dinners, 93, 94; Kenya, 59, 70, 87–88, 92–93; medical teams and hospitals, 89, 90, 91, 92–93; North Africa, 95; partnerships and links with Gülen-affiliated organizations in Africa, 86, 98–99; Ramadan and Eid al-Adha food donations, 86, 89, 90, 91, 93, 96, 99, 130; recipients of assistance (2006-2013), 87–88; scholarships, 90–91, 92; Senegal, 37, 93, 94–95; Somalia, 87–88, 89–91, 93; structure and organization, 85–87; Sudan's Darfur region, 87, 88–89, 93; and TIKA, 89, 99, 119; and the Turkish business community, 36, 73, 92, 94, 98; Uganda, 87–88, 91
Koç, Doğan, 3
Koru, Naci, 55
Küçük, Ismail, 61
Kurdistan Workers' Party, 120
KYM. *See Kimse Yok Mu* (KYM)

Leadership (Abuja, Nigeria newspaper), 133
Lesotho, 46, 93
Liberia: Ebru TV, 108; *Hizmet* dialogue center, 72
Libya: *Hizmet* schools, 45, 46, 131; KYM programs, 95
Light Academy (Uganda), 54
Light Academy schools (Kenya), 36, 45, 54, 59, 60–62
Light Academy Schools Alumni Association (Kenya), 61–62
London School of Economics, 4

Madagascar: *Hizmet* dialogue center, 76; *Hizmet* schools, 45; KYM partnerships in, 86
madrasas, 9, 14, 43–44, 48
Mahama, John Dramani, 32, 50
Makgoba, Thabo, i–ii
Making Peace in and with the World: The Gülen Movement and Eco-Justice (Kim and Raines, eds.), 5
Malawi: al-Qaeda in, 52–53; *Hizmet* schools, 52–53
Mali: African extremist movements, 133, 134; *Hizmet* dialogue center, 72; *Hizmet* schools, 51, 56, 94, 133; *Hizmet*-related local Turkish business associations, 39; KYM activities, 93, 94
Mali-Turkish Businessmen's Association, 39
Mandela, Nelson, 120
Marmara Health Federation, 92, 96
Masons, 23
Mauritania: Islamic Bank, 41; KYM activities, 93, 94
Mauritius Chamber of Commerce and Industry, 33
Mavi Marmara crisis (2010), 119
Mbaye, Abdoul, 81
media and outreach programs, Gülen-affiliated, 101–13; the Abant Platform, 80, 109–11; and the AKP government-*Hizmet* split, 101, 113, 119, 121, 124; Arabic language, 3, 83, 102–4, 106, 107, 108–9, 112, 113; book publishing, 2–3, 101, 106–7, 113; books of Gülen in translation, 3, 79, 106–7; endorsement of Erdoğan's constitutional referendum, 119–20; and Gülen conferences, 4, 18, 81, 83, 102, 103, 105, 109–12, 113; and *Hizmet* dialogue centers, 71, 72, 102, 109; and *Hizmet* discussion groups in Africa, 112; Internet websites, 105–6; magazines, journals, newspapers, 78, 102–6, 107, 113; praise for *Hizmet* schools in Africa, 50, 110, 111; television channels, 101, 107–9, 113. See also conferences, Gülen Movement; *Hizmet* dialogue centers in Africa; Journalists and Writers Foundation (JWF)
Meral, Riza Nur, 28, 29, 31, 55
The Messenger of God: Muhammad (Gülen), 3, 79, 106–7

Mevlana University (Turkey), 65
Michel, Thomas, 71
Mkhize, Hlengiwe, 51, 75
Mohammed Al Fatih (MAF) Company schools (Morocco), 45, 67–69
Mohamud, Hassan Sheikh, 33
Mormons, 23
Morocco: as Arab country with *Hizmet* presence, 131–33; disciplinary system in *Hizmet* schools, 67–68; *Hizmet* dialogue center, 82–83; *Hizmet* discussion groups in Casablanca, 112; *Hizmet* schools, 45, 46, 49, 67–69, 70, 131–32; *Hizmet*-related local Turkish business associations, 38; TUSKON's bilateral activity in, 32
Mozambique: *Hizmet*-related local Turkish business associations, 39; TUSKON's bilateral activity in, 33, 39
Mozambique-Turkey Trade and Investment Forum (2012), 39
Muhammadiya (Indonesian organization), 23
Mulago Research Hospital (Uganda), 91
Museveni, Yoweri, 33, 50
Muslim Citizens of the Globalized World: Contributions of the Gülen Movement (Hunt and Aslandoğan, eds.), 4
Muslim Judicial Council (South Africa), 74
The Muslim World (journal), 4
Muslim World in Transition: Contributions of the Gülen Movement (Yilmaz, ed.), 4
Mwangi, David, 61–62
Mwinyi, Ali Hassan, 51

Namibia, 46
The Nation (Lagos, Nigeria newspaper), 80–81
Nejashi Ethio-Turkish International Schools (Ethiopia), 27, 45, 110
The New Turkish Republic: Turkey as a Pivotal State in the Muslim World (Fuller), 4
Niagara Foundation, 18
Niger: *Hizmet* schools, 54; *Hizmet*-related local Turkish business associations, 39; Islamic Bank, 41; KYM activities, 88, 93; the Turkish government's political and aid relationship with, 126
Nigeria: Boko Haram terrorist activity, 63, 65, 70, 79, 81, 133–34; Ebru TV, 108; *Hizmet* dialogue centers, 78–81, 111; *Hizmet* humanitarian activities, 97–98; *Hizmet* schools, 45, 46, 51–52, 53, 54,

62–65, 70, 80, 133; *Hizmet*-related local Turkish business associations, 36–37; National Mosque (Abuja), 78; Nizamiye Hospital (Abuja), 80, 97–98; praise for *Hizmet*, 78–79; translations of Gülen's books into Hausa, 79, 106–7; Turkish embassy, 48; TUSKON's bilateral activity in, 32, 37
Nigeria Association of Women Journalists, 80
Nigerian Association of Chambers of Commerce, Industry, Mines and Agriculture, 36
Nigerian Investment Promotion Commission, 36
Nigerian Turkish International Colleges (NTIC schools), 45, 54, 62–64, 80
Nigerian Turkish Nile University, 45, 62, 64–65, 80
Nile Foundation (Somalia), 45, 53, 89–90
Nile Humanitarian Development Agency (Uganda), 86
Nilüfer: Centre de Langues et de Culture in Morocco, 69, 82–83
Nizamiye Al-Azhar Institute (South Africa), 49, 58
Nizamiye Hospital (Abuja, Nigeria), 80, 97–98
Nizamiye Mosque Complex (Midrand, South Africa), 49, 131
Nizamiye Schools (South Africa), 45, 49, 58
non-governmental organizations. *See* humanitarian activities of *Hizmet* in Africa
Nursi, Bediüzzaman Said, 9

Omeriye Educational Foundation and Medical Charitable Trust (Kenya), 59, 93
Ondimba, Ali Bongo, 32, 50
Opus Dei, 23
Organization of Islamic Cooperation, 110
Özal, Turgut, 10
Özdalga, Elisabeth, 22
Öztürk, Hasan, 88

Pandya, Sophia, 5
Parmaksiz, Hussein, 36
Peace Islands Institute, 18, 111
People against Gangsterism and Drugs (PAGAD) (South Africa), 75–76

al-Qaeda, 52–53, 133
al-Qaeda in the Islamic Maghreb, 133, 134

Le Quotidien (Senegalese daily newspaper), 82, 104

Rainbow Charitable Association (Ethiopia), 36, 73, 92
Rainbow Intercultural Dialogue Center (Monrovia, Liberia), 72
Raines, John, 5
Rasool, Ebrahim, 2, 33–34, 74, 75–76
Ravinala Culture and Dialogue Institute at Antananarivo State University (Madagascar), 76
Respect Foundation (Kenya), 76–78
Revista Cascada (Spanish-language magazine), 104, 107
Rice University's Boniuk Center for the Study and Advancement of Religious Tolerance, 4
Ridge, Stanley, 75
Rumi, Jalaladdin, 136
Rumi Forum (Washington, D.C.), iii, 2, 18, 71
Rwanda: *Hizmet* schools, 45; TUSKON's bilateral activity in, 33

Sabanci University's Istanbul Policy Center, 30
Şafak École Internationale Turco-Congolaise (DRC), 45
Salafism, Islamic, 3, 84, 104, 133
Salahaldin International School (Cairo, Egypt), 49
Samanyolu Broadcasting Company (SBC), 101, 107, 108, 109, 125
Sambi, Ahmed Abdullah Mohammad, 110
São Tomé and Principe, 46
Saudi Arabia, 131
School of Oriental and African Studies at the University of London, 4
schools in Africa, Gülen-affiliated, 6, 12–14, 20, 43–70, 137–47; AKP leaders' visits to, 54–55, 118; AKP-led government closures, 55–56, 121, 124–25, 126; Arab countries, 46, 67, 131–32; arrival in Africa, 46, 48, 65; class sizes, 69; criticisms of, 14, 25, 26, 49, 52–53; disciplinary systems (Morocco), 67–68; financing and links to Turkish business community, 28–29, 34, 36, 37, 45, 47–48, 50; girls' education, 15–16, 49, 59, 60, 62, 63, 66, 69; and Gülen's educational philosophy, 12–14, 43–45; as

insufficiently Islamic, 49, 53; and Islam, 13, 43–44, 48–49, 61, 130; and Islamic extremists, 63, 65, 70, 133, 134; and *madrasas*, 43–44, 48; names and naming themes, 43, 45; and non-Muslims, 13, 48–49, 130; numbers of, 43, 46, 48; parents' involvement, 13, 47, 57, 62, 63, 67, 68; praise and testimonials for, 50–52, 67, 110, 111, 126; in predominantly Muslim countries, 46, 130; profits, 47, 66, 69; science curricula, 14, 44; teacher salaries, 47, 52, 53; teachers, 13, 44, 52, 53, 57, 66, 67–68; and tolerance, 15–16, 44; and Turkish embassies, 48, 54, 118; and TUSKON, 28–29, 47, 50

science: Gülen's views on religion and, 14–15, 44; *Hizmet* schools and science curricula, 14, 44

Scientology, 23

Senal, Selahattin, 38

Senegal: daily paper *Le Quotidien*, 52, 82, 104; Ebru TV, 108; eye hospital in Dakar, 37–38, 97; *Hizmet* dialogue center, 81–82; *Hizmet* media and outreach, 82, 104; *Hizmet* schools, 28, 37, 45, 46, 49, 52, 53, 54, 65–67, 70; *Hizmet*-related local Turkish business associations, 37–38, 94; Islamic finance and Tamweel Africa Holding (TAH), 40–41; Islamic Salafism, 104; KYM humanitarian activities, 37, 93, 94–95; Turkish embassy, 48; TUSKON's bilateral activity in, 28

Senegalese-Turkish Businessmen's Association (*Kardeslik*), 37–38, 94

Senghor, Leopold Sedar, 81

Seychelles, 46, 93

al-Shabaab in Somalia, 90–91, 133, 134

Shein, Ali Mohamed, 33

Shia Ismaili Islam, 24

Sierra Leone, 93

Sizinti magazine, 10, 107

Soka Gakkai International, 23

Soltes, Ori Z., 3

Somalia: extremist al-Shabaab movement, 90–91, 133, 134; *Hizmet* schools, 45, 53, 89–90, 133; KYM humanitarian activities, 87–88, 89–91, 93; Turkish embassy, 89; the Turkish government's political and aid relationship with, 126; TUSKON's bilateral activity in, 33

Somali-Turkish Businessmen's Association, 38

South Africa: *Hizmet* dialogue center, 4–5, 73–76; *Hizmet* in the Western Cape, 2, 33–34, 74–75; *Hizmet* Islamic schools, 45, 48, 49, 56, 58; *Hizmet* non-Islamic schools, 56–58; *Hizmet* schools, 45, 46, 48, 49, 50, 51, 52, 54, 56–58, 69–70, 130; *Hizmet*-related local Turkish business associations, 35, 73–74; lack of awareness of/familiarity with Gülen, 129–30; Nizamiye Mosque Complex at Midrand, 49, 131; Turkish embassy, 48, 119; TUSKON's bilateral activity in, 33–34

South African Council of Churches, 74

South African Turkish Business Association (SATBA), 35, 73–74

Southern Methodist University's Graduate Program in Religious Studies, 4

St. Augustine College of South Africa, 74, 75

Star International (Cape Town, South Africa), 45, 57

Strategic Defamation of Fethullah Gülen: English vs. Turkish (Koç), 3

Sudan: Darfur region, 87, 88–89, 93; *Hizmet* dialogue center, 72; *Hizmet* schools, 45, 49, 131; KYM humanitarian activities, 87, 88–89, 93; Time to Help humanitarian activities, 95; Turkish embassy, 48; the Turkish government's political and aid relationship with, 126

Sudanese-Turkish School (Khartoum), 45, 49

Sufism, 3, 78, 136; Arab Salafist hostility towards, 3, 84, 133; Gülen's, 3, 9, 10, 12, 84, 104, 133; *tekkes* and religious education, 44; Tijani Sufi movement (Nigeria), 78

Sultan of Sokoto, 78

SURAT Educational Institutions Ltd., 62

Swaziland, 93

Tajir, Hassan, 107

Tamweel Africa Holding (TAH), 40–41

Tanzania: *Hizmet* dialogue center, 76; *Hizmet* humanitarian activities, 96, 97; *Hizmet* schools, 45, 46, 51, 76, 97; *Hizmet*-related local Turkish business associations, 35

Tas, Tuncay, 37

Tasçi, Hakan, 29

Teklemariam, Shiferaw, 51, 110, 134
Temizkan, Yusuf, 37
Temple University (Philadelphia), 5
Teshome, Mulatu, 51
Tijani Sufi movement (Nigeria), 78
TIKA. *See* Turkish Cooperation and Coordination Agency (TIKA)
Time magazine, 11–12
Time to Help (*Yardim Zamani Derneği*), 85, 94, 95–96, 98; collaborations with KYM, 96; Denmark branch, 95; German and Belgian branches, 95–96; Kenya, 96; Sudan's Darfur region, 95
Tittensor, David, 13
Today's Zaman (English-language newspaper), 5, 18, 30, 40, 72, 81, 104–5; and the AKP government-*Hizmet* split, 124; and Bank Asya, 40; coverage of TUSKON, 30; on *Hizmet* dialogue centers in Mali, 72
Togo, 93
Tol, Gönül, 123n
Toward an Islamic Enlightenment: The Gülen Movement (Yavuz), 5, 9–10n
Tradition Witnessing the Modern Age: An Analysis of the Gülen Movement (Ergene), 3
Tughra Books (New York City), 2–3, 102, 106
Tunisia: Gülen-affiliated media, conferences, and outreach programs, 103–4; and *Hizmet* schools, 46, 51, 131; KYM programs, 95
Turkey-Africa Seminar (2011), 30
Turkey-Africa Trade Bridge (2011), 30
Turkey-Africa Women Entrepreneurs Trade Bridge (2014), 31
Turkey-Benin Trade and Investment Forum (2012), 32
Turkey-East Africa Trade Bridge (2014), 30
Turkey-Gabon Trade and Investment Forum (2012), 32
Turkey-Ghana Trade and Investment Forum (2013), 32
Turkey-Morocco Textile Business Forum (2013), 32
Turkey-Morocco Trade Bridge (2011), 32
Turkey-Morocco Trade Forum (2010), 32
Turkey-Nigeria Trade and Investment Forum (2011 and 2013), 32
Turkey-Rwanda Trade and Investment Forum (2012), 33
Turkey's Foreign Economic Relations Board (DEiK), 34
Turkey-Somalia Trade and Investment Forum (2012), 33
Turkey-South Africa Business Forum (2010 and 2012), 33
Turkey-Uganda Business Forum (2010), 33
Turkey-West Africa Trade Bridge (2014), 30–31, 47
Turkish Airways, 89, 127
Turkish and Cameroonian Businessmen's Association (TURCABA), 39
Turkish business community in Africa, 22–23, 27–42, 129; business organizations with no relationship to *Hizmet*, 31; donor funding for *Hizmet* projects, 22–23, 27, 47, 72–73; and *Hizmet* dialogue centers, 72–73; and *Hizmet* discussion groups, 112; and *Hizmet* schools (support and financing), 28–29, 34, 36, 37, 45, 47–48, 50; and Islamic banking, 39–41, 42; and local Turkish business associations, 34–39; and Turkish business councils, 34; TUSKON, 27–31, 32–34, 37, 38–39, 129. *See also* Bank Asya; TUSKON (Confederation of Businessmen and Industrialists of Turkey)
Turkish Cooperation and Coordination Agency (TIKA), 89, 96, 97, 99, 119
Turkish government. *See* AKP-led Turkish government; embassies, Turkish
Turkish Industry and Business Association (TÜSIAD), 31
Turkish Islam and the Secular State: The Gülen Movement (Yavuz and Esposito, eds.), 4
Turkish Journal of Politics, 102
Turkish Review, 102
Turkish-African Foreign Trade Bridge (2006), 30
Turkish-Egyptian Businessmen's Association, 38
Turkish-Kenya Businessmen's Association, 35–36
Turkish-Kenyan Business Council, 34
Turkish-Moroccan Businessmen's Association (TÜFIAD), 38
Turkish-Sudanese Business Council, 34
Turquoise Harmony Institute (South Africa), 4–5, 73–76; critics, 74; distribution of food packages to the needy, 74–75; funding, 73; impact, 75–76; interactions

with other South African religious groups, 74, 75; lectures, 74; panel on relevance of the Gülen Movement to South Africa (2010), 4–5, 74; praise and testimonials to, 75–76; professional staff and volunteers, 73; publications, 4–5; seasonal *Iftar* dinners, 74, 75

TUSKON (Confederation of Businessmen and Industrialists of Turkey), 27–31, 32–34, 37, 38–39, 129; affiliations with *Hizmet*, 28–30; and the AKP-led Turkish government, 28–29, 118; bilateral activity in Africa, 32–34, 127; events, trade bridges, and investment forums, 27–28, 30–31, 32–34, 47; goals, 27; and *Hizmet* schools in Africa, 28–29, 47, 50; offices outside Turkey, 27; partnerships with *Hizmet*-related local Turkish business associations, 37, 38–39; similar business organizations with no relationship to *Hizmet*, 31

TUSKON World Trade Summit (2013), 30

Tzu Chi Charitable Foundation, 23

Ufuk Dialogue Foundation (Nigeria), 78–81, 111

Ufuk Doctors Association, 96–97

Uganda: *Hizmet* schools in, 50, 54; *Hizmet*-related local Turkish business associations, 39; KYM humanitarian activities, 87–88, 91; KYM partnerships in, 86; TUSKON's bilateral activity in, 29, 33, 39

Uganda-Turkey Business Association (UTBA), 39

Understanding Fethullah Gülen (JWF), 3, 18

United Nations: Economic and Social Council, 85; JWF-sponsored panel discussions at, 111

University of Algiers, Faculty of Islamic Sciences, 112

U.S. Central Intelligence Agency (CIA), 20, 24, 52–53

U.S. Department of Homeland Security, 11

U.S. Department of State, 125

U.S. National Intelligence Council, 4, 20

Valkenburg, Pim, 18
van Heerden, Michael, 74, 75

Wagner, Walter, 3

The Wall Street Journal, 123–24

Washington Institute for Near East Policy, Turkish Research Program at, 127

women: girls' education in Gülen-affiliated schools, 15–16, 49, 59, 60, 62, 63, 66, 69; Gülen's educational philosophy, 15–16; KYM humanitarian programs and Turkish women, 95; TUSKON and African women entrepreneurs, 31

World Businesswomen's Association, 95

Wrestling with Free Speech, Religious Freedom, and Democracy in Turkey (Harrington), 3–4

Yağmur (magazine), 107

YarAdua, Umaru Musa, 62

Yavuz, M. Hakan, 4, 5, 9–10n, 11; on criticisms of Gülen's ideas, 24–25; on Gülen-affiliated schools, 14; on Gülen's goals for interfaith dialogue, 17; on Gülen's Islamic philosophy, 12; on link between TUSKON and *Hizmet*, 28; on three circles of Gülen Movement followers, 21–22; *Toward an Islamic Enlightenment* (2013), 5, 9–10n

Yavuz Selim Anatolian School (Gambia), 55

Yavuz Selim Schools (Senegal), 45, 49, 53, 54, 65

Yeni Ümit (magazine), 103–4, 107

Yesil, Mustafa, 116

Yildiz Technical University (Istanbul), 64

Yilmaz, Ihsan, 4, 120

Zaman (Turkish-language newspaper), 18, 30, 40, 81, 105. See also *Today's Zaman* (English-language newspaper)

Zaman Media Group, 105

Zambia, *Hizmet* schools in, 45, 50, 58

Zanzibar: *Hizmet* humanitarian activities, 96; *Hizmet* schools, 96; TUSKON's bilateral activity in, 33

Zemheri, Yavuz, 36

Zenawi, Meles, 50

Zuma, Jacob, 50, 131

BOOKS THAT BELONG ON YOUR SHELF
MORE BOOKS YOU LOVE TO READ ARE ON OUR WEBSITE

 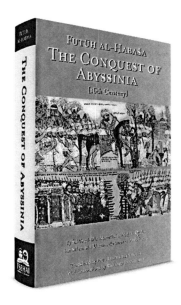

Boko Haram: Islamism, Politics, Security and the State in Nigeria

Edited by: Marc Antoine Pérouse de Montclos

ISBN: 978-1-59907-097-1
Pub. Date: January 2015

"For scholars, government officials, journalists, and civic actors, this book expands our understanding of this enigmatic jihadist movement, its genesis, evolution, and political implications. In light of the global significance of militant Islam, the book is indispensable for students of Nigeria, Africa, Muslim societies, and armed conflicts."

—**Richard Joseph**, John Evans Professor of International History and Politics, Northwestern University

The Conquest of Abyssinia: Futuh Al-Habasa

Translated by: Paul L. Stenhouse
Annotation by: Richard Pankhurst

ISBN: 0-9723172-5-2
Pub. Date: May 2004

"This is truly a wonderful work, which is destined to remain an indispensable source for the history of Ethiopia and the Horn of Africa during the first half of the tumultuous sixteenth century. Anyone interested in understanding the intensity and brutality of religious war will be rewarded by reading this classic."

—**Mohammed Hassen**, Associate Professor of African History at Georgia State University in Atlanta

www.store.tsehaipublishers.com

CPSIA information can be obtained
at www.ICGtesting.com
Printed in the USA
FSOW01n2031250116
16028FS